Citizenship and Democratic Control in Contemporary Europe

Citizenship and Democratic Control in Contemporary Europe

Edited by

Barbara Einhorn, Mary Kaldor and Zdenek Kavan
Sussex European Institute
University of Sussex, UK

Edward Elgar
Cheltenham, UK • Brookfield, US

Published by
Edward Elgar Publishing Limited
8 Lansdown Place
Cheltenham
Glos GL50 2HU
UK

Edward Elgar Publishing Company
Old Post Road
Brookfield
Vermont 05036
US

British Library Cataloguing in Publication Data
Citizenship and Democratic Control in
Contemporary Europe
  I. Einhorn, Barbara
  321.8094

Library of Congress Cataloguing in Publication Data
Citizenship and democratic control in contemporary Europe / edited by
  Barbara Einhorn, Mary Kaldor, and Zdenek Kavan.
    Includes index.
    1. Europe, Eastern—Politics and government—1989– 2. Europe,
  Eastern—Economic conditions—1989– 3. Post-communism—Europe,
  Eastern. 4. Europe—Economic integration. I. Einhorn, Barbara.
  II. Kaldor, Mary. III. Kavan, Zdenek.
  JN96.C58   1994
  320.947—dc20   94–27893
                                                           CIP

ISBN 1 85898 069 0

Printed and bound in Great Britain by
Hartnolls Limited, Bodmin, Cornwall

Contents

Contributors   vii

Acknowledgements   viii

1.   Introduction   1
      Barbara Einhorn, Mary Kaldor and Zdenek Kavan

Part I

2.   Nation-States, European Institutions and Citizenship   9
      Mary Kaldor

3.   Democracy and Nationalism in Czechoslovakia   24
      Zdenek Kavan

4.   German Identities: the Impact of 'Unification'   40
      Peter Lambert

5.   From the Single European Act to Maastricht: 54
      the Creation of the European Union
      Peter Holmes

6.   Gender and Citizenship in East Central Europe After the   69
      End of State Socialist Policies for Women's 'Emancipation'
      Barbara Einhorn

Part II

7.   Marketisation and Nationalism: A Critical Interface   89
      in the Process of Transformation
      David A. Dyker

8.   Privatisation and Economic Democracy in Hungary   102
      Yudit Kiss

9.   International Business: Global Political Economy and   117
      Eastern Europe
      Sonia El Kahal

Contents

10. A Europe of the Citizen, A Europe of Solidarity?   134
     Social Policy in the European Union
     Crescy Cannan

11. The European Community and the Problems of   150
     Economic Transition in Central and Eastern Europe
     Alasdair Smith

Part III

12. Steering the Public Sphere. Communication Policy in   165
     State Socialism and After
     William Outhwaite

13. The Ideology of the End of Marxism/End of Socialism Thesis: 180
     A Critical, Global Perspective
     John MacLean

14. 'Public Service' and 'Collectivism': the Place of Gender and   197
     Voluntary Work in Different European Traditions
     Jenny Shaw

15. East Central European Media Systems in Transition   214
     Nancy Wood

Index   231

Contributors

Crescy Cannan, Senior Lecturer in Social Policy, School of Cultural and Community Studies, University of Sussex

David Dyker, Reader in Economics, School of European Studies, University of Sussex

Barbara Einhorn, Honorary Research Fellow, School of European Studies, University of Sussex

Sonia El Kahal, Principal Lecturer in International Business, Sheffield Hallam University

Peter Holmes, Senior Lecturer in Economics, School of European Studies, University of Sussex

Mary Kaldor, Jean Monnet Reader in Contemporary European Studies, Sussex European Institute, University of Sussex

Zdenek Kavan, Lecturer in International Relations, School of European Studies, University of Sussex

Yudit Kiss, Researcher, former Research Fellow, Institute of Development Studies, University of Sussex

Peter Lambert, Lecturer in History, University of Aberystwyth

John MacLean, Senior Lecturer in International Relations, School of Social Sciences, University of Sussex

William Outhwaite, Professor of Sociology, School of European Studies, University of Sussex

Jenny Shaw, Lecturer in Sociology, School of Cultural and Community Studies, University of Sussex

Alasdair Smith, Professor of Economics, School of European Studies, University of Sussex

Nancy Wood, Lecturer in Media Studies, School of European Studies, University of Sussex

Acknowledgements

This book emerged out of a series of lunch-time and long weekend seminars organised at the University of Sussex in the aftermath of the 1989 revolutions. The series, which was entitled *Conflict and Co-operation in Europe*, brought together faculty and students interested in both East and West Europe and helped to lay the groundwork for the establishment of the Sussex European Institute. We are extremely grateful to the John D. and Catherine T. MacArthur Foundation for an educational enrichment grant which, among other things, made possible the seminar series.

We would also like to thank all those who took part in the seminars and who contributed to the ideas and perspectives developed in these essays. In particular, we would like to thank Sean Horstead for his assistance in both organising the seminars and editing the book, and Sara Spencer and Indira Konjhodzic for their laborious efforts to transform our discs into camera-ready copy.

1. Introduction

Barbara Einhorn, Mary Kaldor and Zdenek Kavan

The year 1989 is generally considered to be a watershed marking the collapse of communism, the end of the Cold War and the beginning of a transition towards a new system in the East and towards a new international order. But it might be more illuminating to interpret the events of 1989 not so much as a watershed but as one very important episode in a continuing process. This process, which began at least two decades ago, involves the erosion, even disintegration, of the post-war system which had certain common but obviously asymmetric features in East and West, despite the apparent opposition between the capitalist and the state socialist systems. These features included the prominent role played by the state in social, economic and international affairs, planning, paternalism and militarisation, mass production, and the privileged position accorded to organised workers. It is to be noted that the stress put on the revolutions of 1989 in the analysis of contemporary Europe has tended to obscure the impact of the relative decline of social democracy and Keynesianism in the West.

It is often argued that the revolutions of 1989 represent a triumph of democracy over totalitarianism in Europe. Though these revolutions undoubtedly swept away highly undemocratic regimes and brought about conditions in which the construction of democracy is at least possible, it is to be noted that the collapse of state socialism in the East and the relative triumph of neo-liberalism in the West has left two dominant ideologies in place, nationalism and the market, only somewhat qualified by Europeanism. The effect of nationalism and of market ideology on the development and maintenance of democracy is problematic both at the level of the state and Europe. The problem is compounded by the growing internationalisation of economic and social processes and the resulting relocation of crucial decision-making power in institutions other than the nation-state. In these circumstances it is imperative that the nature of democratic society, the conditions for its functioning and its emancipatory potential be critically examined.

1

It is sometimes argued that the revolutions of 1989 contained no new ideas, that they were 'backward looking'. In our view, this is a misperception. The revolutions expressed a critique of the post-war system that had been developing among the new social movements of the 1970s and 1980s in both East and West, and indeed North and South, but which, for a variety of reasons, was most clearly articulated by East European dissident intellectuals. This critique which centred around such concepts as citizenship, civil society and anti-politics did and still does offer an emancipatory potential today when some earlier emancipatory ideas appear to be discredited. In this book we try to develop these conceptions and to demonstrate their continuing relevance to some of the diverse problems which are currently being confronted in both East and West. Paradoxically in the aftermath of 1989 such views were marginalised in the post-communist societies themselves. Hardly any of the former dissidents who led the revolutions remain in power today. The inheritors of the revolutions seem rather to be the nationalists, the neo-liberals, the ambitious entrepreneurs and the Eurocrats. The very notion that these revolutions did not generate any new ideas is part of a discourse that presents 1989 as a watershed that marks the negation of what went before. It is a discourse that helps to legitimate the position of these new elites and to delegitimate critical challenges to them. It is also a discourse that lends itself to the confirmation of the existing dominance of neo-liberalism in the West and to its presentation as the only real alternative.

The revolutions were empowering in the sense that they demonstrated the possibility of overthrowing the established order and offered individuals the chance to assume responsibility for their lives. But the revolutions could not immediately resolve the problem of a general lack of political experience, relative lack of critical understanding of democracy and the long history of authoritarian rule and authoritarian culture. In these circumstances it is not surprising that the institutions of authority were not transformed into fully democratic and empowering ones. The problem of the individual's powerlessness when faced with remote and powerful institutions that so exercised the Eastern dissidents under the communist regimes is reemerging under a new guise and is threatening to stifle the opportunities for the exercise of individual responsibility.

This problematic of the empowerment of the individual in the context of a society characterised by social justice can be viewed in relation to different but related issues.

1. MARKET AND PRIVATISATION

The reestablishment of the market and privatisation as one of the crucial means of bringing it about is often presented as creating space for the exercise of individual responsibility. The neo-liberals oppose the market to the state and emphasise the emancipatory consequences of freeing the individual property owner from dependency on the institutions of the state. Privatisation is understood in this context as creating autonomy and freeing the economy from political interference. Consequently the power of the state to regulate and control the lives of its citizens is dramatically reduced. Social stability and democracy are to be based on a reconstructed middle class and particularly the power of its new entrepreneurial element. It is to be noted that this position does not lead to the construction of citizenship as a powerful basis of empowerment of the individual, partly because it sees citizenship almost exclusively in relation to the state and defined by political and civil rights and duties. Citizenship, in this sense, covers only a smaller aspect of the individual's social existence. Empowerment is individualised through negative liberty and seen as lying in the individual's ability to succeed in competitive, market-based activities. In a market freed from state interference it is the individual's abilities and hard work that are rewarded with success and therefore economic and social power. Yet for those who do not succeed in market activities, this negative liberty constitutes disempowerment.

These processes can be well illustrated by considering the example of the West where the recent dominance of neo-liberal market ideology led to the substantial reduction in the state's involvement in economic and social activity, particularly those associated with the provision of welfare.

2. NATIONALISM AND ETHNICITY

After 1989 nationalism has been presented both as emancipatory and as oppressive. Nationalism is often presented as an ideal form of social construction of collective identity. The emancipatory effect of nationally constructed social solidarity is emphasised and national self-determination is seen as a precondition for democratic existence. The rights of oppressed nations and national minorities are presented as the basic rights without which other rights cannot be democratically exercised. In this context it is worth noting that the defence against supranationalism, including Europeanism, that is inspired by nationalism, often stresses the presumed anti-democratic nature of such supranational organisations. On the other hand nationalism is also used to support anti-democratic policies, to legitimate the position of powerful elites of the nomenklatura or even Thatcherite type, and to legitimate discrimination against 'the other'. In its most extreme form this leads to 'ethnic cleansing'.

3. EUROPE

In contemporary discourses on Europe we again find opposing positions with regard to its emancipatory potential. The dominant position in the West sees Europe as a state in the making. Some see it as a threat to democracy believing that democracy, if it is to work, has to operate on a national basis. Others see it as a rational response to the processes of globalisation as well as having the positive advantage of diluting national conflicts and helping to create social solidarity on a regional basis. In the East, Europe was perceived mainly as a means of returning into the Western fold and of guaranteed emancipation from Soviet dominance.

4. DEMOCRACY

The 'triumph' of democracy in 1989 and since has raised important questions about the nature of democracy and its emancipatory potential. On the one hand democracy is presented as a set of formal rights, mainly civil and political, and institutions which guarantee ordered competition for power and which also limit the exercise of this power. The citizen is akin to a consumer who can freely choose from the range of options on offer but whose participation in the political community's decision-making is otherwise very limited. The alternative view of democracy is concerned with the empowerment of all individuals to take control of their own lives and, therefore, to be able to participate in and to affect the creation of public policies that will affect them. This concept of democracy is centred round the concept of democratic and active citizenship operating within the context of democratic political culture. The citizen is not only empowered through the provision of spaces for participation but (s)he claims power through action. It is this concept of democratic and active citizenship that provides the central theme for this book.

This concept of citizenship has certain corollaries. First, it gives a new meaning to the concept of civil society. Civil society is not simply used here in its original eighteenth-century meaning, as the rule of law as opposed to anarchy as well as arbitrary rule, civilisation as opposed to nature. Rather, civil society is the medium through which individuals become citizens, through which they become members of the political community and participate in public life. Civil society is composed of independent, autonomous, self-organised groups through which ideas and criticisms can be articulated, and which can, if necessary, negotiate with government and other social institutions.

Second, this concept of civil society is associated with the concept of anti-politics. Civil society is independent of, although not in opposition to, the state and other political institutions, including political parties. Civil society is a way of exerting democratic control over the state. Although political parties sometimes act as 'bottom-up' organisations which provide a medium for expressing grievances and criticisms and for organising political debate, most of them tend to become preoccupied with the capture of political power and largely abandon the role of providing a public forum for the marginal and disaffected. The concept of anti-politics emphasises the importance of remaining outside the 'power game' so as to be able to express unpopular views and to challenge the prevailing orthodoxy. It is important to realise that these orthodoxies include not just the dominant political ideologies, but, crucially, the constantly reproduced prevailing notions of rationality, knowledge and professional expertise. In many ways it can be argued that such a civil society is indispensabe to the maintenance of democratic pluralistic political culture without which democracy would be reduced to a regulated competition for power.

Third, civil society and the form of citizenship which is associated with it can also form a basis for the democratic control of international institutions. It is not bound by the state and the concept of sovereignty nor by the concept of ethnos, but by the concept of political community. Indeed, European citizenship, if it is to be empowering and democratic, requires the construction of European civil society. Otherwise no amount of subsidiarity will guarantee democratic control of the European Community.

All the essays in this book, in their different ways, stress the importance of such a concept of citizenship in confronting the problems faced by Europeans, East and West, in the post-Cold War period. The first section deals with politics and political processes. Mary Kaldor's chapter is about the erosion of the nation-state and the need for new political institutions at both international and local levels; such institutions would need to be enabling, providing space for individuals to shape their own environment. Zdenek Kavan and Peter Lambert's chapters deal with the evolution of politics in post-totalitarian transition. Both the break-up of Czechoslovakia and the unification of Germany, dealt with by these authors respectively, have comparable characteristics. Zdenek Kavan also shows how a market ideology, as opposed to a market policy, can function as a form of nationalism. Peter Holmes's chapter is about the European dimension of citizenship and the importance of a trans-European political culture if the development of the European Union is to be sustained. Barbara Einhorn's chapter demonstrates that gender is often the missing ingredient of citizenship and that a dialogue between women in East and West based on the recognition of the differences between European cultures could provide an essential precondition for a reconstructed notion of citizenship.

The second section is about economic and social policy. All the chapters emphasise the need for an approach to economic and social issues that is both internationalist and democratic. David Dyker's chapter demonstrates the way in which nationalism, particularly so-called nomenklatura nationalism, inhibits economic transformation; even those nationalists who favour joining the 'West' and who claim to be 'European' neglect trade with their neighbours which could well be vital for regeneration. Yudit Kiss describes the undemocratic nature of privatisation in Hungary and the problems this poses for transition. Sonia El Kahal argues that the form of transition in Eastern Europe has been determined more by the global discourse of privatisation and deregulation than by autonomous democratic choices. Alasdair Smith is more positive about the transition to the market; he emphasises the importance, despite the difficulties, of enhanced economic integration between East and West. Crescy Cannan's chapter is about the importance of social policy as an element of Europeanism. Notions of citizenship and solidarity offer an essential alternative to earlier paternalistic concepts of welfare.

The last section of the book is about language, ideology and communication. William Outhwaite explores the ideological discourse of state socialism as an 'inverted communicative rationality'. John MacLean suggests that, in the aftermath of 1989, its negation, the ideology of the end of Marxism, also inhibits emancipatory potential. Jenny Shaw and Nancy Wood conclude the book by discussing the need for a democratic public sphere. Jenny Shaw articulates the notion of a public service ethic which addresses those realms in which neither the state nor the market can provide. Nancy Wood describes the trends towards media marketisation/privatisation and the debate about public-funded media. It is in those areas of life which affect communication and discourse, particularly the media, that independent political space is created in which civic activity can exist.

PART I

2. Nation-States, European Institutions and Citizenship

Mary Kaldor

The post-Cold War period is a period of fragmentation and integration in both halves of Europe. Current political struggles are primarily directed towards the creation of new forms of governance. How do we theorise this process? How do we elaborate principles on which to base ideas about new forms of governance? And, in particular, given the current context, what could constitute a form of democratic governance?

I use the term 'democratic' in the broadest sense. I am not referring to formal democratic institutions, for example representative government, elections, free press, independent judiciary, and so on, although these are a necessary condition for democratic governance. Rather, I am referring to the redistribution of political power, that is to say, the ability of the individual to participate (or not as he or she chooses) in key decisions concerning his or her life. The term 'citizenship' has this active connotation, meaning responsibility, participation, empowerment, and so on as in the original Greek sense.

The term 'governance' refers to the process of managing or organising society - a process which involves political institutions as well as other individuals and formal or informal groups. Political institutions include states, international organisations, local and regional governments, and so on. They are administrative units which have varying degrees of legitimacy, namely broadly accepted political power.

In this essay, I shall argue that the nation-state, at least in its nineteenth-century form, is no longer adequate as the dominant form of political institution. New institutions, at local, regional and international levels, will have to supplant the nation-state but not in the form of smaller or larger nation-states, but as new forms of governance. I do not want to suggest that there is no room for national identity or national self-determination, but rather these demands have to be channelled towards new types of political units that are less absolutist and less powerful than the nation-state.

It may seem strange or even paradoxical to argue that the nation-state is anachronistic at the very moment when nationalism is self-evidently on the

9

rise. But the paradox may actually help to explain what is happening. The very fact that national governments are becoming less and less important, that it is increasingly difficult for politicians to implement constructive policies or to influence events, the sense of impotence experienced by many politicians increases the tendency to appeal to an abstract national idea or deeply rooted prejudices against other nations or minorities in order to maintain power positions.

In what follows, I shall first describe the characteristics of the nation-state, then consider the inadequacies of the nation-state as a form of political organisation in the current epoch, and, in the last section, I shall discuss the possibilities for the future.

THE NATURE OF THE NATION-STATE

It is difficult to disentangle the concept of nation from the concept of the nation-state. Definitions of nations vary: a common linguistic group, inhabitants of a particular territory, an ethnic group, a group with shared values or cultural traditions. In practice, a group of human beings that define themselves as a nation usually do so because they are citizens of a particular state, because they are discriminated against by a state, or because of their interest in establishing their own state.

What made the nation-state different from previous forms of political organisations? First of all, the administrative reach of the state was greatly extended. Territory was clearly defined; nation-states had borders rather than vague frontiers and state control over national territory was much greater than under earlier kingdoms or empires. Previously, large tracts of territory were beyond the control of the state - they were chaotic and violent, or sometimes, as in the case of English towns or counties, self-organised.

Second, the concept of sovereignty changed radically. The legitimacy of the nation-state derived from the notion that sovereignty belonged to the people rather than to the King or Emperor. Citizens replaced subjects.[1] Hence the establishment of nation-states was inextricably linked to principles of accountability, self-determination, individual autonomy, and so on.

Who were the citizens? They were members of the nation. A third feature of the nation-state was the homogenisation of national culture, in which the state played a key role. In earlier periods, there were horizontal high cultures generally linked to religion and not to the state, for example, Latin, Persian, Sanskrit or Mandarin Chinese, and a variety of local rural cultures. Cultural diversity was given and, indeed, was an essential feature of a relatively stable social stratification. A person's place in society was largely determined at birth, and identified with cultural background.

The rise of the nation-state was linked to the rise of written vernacular languages. This was made possible by the discovery of print technology which made the written word far more widely accessible. New publications, for example, novels and newspapers and even the bible, in vernacular languages, gave rise to new identities, to new communicative networks. Benedict Anderson uses the term 'imagined community' to describe the way in which people who had never met or who were not related could develop a sense of community because they read the same newspapers or novels.

The spread of language was just what was needed both for expanded administration and for industrial development. The nation-state took over responsibility for the reproduction of culture, particularly education. The national language, generally a dominant dialect, gradually displaced other languages, dialects, and cultures. With the rise of modern society, says Gellner, 'life and work also becomes one long series of encounters with pervasive economic and political bureaucracies. Participation and effective citizenship and employability and dignity all depend on possessing mastery of the literate High Culture which is also the idiom of the political unit in which one lives' (Gellner, 1991, pp. 129-30). Hence, the typical feature of the nation-state was cultural homogenisation and assimilation of lesser cultures.

In Western Europe, the process of nation-building came about organically, over a long period. The development of an 'imagined community' paralleled or even preceded the rise of the nation-states. The first English newspapers appeared during the English Civil War, which also played a key role in extending the administrative reach of the state. In Eastern Europe, these processes were compressed into a short time period. The dynastic empires lasted up to 1918. They were characterised by huge ethnic and linguistic diversity; what held the empires together was religion and loyalty to the dynastic family. Under the impact of Western modernity and the need for greatly extended administration and rapid industrialisation, cultural homogenisation became much more savage in these 'latecomer' efforts at nation-building, so much so that the idea of nation and the principle of nationality became more important than the principle of citizenship. In Western Europe, learning the national language was the way to acquire citizenship and to participate in political and economic life. In Eastern Europe, knowledge of the national language became a criterion of citizenship; those who were not born speaking a particular language were often excluded from political and economic life.

A fourth feature of the nation-state was the establishment of unified currencies under the control of central banks. This was associated with a greatly expanded economic role for the state through regularised taxation, the elimination of internal tariffs, regulations concerning banking, weights and measures, and so on. A central discussion among theorists of the nation-state concerns the relationship between the formation of nation-states and the rise of industrialisation. Undoubtedly these were interconnected phenomena; modern industry requires a modern state and vice versa and both contributed to the evolution of the other. However, it is also the case that economic and political activities became separate activities, both in an analytical and empirical sense, with the rise of capitalism. The nation-state could be said to be compatible with industrialisation in a way that earlier empires were not, but it was also a highly contradictory relationship.

Nation-states were, by and large, established through wars. A final and perhaps most important characteristic of the nation-state was the monopoly of legitimate organised violence - the elimination of private armies, the process of internal pacification, the establishment of regular armies which were distinguished from police forces. The distinction between civil society, the rule of law within states, and the state of nature and the balance of power in the international arena parallels the rise of the nation-state. It was in this period that the notion of Europe began to displace the notion of Christendom. The secularisation of sovereignty meant that the rules of international behaviour were no longer governed by a sense of belonging to a common religious community. Instead, *realpolitik*, the notion of political order governed by power based on force, became the dominant international discourse.

Wars required resources, taxes and soldiers. And these were extracted from the population through a mixture of coercion and consent. Charles Tilly says:

> Recurrently, we find a chain of causation running from: 1) change or expansion in land armies; to 2) new efforts to extract resources from subject populations; to 3) the development of new bureaucracies and administrative innovation; to 4) resistance from the subject population; to 5) renewed coercion; to 6) durable increases in the bulk or extractiveness of the state. (Tilly, 1975, p. 75)

The idea of nation, and the associated idea of an 'other' - an enemy nation, was also forged in war and provided a basis for consent and for legitimacy for expanded administration. National wars belonged to the people in the way that dynastic wars did not. Wars became discontinuous and with the establishment of regular armies, both real and imaginary, wars became an ingrained element of national culture. The notion of 'imagined community' included the remembrance and glorification of past wars and the prospect of future wars.

THE INADEQUACIES OF THE NATION-STATE

The nation-state was by no means an ideal form of political organisation. It did provide a framework for industrialisation but, in other respects, it had major limitations. Moreover industrialisation passed through several phases - textile era, railway era, and so on. The most recent phases -Fordism and post-Fordism - are not as compatible with the nation-state as earlier phases. The nation-state is, at once, too large and too small.

It is both too large and too small for democratic governance. The rise of representative democracy involved a more passive concept of citizenship than in the original Greek sense. Indeed, given the size of the nation-state active citizenship is extremely difficult to organise. Yet, without active participation, especially after the introduction of mass suffrage, representative democracy becomes very vulnerable to populism, that is the appeal to irrational prejudices in order to win votes.

To some extent, the party system offered an opportunity for active citizenship, at least in the West. The political parties offered a medium through which ideas and policies could be discussed. The parties of the left in particular provided a form of political access to ordinary people. However, parties increasingly began to evolve into electoral machines with their own centralised bureaucracies, and their role as mechanisms through which a range of ideas and demands could be debated and articulated has been eroded. At the same time, the 'neutral' expert has become an increasingly influential figure; the ideological content of expertise is obscured and access to alternative 'non-expert' policy approaches is delegitimised.

In the twentieth century, new technologies have facilitated populism. Pre-modern methods of electioneering - public meetings, door-to-door canvassing, the political pamphlet - have increasingly been replaced by advertisements, party political broadcasts and televisual events, designed around marketing techniques, based on opinion poll data. The citizen chooses a candidate in much the same way as he/she chooses a product and the candidate is accordingly packaged, according to image consultants. Policies may be shaped as much by minor fluctuations in opinion polls as by serious debate. This system is an effective way to reproduce the political elite while ignoring the frustration of minorities and denying political access to those outside the political game, as played on television.

Only a few very small countries, perhaps Denmark or the Netherlands, seem to be successful in sustaining democracies which are not merely formal, but involve genuine public participation in decision-making. However, there are problems for small countries as well. Since many current problems are transnational in nature, nation-states do not have the capacity to resolve them - hence the ability to influence decision-making about issues which directly affect the lives of the citizens is also circumscribed by the fact that nation-states are too small.

The nation-state is also too large for cultural diversity. Even though some nation-states did, initially, try to celebrate multiculturalism - for example, in Britain - the dominance of the national language and the sway of national administration gradually eliminated lesser dialects and cultures. In the twentieth century, moreover, new unifying cultures developed in the large nation-states like the USA or the Soviet Union - the unifying culture of materialism or, in the case of the Soviet Union, of a secular Marxist-Leninist ideology. The anonymity and alienation of the mass modernising cultures explains the longing to reclaim older cultural identities, and the trend towards secession, the claim of very small cultural groups to be a nation.

Yet at the same time, the nation-state is too small to preserve national culture. The state can no longer control the flow of information. If print technology created a new national communicative network, then electronic technology, the technology of television, the computer, the fax or the telephone, has created an entirely new set of transnational communicative networks, which are beyond the reach of any one state, and can undermine cultural norms or national regulations.

The nation-state is also too small to manage economic and ecological interdependence or to conduct wars. Over the last two hundred years, there has been a huge increase in trade, migration and the international transfer of finance and/or technology. Multinational companies are often larger than nation-states and control a considerable share of world trade and have at their disposal an almost infinite range of methods for evading national regulations. The idea of a national economy so much favoured by early nationalists, no longer reflects reality. Governments can still influence national economic development through the provision of infrastructure and through national economic policies such as exchange rates, interest rates or fiscal measures. Nevertheless, they have far less influence than only twenty years ago.

The same is true for the environment. Chernobyl demonstrated that radiation does not respect national borders. Nor do acid rain, holes in the ozone layer, the greenhouse effect or the pollution of rivers and seas. These problems can only be resolved internationally.

Yet at the same time, such is the complexity of modern economic and ecological problems that decisions cannot be overcentralised; this is vividly demonstrated by the experience of centrally administered economies. Hence the nation-state is also too large to manage the complexity and diversity of modern society.

The nation-state is also too small for wars. It is often argued that the advent of nuclear weapons means that war can no longer be an instrument of policy since nuclear weapons can not be used. In fact, nuclear weapons are merely the most extreme consequence of a general phenomenon - the application of science and technology to warfare. Especially since the advent of electronics technologies, the accuracy and destructiveness of all weapons have greatly increased. The value of using force to achieve limited or specific objectives, especially against a similarly armed opponent, is becoming questionable. Nation-states have become increasingly reluctant to use force unless casualties to their own side can be minimised, and this is extremely expensive. Just consider what it cost to liberate Kuwait, around $150 billion, several times greater than what the West has provided in economic aid to Eastern Europe.

Yet in part because nation-states are becoming too small for wars, private armies are re-emerging. The new wars in places like Bosnia, Somalia and Northern Ireland are not interstate wars on the Clausewitzean model. Nor are they classic civil wars because there is considerable international involvement - expatriate groups, humanitarian NGO's, outside powers, international peacekeepers, journalists, and so on. In essence, they constitute a profound challenge to the notion that any given national institution can claim a monopoly of legitimate organised violence in a given territory.

War still seems to have a domestic and political value as a spectacle and as a form of organisation. Observed on television, it serves to uphold the national spirit. Experienced first hand, it serves to instil fear and discipline and to uphold authority. But it cannot, in Clausewitz's words 'compel our opponent to fulfil our will', or at least it can only do so at enormous cost in resources and lives.

During the post-Second World War period, new international organisations came into being, or at any rate, their role was greatly extended. These new organisations were mostly intergovernmental. Their power was derived from their member states and the strongest nations dominated the organisations. There were, of course, elements of supranationality in some organisations, notably the European Community.

In international relations literature, the term 'international regime' is used to describe horizontal organisations of states. Of particular importance was the rise of the bloc system which determined the political composition of international organisations; it could be described as an international organising principle. The advent of the bloc system can be viewed as a way of overcoming some of the inadequacies of the nation-state, at least those that arose from the fact that the nation-state was too small. It was a kind of experiment in post-nation-state methods of political organisation.

The bloc system allowed for the creation of bloc economies and it replaced real war by imaginary war, which confirmed the advantages of new forms of war as a spectacle and form of political organisation while avoiding the destructiveness of real war, in much the same way that George Orwell anticipated in *Nineteen Eighty-Four*.

The blocs represented a break with the nation-state in two respects. First, they broke down the administrative sovereignty of the nation-state over national territory. The integration of armed forces into joint command systems meant that no single nation-state except the Soviet Union and the United States, and to a lesser extent Britain and France, had an independent capacity to wage wars. And this symbolic loss of sovereignty was expressed in a real political and administrative interdependence, especially in Western Europe. The blocs both greatly extended administration and, at the same time, weakened exclusive national control.

Second, the national idea was increasingly supplanted by the bloc idea - the defence of ideology rather than of national culture. If nations can be defined as 'imagined communities', blocs were defined by an imaginary war, a perpetual struggle, expressed in a permanent military confrontation, between, in their own terms, the idea of 'socialism' and the idea of 'freedom'. Moveover, unlike the idea of the nation which was inherently limited, the idea of 'freedom' or of 'socialism' was, in principle, universal and not tied to territory.

Of course there were considerable differences between East and West. The Eastern bloc, in many respects, represented a reversion to empire. It was as though the Tsarist empire had combined with the administrative techniques of the nation-state to produce the ultimate expression of administrative extension and cultural homogenisation, namely totalitarianism. It was simply not possible to sustain the Eastern bloc as a closed economy and a closed system of administration and culture. In contrast, the Western bloc could be said to prefigure new transnational political organisation although it also had elements of empire. The role of the blocs in protecting ideology, in some respects, echoed the role of pre-national empires in protecting faith.

If the blocs overcame the limitations of the nation-state that arose from the fact that the nation-state was too small, they could not overcome the problems that arose from the fact that the nation-state was too large. The absence of cultural diversity and democracy was self-evident in the East. In the West, materialism as well as blocism supplanted national culture and the functioning of democracy was constrained by the permanent atmosphere of struggle. The Cold War legitimised secrecy, surveillance and other measures characteristic of wartime. What is more, the tendency for international regimes, especially the blocs, to replace national decision-making without a corresponding internationalisation of democratic procedures, also weakened democratic control.

With the advent of what is known as 'globalisation', the blocs may also be too small. With global communications, it is becoming increasingly difficult to insulate any area from political or economic turbulence in any other part of the world. The Western bloc has not collapsed. But with the collapse of the Eastern bloc it has lost its *raison d'être*, its organising principle. So what replaces the blocs?

FUTURE POLITICAL INSTITUTIONS

The end of the Cold War came about, in part, because of the emergence of a transnational civil society in Europe. By civil society, I do not simply mean the rule of law instead of the rule of force. Nor do I mean everything in society that is not the state. Rather, I mean self-organised autonomous groups and institutions that are actively responsible for public affairs. It was the growth of such a civil society in Eastern Europe in the 1980s, supported and sustained by similar groups and institutions in the West, that penetrated the closed administrative system of the Soviet bloc.

In the aftermath of the Cold War, we are witnessing the emergence of a new sort of nationalism, at least in the East. It is nationalism that builds on the deep-rooted desire for cultural identity and the pervasive dissatisfaction with the previous system but which is used to preserve inherited authoritarian structures and to suppress the newly emerging civil society. It is a nationalism in which cultural self-determination, based on birthright, is much more important than democratic self-determination. This is what is meant by the term ethnicity which was characteristic of 'latecomer' nationalism. Particularly in the Balkans and in the former Soviet republics where there has been little or no democratic experience, it is easy enough to substitute national polarisation for ideological polarisation, the national idea for the socialist idea, nation-states for blocs, as a way of maintaining administrative control and the wartime atmosphere which is characteristic of authoritarianism. In the West, the unexpected difficulties confronted by the post-Maastricht process and the rise of the new Right also seem to indicate the emergence of a new or rediscovered sort of nationalism.

A reversion to nation-states is a dead end. Not only a dead-end in terms of political organisation but maybe in terms of civilisation as well. It is extremely difficult to envisage any solution to deep-rooted economic and ecological problems if nationalism finds its only outlet in culturally homogenising and administratively totalising forms of state power. National polarisation and cultural exclusivism can only lead to violent, destructive and ultimately pointless wars.

What is needed now is to develop proposals and ideas for new kinds of political organisation which can overcome the limitations of both being too large and too small, resolve both international and local problems, and offer a humane outlet for nationalist energies that does not involve the suppression of civil society or the exclusion of minorities. One of the explanations for Europe's historical dynamism is the diversity of political institutions; any innovator who was constrained in one political environment could always move to a different environment. This institutional diversity brought material progress and cultural excellence, but it also brought conflict, imperialism and war. Are there ways in which the advantages of political diversity can be preserved while avoiding the disadvantages?

One answer is that diversity need not be based on territory. The key feature of the nation-state was absolute administrative control over a particular territory. The new post-war international regimes do offer an alternative possibility, namely that administrative control could be based on fields of activity or competence and, moreover, administrative control could be shared. The buzz word in discussions of European institutions today is 'interlocking institutions'. It is possible to envisage various layers of political organisation with different but overlapping responsibilities.

The first layer of political organisation consists of local or regional territorially democratically elected political units, like municipalities or provinces, that have as much responsibility as possible for as wide a field of policy-making as possible, including economic policy and foreign policy. In EC jargon, the principle of subsidiarity would mean that as many decisions as possible are taken by the smallest unit of administration or the lowest layer of political organisation.

One of the arguments for the nation-state was industrialisation and the growth of a national economy. Nowadays, the economy is global and there are undoubtedly requirements for global financial management, global standards and so on. But, at the same time, mass production and mass consumption in a physical sense are less important. The advent of computers means that, instead of the production of standardised products on huge assembly lines, it is possible to produce reprogrammable standardised machines that can cater to a much wider variety of tastes and produce in much smaller quantities. So products and production processes can be organised around local skills and local markets. Hence local economic policies, suited to local conditions, are more likely to succeed than national economic policies which lack local knowledge.

The same kind of argument can be applied to foreign policy. Municipal participation in foreign policy has expanded in recent years with the declaration of nuclear free zones, peace zones and twinning arrangements. Such participation is facilitated by cheap travel and new forms of communication - automatic dialling, faxes and so on.

Unlike nation-states, however, these territorially-based units would not enjoy absolute administrative control. Their power would be limited by agreements at higher layers about certain common standards, such as respect for human rights, common environmental regulations, finances or trade agreements. Just as family life is no longer considered a totally private domain, the same has to be true in the future for territorially-based political units.

The second layer is international organisation, which may be global or regional. Such organisations already exist - the United Nations, International Monetary Fund, the European Union, Conference on Security and Cooperation in Europe (CSCE), General Agreement on Trade and Tariffs, Comecon, and so on. Up to now, their power has been derived largely from the member nation-states. What is needed are international organisations that possess a certain degree of sovereignty and accountability and yet do not become large nation-states. They need to have sovereignty in their areas of competence to interfere, for example, in the activities of local units in order to ensure, say, the observance of human rights. But their fields of competence need to be limited to certain areas - security, trade, environment, human rights - even though they may sometimes overlap. Their role could be described as not so much interventionist as enabling. Their function is to provide conditions for self-governance at local and regional levels. These conditions may be financial, for example through various mechanisms for the redistribution of resources. Or they may be military, through securing protected demilitarised areas in which democratic governance can operate.

Thus these organisations would enhance democratic governance through support for lower tiers of governance as well as for the strengthening of civil society. But they would also have to be democratically organised. The problem is how to ensure democratic accountability beyond accountability to the constituent states. One way is to establish a parliament of constituents units, namely municipalities or provinces. Another way is to establish democratically elected parliaments as in the case of the EC. The problem with this approach is that it could magnify the limitations of mass politics, transferring the techniques of image building, opinion poll manipulation, and so on, to the international level. Also, it is very difficult to engage a wide range of people in international politics. Voter turnout for US federal elections is very low. Voter turnout for European Parliamentary elections is only 30 per cent.

Another solution, which ought to be combined with a parliamentary system of some kind, is formal participation by relevant Non-Governmental Organisations (NGOs). This is rather similar to something proposed by Hannah Arendt in *On Revolution*. She is critical of the principle of universal suffrage because of its homogenising tendencies. She proposes that 'normal' politics should be complemented by a new form of politics based on voluntary associations, 'islands in the sea' of mass politics. She talks about the development of new 'aristocratic' elites to revive republicanism, but who are self-selected and self-organised. 'What the US needs', she says is 'a completely different principle of organisation, which begins from below, continues upward, and finally leads to a parliament .... Since the country is too big for all of us to come together and determine our fate, we need a number of political spaces within it' (quoted in Isaacs, 1994).

In a sense, Hannah Arendt's self-selected 'aristocracy' could be constituted by the new social movements that emerged in the 1970s and 1980s. One of the interesting features of the new social movements is their transnational character, in contrast to earlier emancipatory movements, say, labour movements, which aimed at national politics. These movements partly arose in order to address issues that were not addressed by existing political parties - peace, green, gender or human rights issues. And partly because, even in the West, parties cannot offer a site for genuine political debate because of their preoccupation with electoral politics. This is what Vaclav Havel meant by 'speaking the truth'. These movements have been rather unsuccessful at transforming themselves into political parties, even in post-1989 Eastern Europe. But in contrast to political parties, new social movements or NGOs like Amnesty International, Greenpeace or the Helsinki Citizens Assembly (HCA), have transnational constituencies.

The concerns of the new movements do parallel the concerns of international organisations. Hence, it could make sense to formalise their participation. Already, several international organisations pay lip service to the role of the NGOs - the UN, the CSCE or the Council of Europe. The Council of Europe has gone furthest in establishing consultative status for NGOs. The HCA has such a status and it does confer some real benefits such as joint seminars and joint activities. But in the case of the UN and the CSCE, NGO participation merely means parallel space and the occasional meeting with the media or with national delegations. The new social movements have to be recognised as organisations which specialise in particular issues and are genuinely concerned with the public interest. They offer an alternative to the so-called 'neutral' expert by providing a medium through which views on specialised issues can be expressed. Of course, they also tend to be confined to a narrow strata of society, mainly educated groups. Moreover, there is and must be a plurality of views about what constitutes the public interest and international organisations, however constituted, need to debate that plurality of views in order to improve the quality of decision-making. Hence the problem of how to recognise particular organisations as appropriate partners and how to reach out to a wider spectrum of people has to be addressed.

The third and final layer consists of national units. They could be viewed as the repositories of national culture with responsibilities for language and traditions. The national units might be territorially based units roughly corresponding to their present territorial sway or on a par with local and regional units. But they would not be nation-states in the traditional sense because administrative control would be limited both by international organisations and by local units.

It might also be possible to envisage national units that are not necessarily territorially-based. The new nationalism is actually transnational in character. It was always the case that national movements were able to call on the support of exiles. Today that element in national movements is much more important for two reasons. One is the desire of large groups of expatriates in new nations, like the United States, Australia or Canada, to reassert their cultural identities. (Perhaps this results from the longing to escape the anonymity conferred by a unifying materialist culture.) The other is the ease of communication - the speed at which expatriate groups can provide money, ideas, arms, advice, techniques, and so on. The role of Tyminski in Poland, Canadian mercenaries in Croatia, or Irish American support for the IRA are all examples of this kind of influence and the emergence of what might be called diaspora nationalism.

Why should not national units in fact become transnational organisations? They could have offices in the 'homeland', the national capital perhaps. But they could provide cultural services - language teaching, musical festivals and so on - to all nationals wherever they are based. This is, for example, how the Scottish clans work. The heads of the clans still consider themselves responsible for clansmen in America, Canada and Australia. And there are some nations, for example the Roma, that have no fixed territory and yet desire something more than a voluntary organisation to protect their rights and cultures.

National units might even continue to be responsible for armies. They are after all cultural relics of the nation - Scottish bagpipers or Croatian National Guardsmen in Hungarian uniforms. But these armies would have to be integrated into an international security system - the CSCE, an expanded NATO, the UN. And a network of arms control agreements, inspection regimes and confidence-building measures would limit the independent capacity to wage war.

Such a layering of political institutions raises the question as to which political unit would an individual belong. Can he or she choose one or several political units? Can he or she choose to whom he or she pays taxes? There is no reason why an individual cannot define his or her political identity both in terms of a local unit, where he or she lives, and in terms of one or more national units, and schemes could be devised for sharing out taxes and for voting.

What would this imply for the concept of citizenship? The passive concept of citizenship tends to mean nationality, the right to a passport, the right to receive welfare benefits. For democratic governance, citizenship has to have an active connotation again; it has to mean the possession of sovereignty, responsibility for public affairs and participation in civil society. But this can no longer be equated with nationality. Democratic governance requires a transnational civil society both in the sense of a transnational rule of law and in the sense of self-organisation. A citizen has to have several political identities, one of which may be national but others have to be shaped by a globalist political culture. This is a complex and difficult agenda. Active citizenship implies an uphill struggle against forms of authoritarianism that inevitably tend to be associated with the attempt to build traditional exclusive nation-states in the current interdependent world.

NOTE

1. British nationals remain formally 'subjects' but with the development of a constitutional monarchy, their status as subjects began to be transformed.

REFERENCES

Gellner, Ernest (1991), 'Nationalism and Politics in Eastern Europe', *New Left Review,* September-October.

Isaacs, Jeffrey C. (1994), 'Oases in the Desert: Hannah Arendt on Democratic Politics', *American Political Science Review*, Vol. 88, No. 1, March.

Tilly, C. (1975), 'Reflections on the history of European state-making' in Tilly, ed., *The Formation of Nation-states in Western Europe,* Princeton University Press.

3. Democracy and Nationalism in Czechoslovakia

Zdenek Kavan

On 17 November 1989, a student demonstration was held in Prague commemorating the fiftieth anniversary of the death of Jan Opletal, a medical student shot by the Nazis at an anti-German demonstration. This memorial demonstration, and particularly the violence used against the peaceful demonstrators by the security forces, sparked off the 'revolution' which was to sweep away the communist regime which had held power in Czechoslovakia for over forty years in just a few weeks (see Wheaton and Kavan, 1992, for a detailed account). By the end of the year a post-communist government was in power and the process of transition towards a Western-oriented, market-based democracy had begun. Almost exactly three years later, on 1 January 1993, Czechoslovakia ceased to exist and was succeeded by two new states, the Czech Republic and Slovakia. This paper examines the transition process and why it led to the disintegration of the Czechoslovak state along national lines within such a relatively short period of time. It will argue that nationalism, though an important cause of the disintegration of the Czechoslovak state, was not the primary cause. Rather, the existing national differences were exacerbated by the fact that conflicts of interests, policies and outlooks that partly arose from and partly accompanied the process of transition towards democracy and a market economy were managed within quite narrow boundaries of legitimate disagreement. What is meant by the boundaries of legitimate disagreement here is the range of ideas, claims, demands and interests that can be voiced legitimately, that is those that society recognises as having a rightful status. It defines the range of tolerance of differences and disempowers interests and claims outside of that range. It also establishes the parameters for the legitimation of governments. It was the relative lack of practical experience with the management of democracy and the long history of authoritarian rule that mitigated against the widening of these boundaries. In these circumstances nationalism came to be used more widely by certain sections of the new elites as the source of legitimation of their interests and policy positions and the source of delegitimation of the interests and policy positions of their opponent.

The impact of previous history on the transition process necessitates that at least a brief summary be given of the state of Czechoslovak society at the time of the collapse of the communist regime. Twenty years of a 'normalised' regime in which the authorities tended to perceive any change and any reform as potentially dangerous and destabilising produced a largely alienated and disillusioned society, particularly in the Czech part of the republic, in which the bulk of the population retreated into the private sphere. This retreat manifested itself by preoccupation with the welfare of one's family, the most visible signs of which were the myriads of weekend cottages that mushroomed all over the countryside. Not only did the building and maintenance of these cottages consume a large part of the leisure time and resources of the average citizen but the weekend and holiday escape into these cottages was a real as well as a symbolic escape from the oppressive realities of urban social existence.

The survival of the regime was based not on its legitimacy but on the conformist apathy it generated. This apathy was maintained not only through the fear of punishment of non-conformist behaviour, and here the treatment of dissidents served as a powerful deterrent, but also through the lack of popular belief in the reformability of the communist system and the widespread sense of the futility of trying to achieve a change for the better. The crushing of reformist hopes through the Soviet intervention and the subsequent process of 'normalisation' profoundly affected the outlook of most Czechs and Slovaks. At the core of the 'normalised' regime's survival, however, lay a kind of social contract. In exchange for the citizens' non-interference in the process of government, the state socialist authorities granted them the basic security of a job that did not demand hard work and a bearable standard of living. One of the most far-reaching implications of this contract was that the conforming individual was largely absolved of the need to take responsibility. Civil society in contradistinction to the state was largely absent and with it any chance of exercising genuine active citizenship.

Overt opposition to the regime was restricted to a relatively isolated group of dissidents, Charter 77, indirectly supported by the growth of a counterculture, particularly among the young, in the 1980s. This isolation of the Charter was not due just to the efforts of the regime to keep them so, but also to the way that Charter 77 challenged the implicit social contract. 'Living in truth' as an example of moral integrity, of the refusal to participate in the public endorsement of the institutionalized lie, presented a challenge not just to the government but also to the ordinary people. As Kusy has pointed out, the people had something to lose:

> [The] misgivings of the nation towards the Charter increase where the Charter affects people's consciences directly. Look at it this way: this exclusive association of Chartists has decided to live from now on in truth, to struggle against evil and wrong doing. Some may have what it takes, but we, the vast majority of the nation, cannot afford such a luxury. We have children, we are building houses and cottages ... we're paying off a debt, we want a peaceful old age ... [Moreover] ... by demanding that the regime consistently obey its own laws, you necessarily interfere in our private sphere as well. If the state organs began to function as they ought, then we too would have to work as we ought; if they stopped stealing wholesale from the nation, they would stop us doing it in retail; if they stopped pretending that the plans were being fulfilled, then it would be up to us to fulfil them in fact. If they started taking seriously those ideals of socialist man, socialist work relations, socialist competition, the whole real-socialist ideology, we, and we alone would be the ones to suffer. (Kusy in Havel, 1985, pp. 168-9)

The national question, particularly the relations between the Czechs and the Slovaks, was never fully resolved. Conflicts over the nature of the common state and over the respective legitimate national aspirations of the Czechs and the Slovaks go back to the creation of modern Czechoslovakia in 1918. There was no symmetry to their relations. Interwar Czechoslovakia was a unitary state based on the Czech assumption of common Czechoslovak nationhood, which in practice meant that the Slovaks were expected to adopt Czech culture and identity. Dissatisfied claims by Slovak nationalists created a potential for disintegration aptly illustrated by the emergence of a puppet Slovak state during the Second World War under German tutelage. Various changes took place after 1945, which involved a degree of recognition of Slovak nationhood and its rightful claim to political recognition and a degree of autonomy culminating in the federalisation of the state in 1968. However, this process was severely circumscribed by the fact that Czechoslovakia remained a communist state which, in spite of the important constitutional changes, remained de facto highly centralised. The leadership of the Communist Party in Prague continued to make binding policy decisions for both republics. At the same time, however, the originally very great economic and social differences between the two parts of the country were significantly eroded through Slovakia's rapid industrialisation under the communist regime and through the common experience that this regime generated. In the late 1980s, although there was scope and potential for national resentments and conflicts they were not, in fact, manifesting themselves very acutely.

The revolution that swept away the communist regime in 1989 came suddenly. In spite of the relative growth of opposition to the regime throughout 1988-89 it was also experienced as unexpected by most of its protagonists. Although mass demonstrations did take place in Prague and some of the other major urban centres and these provided the last push to a regime that was largely disintegrating from within, neither the extent of the weakness of the regime nor the relative ease with which it would be toppled were widely anticipated. The failure of economic policy and the inability of an illegitimate government to introduce necessary changes which would require a degree of sacrifice on the part of the people and thus undermine the social contract, the absence of political know-how on the part of the authorities, the loss of the Soviet commitment to bolster up the regime come what may and the resulting loss of credibility of the threat of Soviet intervention, and the dramatic changes in the neighbouring East European countries, all contributed to the regime's massive loss of nerve. The result was that the collapse of the regime was both swift and peaceful. Despite the large numbers taking part in the demonstrations, the orderly transfer of power to post-communist authority was negotiated by a relatively small number of people drawn mainly from among the ranks of the dissidents. The appearance of a civic movement, the Civic Forum, masked a relative absence of a broadly based democratisation.

The new transitional authorities were drawn from four groups of people: dissident circles; supporters of dissent who had not, however, actively joined and participated in dissident activity; others, mostly ambitious professionals, who joined the revolution after its outbreak; and finally, some less compromised members of the old communist regime. Of these groups it was the dissidents who, at least partly due to the prestige that their former dissidence was now giving them, came to be in a position of dominance. Their influence, however, for reasons that will be elaborated below, soon declined and was gradually replaced by that of the professionals and new ambitious politicians. The language and strategy of the leading dissidents such as Vaclav Havel and Jiri Dientsbier, with its emphasis on citizenship and civil society was partly adopted by these new politicians but became transformed in the process. The precepts of anti-politics were soon challenged and overturned.

Initially a broad, general agreement existed among both the new elites and the majority of the people on the goals to be pursued and achieved. These were the construction of a market economy and a pluralist democracy, 'return' to Europe, and a reconstruction of civil society. This consensus was based on some limitations, however. 'The lack of any recent history of democratic public discourse, the misuse of language under the old regime, and the absence of institutions and practices to which the discourse could refer confounded the problem of establishing an adequate degree of shared public understanding of certain central terms' (Wheaton and Kavan,

1992, p. 128). Thus terms such as 'democracy' and market were often treated in a contradictory sense or as simple negations of their communist opposites (leading role of the party and centrally planned economy). The process of giving real content to these terms and goals proved to be conflictual, and quickly shattered the illusion of unity. This conflictual process soon came to be linked with the national problematic.

ECONOMIC REFORM

Major disagreements soon emerged between the economic radicals of the neo-liberal and monetarist kind and the Keynesians and social democrats. Although a market economy was the accepted goal there were bitter disagreements about the speed of transition and, to a lesser extent, its process, particularly as to the question of whether liberalisation of prices should precede de-monopolisation or vice versa. The main fear of the opponents of fast transformation was that the liberalisation of prices and hence the rapid introduction of the market mechanism would bring both rapid inflation and rising unemployment. They feared the potentially prohibitive social costs and argued that the market, in any case, must be tempered by social considerations as well as those of justice. The radicals emphasised the rationality of the market and the impossibility of finding a functioning alternative for making economic choices. As to the social consequences, the radicals argued that they may indeed be somewhat worse in the short term if the radical programme was adopted but in the medium to long term the social consequences would be much better. The additional advantage of the radical strategy would be, in their view, that in the short term people would be prepared to make sacrifices in the euphoria of the immediate post-communist period but that the willingness to accept such sacrifices might soon dissipate.

This contest soon began to have repercussions for the national question as well as the construction of democracy. The victory of the radicals led by Vaclav Klaus and Vladimir Dlouhy (Ministers of Finance and Planning respectively) at the federal level and in the Czech Republic was not duplicated in Slovakia. There the much more outdated industrial structure which resulted from the communist form of industrialisation with its emphasis on heavy industry, with a disproportionately high allocation of defence industries to Slovakia, made the economy much more vulnerable to the negative consequences of the new economic conditions that arose out of the virtual collapse of the Soviet and other East European markets. The difficulty of finding alternative customers contributed significantly to declining exports and consequently to the rising unemployment (this was to reach 12 per cent in Slovakia in 1992 as against 4 per cent in the Czech Republic). It is not surprising that in Slovakia a strategy demanding a slower approach, continuing state subsidies and cushioning from the negative impact of transition, proved more popular. At the same time the disparities between the Czech and Slovak positions raised the question of the power and role of federal institutions.

The impact on the development of democracy was twofold. First it began to damage the unity of the ruling Civic Forum (more about that below) and second it affected the construction of the public discourse. The public debate about economic transformation was characterised by a relatively low level of tolerance and by the language of delegitimation, particularly from the neo-liberals, which was not conducive to compromise construction. 'There is no third way', 'anyone who wishes to retain an important role for the state is an opponent of reforms, if not a socialist' were arguments frequently used to delegitimise opponents. Usage of the language of exaggeration and delegitimation was frankly acknowledged by Klaus: 'In order to move the pendulum by a single centimeter to the right, I must first shift it in my efforts at argument by at least two kilometers ... I clearly cannot use the argument of those more or less left-wing economists and politicians who support state intervention, but I use the argument appropriate to the direction required' (Wheaton and Kavan, 1992, p. 162). Opponents were further delegitimised by associating them with the 1968 reforms, or questioning the professional expertise of those who as dissidents had been unable to practise their profession for the previous two decades. Economics is a hard science, it was argued, and those not on the cutting edge of it should not be paid much attention. The authoritative role of the professionals, this time *vis-à-vis* the general public, is exemplified by Dlouhy in an illuminating statement about the relationship between economic policy and democracy.

> In the world, an economic program is usually associated with the electoral cycle, that is, with a political party or coalition. These parties do not usually submit such programs to the 'working people' for widespread discussion. Their programs tend to be formulated by experts, and the elected government then simply implements them. The democratic control of its implementation is then guaranteed by Parliament and the plurality of political parties. (Wheaton and Kavan, 1992, p. 163)

To be fair, the simplicity and forcefulness of the neo-liberals' message and their appeal to the authority of expertise fell on fertile ground. Most people, unfamiliar with public debates and particularly with those concerning economic policy, found the issues puzzling and tended to respond to clear and authoritative propositions. Klaus in particular soon became one of the most respected and popular politicians in the country.

Though the radicals emerged victorious from this contest of economic strategies in the federal institutions this did not mean that the actual economic policy implemented genuinely reflected the public rhetoric. Klaus, as Minister of Finance and subsequently as the Czech Prime Minister, pursued a policy somewhat at odds with his publicly stated commitment to economic neo-liberalism. The role of the state in maintaining support for the industry in particular remained very much part of this policy. However, the aspect of the public economic policy debate that vitally concerns us here is the way that the use of deliberate strategy of exaggeration and delegitimation contributed to the narrowing of the boundaries of legitimate consensus building. The impact of this on the unity of a broad-based civic movement, the Civic Forum, was not long delayed.

POLITICAL REFORM

The first post-communist elections held in June 1990 brought to power civic movements at the federal level as well as in both republics (Civic Forum and Public Against Violence, respectively). Cracks had already, though, begun to appear even before the elections and by the end of the year the Civic Forum in particular was facing a crisis. The disagreements concerning economic policy were developing into disagreements about the nature of the Civic Forum. The radicals, led by Klaus, impatient with the divisions within the movement, with the cumbersome process of consensus construction and with the lack of power of the leadership to discipline its elected members of parliament to stick to the 'party line', argued for the Civic Forum to be speedily transformed into a political party of a more homogeneous nature. The resulting party would not be an important forum for policy-making and public debate, but its central function would be to act as a disciplined executor of government decisions. To ensure the party's homogeneity and define its electoral focus clearly as lying on the centre-right, all those group and individual members of the Civic Forum outside of these boundaries were to be purged. The opponents of this view argued that for the foreseeable future democratic politics ought to be based on civic movements, as the majority of the population remained deeply suspicious of the 'party principle' and, in any case, their inexperience with party politics would make them vulnerable to populist appeals.

In a crucial sense the dispute about the future of the Civic Forum represented a conflict between two conceptions of democratic politics. The radicals, concerned less with issues of ethics and justice, impatient with the legacy of 'anti-political politics', and concerned mainly with policy-making and the effectiveness of policies, perceived politics largely in terms of a struggle for power and democratic politics as a pluralist system of struggle for power. Parties were instruments for mobilising electoral support. Their opponents, drawn mainly from the ranks of former dissidents, perceived civil society to be the crucial element of the democratic process and that process to be not only about competition but also about consensus, not only about interests but also about ethics. President Havel expressed his position in the following terms:

> I am not against political parties ... I am against the excessive influence of parties in the system of political power. ... Excessive emphasis on political parties can have many unfortunate consequences. For example, loyalty to the party leadership or the party apparatus can count for more than the will of the electorate or the abilities of the politician. ... Ideas, no matter how absurd, are touted purely to gain favour with the electorate. (Havel, 1992, pp. 53-5)

The victory of Vaclav Klaus in the contest for the leadership of the Civic Forum in October 1990 presaged the disintegration of the Civic Forum into several parties, the largest of which was led by Klaus himself. This process heralded a shift towards party politics and competition, and weakened consensus building. In the right-wing parties that emerged from the Civic Forum, being a former dissident no longer counted as a political advantage. The shift of power towards the right, completed at the next elections in June 1992, heralded a gradual but accelerating decline in the influence of the former dissidents and meant a virtually total defeat for the 'anti-political politics' conception.

An important part of this process of conflictual politics and the marginalisation of former dissidents was the total delegitimation of the previous communist regime. Legislation was used to specify that that regime had been a criminal one and other legislative acts, for instance the restitution law, were formulated to delegitimise all actions of the communist regime including the reforms of 1968. It was important for the new Right to proclaim the unreformability of socialism and a total dissociation from it. The dissidents, among whose number were a great many former reform communists, whose activities had brought them into contact with the communist regime in various forms, were made vulnerable to this process of delegitimation. Paradoxically, it implied that anybody who engaged in dissenting activity under the old regime was seen as less reliable and less suitable for positions of responsibility than those who had engaged in no political activity before 1989. In fact, only a handful of former dissidents retained positions of political influence after the 1992 elections.

The emergence of a great number of new parties, quite often with scarcely discernible real differences between them and with little experience of party politics, exacerbated the problem, thus further narrowing down the parameters of legitimate debate. New parties, partly as vehicles for the ambitions of new politicians, sought to carve out a niche for themselves within a rather narrow spectrum of ideological positions, by grossly exaggerating the significance of quite often very minor differences between them and by engaging in the process of not just distancing themselves from their competitors but of trying to delegitimise them. Thus accusations of communist sympathies were hurled at social democrats as well as at some social liberals. Politics was seen more and more as a virile business and compromise as a sign of weakness.

Developments in Slovakia did not quite follow the same path. Although the Civic Forum's sister organisation, Public Against Violence, emerged victorious from the 1990 elections, it was less clearly associated with the old dissident political culture. There had, indeed, been relatively few dissidents in Slovakia. The major difference between the two civic movements was that the Slovak one was more prone to overt forms of nationalism, and was less committed to a non-ethnic conceptualisation of citizenship. Only one Slovak party, the Slovak National Party, had an overtly nationalist programme and advocated Slovak independence, and this party did relatively badly in the 1990 elections. None the less, most Slovak parties came to adopt positions sympathetic to nationalism. There seemed to be two main reasons for this. The first was to do with the perception of a lack of symmetry in the relations between the Czechs and the Slovaks. For the Czechs, the argument went, Czechoslovakia was a reconstitution of their historical state and created no problems for their already well-established national identity. The Slovaks had no such securely established identity buttressed by the experience of statehood. Many argued that such an identity could only be secured on the basis of experiencing a degree of independence. Related to that was the feeling that the Czechs showed little understanding of this Slovak ambition. Jozef Miklosko, chairman of the Slovak Parliament, claimed that 'the Czechs do not feel any problem with unfulfilled statehood. The ordinary Czech identifies more or less with the federal structure and feels no bitterness. We need to deal with this question very sensitively. I talked about it several times with President Havel and he grasped the fact that it is a serious existential problem for the Slovak nation' (quoted in Wheaton and Kavan, 1992, p. 170; also see Havel, 1992, p. 26). Many felt that traditionally Prague showed little sensitivity to Slovak concerns and interests. It has to be said, though, that the attempts of the Slovak nationalists to celebrate the Slovak fascist state that briefly existed during the Second World War was unlikely to generate much sensitivity and sympathy among the Czechs.

However, the strength and actual content of Slovak nationalism were not that easy to establish. As mentioned above, separatism remained a distinctly unpopular option and the demands for independence quite often had a largely symbolic function, where the symbols of independence were more important than the actual content of this independence. The common state was to be based on the recognition that sovereignty lay with the constituent republics and the power of the federal centre was dependent on the consent of both republics. This led to the insistence that a basic contract between the republics be drawn which would determine their mutual relations and upon which the constitution would rest. To the practical and legalistic Czechs the idea of the contract being above the constitution was, of course, unacceptable (about which more below).

As suggested above, the relationship between the ethnic and the civic principles was rather more ambiguous in Slovakia than in the Czech lands. Even the Public Against Violence civic movement recognised the importance of the national issue. What is more the movement, like the Civic Forum in the Czech lands, could not sustain its unity for very long. The cause of the disintegration of this movement was partly a disagreement about economic reform and the extent of the role of the state, but mostly concerned the figure of its first Prime Minister, Vladimir Meciar. Meciar's populism, ruthlessness and dedication to power created a great deal of resentment and mistrust among the leadership of the movement. They engineered his fall from office in April 1991 but thereby created a situation of considerable political instability. Meciar remained by far the most popular politician in Slovakia (opinion polls suggested that at the time of his fall from office he had the support of more than 80 per cent of all Slovaks, see Gal, 1992, p. 32) and he took with him into opposition the majority of the movement. The minority of the movement formed an unstable coalition with the Christian Democrats. Meciar's new movement developed a stronger nationalist and social character. Meciar's own position shifted, partly due to his perception that his fall was plotted in Prague, from a relatively pro-federalist position to a more strongly nationalist one. Perhaps, though, it would be fair to conclude that, given that the only consistency that Meciar displayed was the ambition to gain and keep power, his shift towards nationalism and use of much stronger nationalist rhetoric was purely tactical. It is to be noted, however, that all Slovak parties used nationalism in various forms without, with the exception of the Slovak National Party, showing much consistency, particularly as far as their attitude towards the federation was concerned.

The issue of the Hungarian minority in Slovakia further complicated the conflict between the ethnic and the civic principles. The dispute about the language laws demonstrated the difficulty most Slovaks had with trying to reconcile these principles. This confusion is well illustrated in the first Constitution of independent Slovakia where the preamble refers to 'We, the Slovak nation ... proceeding from the natural right of nations to self-determination, together with members of national minorities and ethnic groups living on the territory of the Slovak Republic ... we, citizens of the Slovak Republic'.

Disputes about economic policy were much less acute in Slovakia. The majority of parties, including the Christian Democrats on the Right, believed in the state having a considerable role to play in the management of the economy, and only a small minority supported Klaus's programme of rapid liberalisation and privatisation.

Furthermore, the Slovaks having been less dissatisfied with the communist regime than the Czechs had been were less prone to use and respond to the strategy of total delegitimation of everything associated with that regime. A good example is the more moderate approach there to 'lustration' (cleansing of state institutions and the media from certain categories of 'collaborators'). Radical anti-communism and economic rationality associated with neo-liberalism were not as readily available as means of legitimation of new authorities in Slovakia and this enhanced the role of nationalism in the process of legitimation there.

EUROPE

The 'return to Europe' had both symbolic and practical significance. The symbolic side had to do with the perception of national identity and for the Czechs in particular it signified their belonging to the West. This Western orientation had a strongly negative meaning, that is it was seen as the opposite to the East. Europe represented values and practices associated with individualism, democracy, the rule of law, human rights and liberty. The forty years of communism could be then comprehended as having been alien to the real national identity and as the result of a form of colonisation. The Slovaks had a less negative view of the previous regime and less of a myth of Westernness to uphold. For the Slovaks 'return to Europe' was less to do with their own identity and more to do with an eventual step to be undertaken after the establishment of a strong Slovakia. It is worth noting that the Czech media abounded with references to Central Europe as the location of the Republic whereas in Slovakia the term was used very infrequently. Slovaks tended to look at Central Europe and their place in it as a bridge between East and West, whereas for the Czechs Central Europe was a means of associating with the West (Svitek, 1991). It is interesting to note, in this respect, that after the disintegration of Czechoslovakia leading Czech politicians, including the new Prime Minister, Vaclav Klaus, proclaimed that without Slovakia the Czech Republic was no longer part of Central Europe but belonged to Western Europe.

On the more practical side 'return to Europe' was soon understood to mean membership of and integration into Western European institutions such as the EU and NATO. Two aspects of this are of interest here. The first is the way in which the goal of entry was presumed to dictate certain policies which in turn legitimised the position of particular political forces. A similar process of legitimation of particular policies involved other international organisations such as the IMF or the World Bank. The second aspect involved the growing perception of some radicals in the Czech Republic that entry into the EU would be much easier and speedier without Slovakia for both economic and strategic reasons.

CITIZENSHIP AND CIVIL SOCIETY

It is clear from the preceding discussion that major differences concerning the nature of citizenship, particularly concerning its ethnic or civic basis, developed both in Slovakia and the Czech lands. This section, however, will be concerned with the contrast between the conception of citizenship held by the dominant right-of-centre liberals and those who rooted citizenship in civil society.

The influential and popular Czech liberal philosopher, Vaclav Belohradsky, described citizenship in the following terms:

citizenship is a contract which guarantees all members of society the same rights. ... The crucial characteristic of citizenship is the right to act according to one's reason and conscience in free cooperation or competition with all other citizens. This right is guaranteed by the state. An important consequence of this citizens' contract is the legitimacy of a certain degree of class difference, because this difference arises out of varying success in enterprise, different abilities and different efforts undertaken by equal citizens. ... The content of citizenship in this sense could be described as freedom from pressure by external powers, be they the past or the will of the sovereign. Man, however, must be not only 'free from oppression', but also 'free to achieve his aims' and this 'freedom to' is realized in the market, where the citizen acts as a free owner ... in such a way as to gain cooperation from other people on the basis of a mutually beneficial exchange. 'Freedom to' is therefore a private matter, the result of our abilities. (Belohradsky, 1992, p. 83)

This echoes the position adopted by the main liberal parties in the Czech Republic well. It posits the separation of the state and the market and describes citizenship as defining the relationship between the individual member of society and the state. Good society is deemed to consist of free, self-determining and self-interested individuals who assume full responsibility for their own lives. It is not surprising, therefore, to see these parties adopting a position largely hostile to the codification of economic and quite a large measure of social rights. The effect of this restricted notion of citizenship on the weaker members of society or on women is that it legitimates their disempowerment (see Barbara Einhorn's chapter in this volume).

It is also a position which sees the role of civic movements in democracy to be at best relatively peripheral. Belohradsky again: 'the Civic Forum created with its anti-political politics a regime (which defines the framework of government), and personalized shared rules for the struggle for power and thus opened up the space for "political politics". But into this space it (the Civic Forum) must not enter as a civic movement, because it would constitute a rule of the regime, and the difference between regime and government would disappear again from public consciousness' (Belohradsky, 1992, p. 34).

The alternative views of citizenship which granted it economic and social dimensions tended to be marginalised in the Czech lands and given a more organically ethnic content in Slovakia. This marginalisation was not only due to the popularity of neo-liberalism but also to the fact that there was practically no dissension from the proposition that the state and the market should be separated. The association of the state's involvement with the market tended to be associated with the previous, communist regime and subjected to a simple process of negation. That politics was the sphere which was virtually fully occupied by political parties and that political involvement of individual citizens was to be largely channelled through these political parties became the new orthodoxy. The marginalisation of citizens' movements helped, however, to create a certain degree of separation between the average citizen and political power. A degree of disillusionment with politics was to that extent inevitable.

It is interesting to note that the neo-liberals' prioritisation of the market as a repository of liberty when coupled with the experience of associating with the EU led to the reconsideration of the value of nationality and nationalism. After independence the Prime Minister of the Czech Republic, Vaclav Klaus, stated that in the light of new experiences it was necessary 'to re-evaluate the original, too simplistic rejection of nationalism and acknowledge (and not be ashamed of) the legitimacy of national feelings'

(*Hospodarske noviny*, 22 December 1993). This is because European integration ought to be about the creation of a free market and not about the creation of a society. Given, he claimed, that immanent internationalism growing from below is not a realisable alternative, nationalism would constitute a powerful defence against an artificial, bureaucratic supranationalism from above.

CZECH-SLOVAK, RELATIONS AND THE END OF CZECHOSLOVAKIA

From the preceding sections it is clear that post-communist relations between the Czechs and Slovaks were wrought with some difficulties. The difficulties of resolving conflicts over policies were compounded by the constitution inherited from the communist regime. This constitution protected each nation against an imposition of policies by the other by requiring a qualified majority in both parts of the Federal Assembly which in effect meant that legislation could be blocked by a national group voting as a bloc. This, of course, had little real effect under communism but now led to frequent paralysis of parliament. The frequent use of this blocking power stopped or delayed the passage of important legislation even in areas where no real disagreements existed. It also helped to establish a habit of confrontation and non-cooperation rather than consensus building and led both sides to the recognition that the federal system in its existing form was dysfunctional.

A considerable amount of time was spent through the duration of the first elected post-communist government on debates and negotiations concerning a new constitutional allocation of power to the federal and republican institutions respectively. These negotiations failed to find a solution to the seeming contradiction between the aims of maximising the power of the republics and having a functional federal government capable of making decisions in defined areas of policy-making. The next and crucial elections in June 1992 were approached without an agreement on this issue. The possibility of the country splitting had already been raised. Havel, for instance, stated in March 1991 'rather than have a nonfunctioning federation that is felt to be an obstacle to the development of the republic, it is better to have two independent republics' (quoted in Wheaton and Kavan, 1992, p. 171). At the same time, however, none of the political parties, with the exception of the Slovak National Party, approached the elections with the specified aim of separation. Given that this party only secured less than 10 per cent of the vote in Slovakia (9.4 per cent for the Federal Assembly and 7.9 per cent for the Slovak National Council) this 'confirmed that there was little support even among Slovaks for separatism' (Wightman, 1993, p. 60). In fact throughout the year preceding the elections opinion polls consistently showed that support for full independence was relatively low in both republics. Nevertheless, the election result which brought a right-of-centre coalition under the leadership of Vaclav Klaus to power in the Czech Republic and a left-of-centre nationalist government under the leadership of Vladimir Meciar to power in Slovakia, made the separation virtually inevitable. The new Czech government's demand that the federal government had to have controlling power over economic policy and that this policy had to apply to the whole country was unacceptable to the Slovaks. The Slovak preference for a confederation with a weak central authority was dismissed as impracticable. There is little doubt that the Czech government was swayed by considerations of the potential coalition between the Czech Left and the Slovaks. Without the Slovaks the Czech Right could look forward to having a virtually unchallengeable position. The post-election negotiations between the two governments were largely concerned with the process of peaceful separation. It is noteworthy that these negotiations were conducted without much regard for the feelings of the electorate. The refusal to hold a referendum on the question of the continued existence of the state is particularly relevant here. The argument that the election did not provide the sanction for the government to bring about the end of Czechoslovakia was dismissed, and Klaus argued that a referendum would not achieve anything because even if the electorate voted against the splitting of the country the intractable problem of how to maintain it would still remain, and in any case the outcome could not be enforced peacefully because the Slovaks were committed to independence (see Draper, 1993, p.24 and Klimova, 1993, p. 50). The end of Czechoslovakia was decided by politicians and not by the electorate.

REFERENCES

Belohradsky, Vaclav (1992), *Kapitalismus a obcanske ctnosti*, Prague: Ceskoslovensky spisovatel.
Draper, Theodore (1993), 'The End of Czechoslovakia', in *The New York Review of Books*, 28 January 1993.
Gal, Fedor a kolektiv (1992), *Dnesni krize Cesko-Slovenskych vztahu*, Prague: Sociologicke nakladatelstvi.
Havel, Vaclav et al. (1985), *The Power of the Powerless*, London: Hutchinson.
Havel, Vaclav (1992), *Summer Meditations*, London: Faber & Faber.
Klaus, Vaclav (1993), *Rok, malo ci mnoho v dejinach zeme*, Prague: Repro-Media.
Klimova, Rita (1993), 'The End of Czechoslovakia: An Exchange', in *The New York Review of Books*, vol. XL, no. 7, 8 April 1993.

Kusy, Miroslav (1985), 'Chartism and "real socialism"', in Havel, Vaclav et al., *The Power of the Powerless,* London: Hutchinson.

Prins, Gwyn (1990), *Spring in Winter,* Manchester: Manchester University Press.

Svitek, Jiri (1991), 'Tisk ocima politologu', in *Reporter,* 3 July 1991.

Urban, Jan (1991), *Democracy and Nationalism in Central and Eastern Europe*, London: The David Davies Memorial Institute of International Studies.

Wheaton, Bernard and Kavan, Zdenek (1992), *The Velvet Revolution, Czechoslovakia, 1988-1991,* Boulder: Westview Press.

Wightman, Gordon (1993), 'The Czech and Slovak Republics', in White, S., Batt, J. and Lewis, P.G. (eds), *Developments in East European Politics*, London: Macmillan.

4. German Identities: the Impact of 'Unification'

Peter Lambert

In the aftermath of the rapid - and almost uncontested - unification of the two German states in 1990, the condition and prospects of democracy in Germany have demanded substantial reevaluation. Virtually without exception, analyses written before the autumn of 1989 were predicated on the continuing separate development of the two German states. Where German unification was addressed at all, it was usually to consign such a possibility to the never-never and occasionally even to warn against it as a threat to (West) German democracy.

There are indeed specific East German factors playing a part in a retreat from democratic politics since mid-1990. In the five new *Länder*, the democratic parties face undeniable problems. They have failed either to recruit a mass membership or to build stable constituencies of mass electoral support. These difficulties in a nascent parliamentary order have coincided with West German anxieties lest their era of prosperity be drawing to a close and with a phenomenon popularly described variously as 'vexation' with parties or indeed with politics (*Partei-* or *Politikverdrossenheit*).

The election results of 1990, in which the *Volksparteien* (people's parties, or parties appealing to the whole electorate) had dominated the West German electoral landscape even more completely than they had the East, seemed to signal that a unified Germany would repeat political patterns that had pertained prior to the emergence of new challenges by the Greens and the far right *Republikaner*. Both these parties had suffered marked setbacks in the 1990 election. However, it soon became evident that voting in that year was as poor an indicator of underlying political trends in the old as in the new *Länder*. It may appear premature to postulate a new crisis of legitimacy affecting the West German political system, but some commentators have gone still further than that, finding a crisis in West German identity. 'The Holy Trinity of post-war German identity, increasing prosperity, large, integrative *Volksparteien*, citizens voting in massive numbers, has broken' (*Der Spiegel*, 13, 1993: p. 142).

Politikverdrossenheit has multiple causes. It is not only a result of the agglomeration of corruption scandals which have plagued the FRG for over a decade now, much as their increasing density will assuredly have added to the irritability of the electorate. Equally clearly, the mood of disenchantment is bound up with the process and costs of unification.

Have recent political and social developments in Germany therefore borne out the worst fears of the detractors of unification? Below, this question will be addressed in relation to three specific issues. First, I will ask how far more than four decades of separate development of the two German societies contributed to the problems encountered in attempts to forge a unified party political culture. Second, I will attempt an interim appraisal of the condition of civil society in the new *Länder*. Here, a sharp distinction should be drawn between sub-cultures of dissent which developed within the GDR on the one hand, and evidence of a far broader range of identifiably working class self-activity on the other. Dissent has attracted considerable scholarly and political interest, although whether the experiences and perceptions of the dissidents have anything to offer to a unified Germany remains a subject of heated controversy. The existence of a very different kind of seed of civil society under communist rule has, by contrast, been all but overlooked: in a grey area somewhere between state control and free association, much of the GDR's population shared a social life beyond the home and outside the ruling party. Through it, East German factory workers developed a sense of community. It may not of itself have provided a sufficient condition for the emergence of a sense of civic duty so markedly lacking in the GDR in general. However, it might plausibly be viewed as a necessary precondition, so that its disappearance virtually without trace and without substitute should nevertheless give cause for concern. Third, a facet of the suspicions regarding unification entertained especially by many left-wing intellectuals in the old FRG deserves discrete comment. This was the fear that the event would lead to a reversion to 'pre-political' discourses: to an integral nationalism, founded on revisionist renderings of German history and on a primacy of ethnicity, which would distort political practices and negate 'modern' trends in the direction of a more open republican consciousness.

Difficulties encountered in the process of trying to establish democratic, pluralist party politics in the new Länder originate in the historical experience of the GDR but, in crucial ways, are exacerbated by an insistence that the parties be national in their organisation and appeal. Of the various bloc parties which operated beside and beneath the ruling SED (*Sozialistische Einheitspartei Deutschlands*, Socialist Unity Party of Germany) in the GDR, two, the CDU (*Christlich Demokratische Union*,

Christian Democratic Union) and the Liberal Democratic Party, predated both the founding of the state and the formation of their 'sister' parties in the western zones of occupation after the Second World War. They were thus genuinely rooted in indigenous political traditions. For the regime, they fulfilled a variety of important functions. They masked the reality of one-party rule; secured intra-systemic mobilisation of sections of the population in which the parties of the labour movement had no historic experience of organisation; acted as a 'conveyor belt' supplying the SED with information respecting their supporters' mood and reactions to regime policies (Oeser, 1980/81:2). Occasionally, and only over issues chosen by the regime, they were allowed a measure of independence to articulate their members' views even in opposition to a specific SED policy, and thus served the interests of their communist masters again, as safety valves reducing social tensions by the very fact of airing grievances. So there was a grim irony for the SED when, in the course of the revolution of 1989, these bloc parties showed some alacrity in removing tainted leaders, disavowing their heritage of collaboration and contributing to the demise of communist rule. This had significant consequences for the outcome of both the free election in the GDR in March 1990 and the first election in the expanded FRG in December 1990. These parties' West German counterparts now found it expedient to regard them as sister parties indeed, and to move rapidly toward organisational unification.

It is tempting to view the victory of the CDU and its Bonn coalition partner, the FDP (*Freie Demokratische Partei*, Free Democratic Party) on East German soil merely as a triumph of western campaign financing and style over impoverished and inexperienced parties and politicians, and as a kind of plebiscite on the pace of unification. Certainly, it was indeed the presence of Helmut Kohl and not that of the newly elected leader of the eastern CDU, Lothar de Maizière, which dominated the hustings in East Germany's first and last free elections. Equally clearly, the complaints of members of the civic movement that a genuine expression of the democratic will of the citizens of the GDR would be ill-served by an influx of western party resources and politicians were ignored, to the great detriment of the partisan interests of the protestors. However, were these the only factors at issue, it might have been supposed that the right-wing German Social Union, backed by the CSU (*Christlich-Soziale Union*, Christian Social Union) in its attempt to break out of its Bavarian stronghold, would have enjoyed considerable success at the polls, whereas it in fact met with abject failure. So the one really unique advantage enjoyed by the CDU and the Free Democrats in East Germany lay in their ability to underpin the aid and democratic authentication provided by Bonn politicians with still highly serviceable networks and a mass membership bequeathed by the functioning of the old regime.

In the Federal Republic, the highly centralised nature of election campaigns is exaggerated by their tendency to function as popularity polls for contending candidates for the Chancellorship. Even there, however, regional disparities in votes cast strongly reflect divergencies in membership of the parties. For the Social Democrats in East Germany, this implied an obstacle to success no less serious than the want of enthusiasm for unification displayed by some of their western leaders. While the eastern SPD (*Sozial Demokratische Partei Deutschlands*, Social Democratic Party of Germany) was at least no less successful in attracting new members than was the CDU (Sylvia, 1993: p. 251), and was able to benefit both from the financial generosity of its western relative and from the high public profile in the GDR of Willi Brandt, it was obliged to build a membership from scratch. The forced merger between the Communist Party and Social Democrats through which the SED had been formed had been succeeded by the announcement that the SED would transform itself into a 'party of a new type'. This rapidly proved to mean its reduction to a Soviet-style 'democratic centralist' cadre organisation. The change was put into effect via the Stalinist purges from the new party of its social democratic components and entailed slavish adherence to all the Kremlin's doctrines. So social democratic traditions cannot be said to have contributed greatly to the nature of the regime, its traces more comprehensively eradicated than were those of the CDU or of liberalism.

Refounded in early October 1989, the latterday eastern social democracy bears little resemblance either to the virtually exclusively working-class composition of its pre-SED ancestor or to the integrative Volkspartei which the western SPD had become, and now strives to remain. Its roots lie in the civic movement of the GDR, and particularly in those dissident groups most closely bound up with the Protestant Church. In key respects, it continues to articulate the politics of a political ghetto, notably in its refusal to countenance within its own ranks any of the one-fifth of the East German population who had been members of any of the bloc parties under the old order, and thus creates tensions both with its potential constituency in the new *Länder* and with western Social Democrats habituated to making ideological compromises in the quest for office.

The eastern SPD is paralysed by paradoxes of its own making. Spasmodically prepared to represent perceived East German interests, it does so even where this means supporting the initiatives of the Bonn coalition and alienating western Social Democrats (Sylvia, 1993: pp. 38-9). Manifestly hostile to collectivist practices which appear to betray continuities with the regimented politics of the old regime, it is chary of trade unionism yet still expounds doctrines of social justice and solidarity. It remains mistrustful of a working class which had seemed docile through years of dictatorship. In East Germany, workers now readily embrace free trade unions while they largely reject socialism; Social Democrats suspect workers' organisations yet cling to socialist ideals. Nor has the eastern SPD succeeded in establishing a presence in extra-parliamentary pressure-group politics and single-issue campaigns since unification. In such activities, the Greens and former dissident groups, whose formal unification did not take place until 1993, vie with their old antagonists in the PDS (Partei des *Demokratischen Sozialismus*, Party of Democratic Socialism) for prominence. Thus, the problems encountered by the SPD in eastern Germany cannot be ascribed simply or directly to a political 'colonisation' by the West. Intriguingly, as I will go on to argue, the SPD's decision to reject erstwhile members of bloc parties has by no means rendered it immune to the GDR's problems of 'coming to terms with the past'.

By dint of having placed so great an emphasis on the introduction of a culture of pluralist party politics, and purposively neglected a civic movement out of touch with the aspirations and practices of German national integration, the East German clients of West German parties rendered their own shortcomings all the more transparent. Yet the marginalisation of the civic movement represents a shift in East German politics which was not just an enforced accommodation with a 'western' model, but was enthusiastically endorsed by some of the most prominent activists of the GDR's independent citizens' groups of the 1980s. Shortly after taking office as a Cabinet Minister immediately after the March 1990 elections, Rainer Eppelmann, long a central figure in the GDR's independent peace groups, justified the marginalisation of the civic movements. These, he opined, would 'always be necessary for the lime tree at the corner and for the clean table in the village. But concerning the big political decisions they are no more than folklore' (Philipsen, 1993: p. 56). The denigration of the future role of civic movements has been reinforced by endeavours, reaching in to the domain of scholarly debate, retrospectively to diminish the contribution of these movements to the revolution of 1989 itself. Instead, the role of the waves of emigrants has received pride of place (Naimark, 1992: p. 93 *et passim*). What, then, was the real condition of a civil society in the former GDR, and will its legacy in any sense affect the expanded FRG?

It has become something of a commonplace to assert that the real 'achievement' of the communist order in East-Central Europe was the withering away not of the state but of society. Fred Klinger paints a bleak picture of life in a working-class block of flats in the 'model' town of Eisenhüttenstadt, itself the product of the GDR's first five-year plan. The inhabitants of the block are described as living in an evironment of 'human isolation and distance from their neighbours' whom they 'systematically avoid. ... People mistrust each other ... each preserves his small opportunities and tries to guard against denunciation' (Klinger, 1993: p. 155). Yet, and herein lies the really disturbing message contained in Klinger's observations, what he is describing is not life in the 'society of nooks and crannies' of the old GDR, but the contemporay disintegration of a working-class community in the unified Germany.

In crucial respects, the depiction of the former GDR as a *Nischengesellschaft* (society of nooks and crannies) is profoundly misleading. For this was also a society of groups, of social clubs, and cultural and sporting organisations. These constituted a kind of civil society which was, to be sure, barely even autonomous in relation to the state, and yet was very unevenly regulated by it. If the network of officially sanctioned civic groups bore the stamp of the regime's strategies of socialisation, they were nevertheless not wholly permeated with propaganda. In 1988, the clubhouse of the employees of the Walter Ulbricht Works at Leuna not only offered lectures on such themes as 'Are Marx and Engels still relevant today?', 'What is a Socialist Personality?' and 'The Siberian Experience: past, present and future', but also ran theatre and film clubs, choirs and brass bands, stamp collectors' and painters' clubs and organised Saturday garden parties throughout the summer.[1] Frequently organised under the auspices of the GDR's vast industrial conglomerates and its trade unions rather than under the direct tutelage of the SED, these activities may well have owed their success in part to the traditions of the German labour movement's sub-culture which, in Imperial Germany, had also exhibited tensions between the Social Democratic Party's wish politically to educate its constituency and workers' desire for recreation and entertainment.

This 'official' civil society furthermore offered some scope for forms of cultural activity which the regime frowned upon. The industrial enterprises' cultural endeavours were, for instance, vital to the punk music sub-culture (which flourished during the last decade of the GDR's existence and which was to play a significant part in the revolution of 1989), providing grants and venues for bands in whose path the regime placed a variety of obstacles (Watson, 1993). Of the three weekly discos run by the Ulbricht Works, one also featured live performances and a second advertised a punk element in its repertoire. If East German youth showed an aversion to over-socialisation and the compulsory participation in large group activities which is now contributing to the atomisation of eastern German society, then it would nevertheless be dangerous to underestimate the importance of the six thousand discos and nearly ten thousand clubs which were at young people's disposal (Grote and Kienbaum, 1991: p. 468).

The FDJ, the GDR's official youth movement, may primarily have served the interests of the regime in training new generations of cadres, but it is remembered with a measure of nostalgia even by a group of young neo-Nazis interviewed by *Der Spiegel* (50, 1992: p. 26), who recall that alongside the 'false ideals' promoted by the regime's 'Young Pioneers', cheap discos, youth clubs and travel opportunities kept youth reasonably happily occupied. The group of workers encountered by Klinger in Eisenhüttenstadt 'openly glorified' aspects of their socialisation in the GDR. Fond memories were preserved, not indeed of officious indoctrination, as they were at pains to emphasise, but of the 'fun of being together'. Albums documenting sporting successes, celebratory gatherings and also residents' elections to the local committee of the National Front were brought forth and lovingly poured over in the presence of the academic visitor. Only in these reminiscences about the 'good old days' were these new citizens of the Federal Republic able temporarily to overcome their sense of mutual alienation (Klinger, 1993: p. 154ff). But these are scarcely reflections which could hope to meet with much sympathy or understanding in the old *Länder* of the Federal Republic, nor, indeed, among the 40,000 or so citizens whose refusal to conform led them into civic movement activism.

And yet, at least until their secularisation in the late 1980s, most of the civic groups cannot be said to have been independent of the state either. In fact, they had depended on space and facilities afforded by the Protestant Church whose relatively privileged position in East German society was contingent in turn on maintaining good relations with the regime and assuming the posture of a 'Church within Socialism'. And if it opened (some) of its doors to peace, environmental, human rights and women's groups, the Church sought also to use the same doors to confine the activities of the dissidents, to keep them off the streets and out of sight of a wider public, and so again served the needs of the SED by guiding discontent into channels where it could do little real harm.

The dead hand of the Stasi archives seems capable of generating almost as much fear today as the living state security service ever did in the GDR under Erich Honecker In Magdeburg, a newly elected trade union branch secretary spoke with pride of relative success in preserving a tolerable atmosphere in his workplace, 'preventing any kind of "reputational lynching"' (Philipsen, 1993: p. 290). The implication is clear: such a willingness to proceed with discretion in the matter of the Stasi is highly exceptional.

On one level, the round of purges presently being endured in eastern Germany can be viewed as a necessary component of a West German strategy of (internal) colonisation. Cultural producers and political leaders of the former GDR bore the brunt of what some commentators have seen as an orchestrated campaign designed to eradicate all vestiges of an independent East German identity (Rosenberg, 1991). Ibrahim Böhme, first leader of the Social Democrats in the East, and Lothar de Maizière, last (and only democratically elected) Prime Minister of the GDR who was briefly to hold a seat in Helmut Kohl's Cabinet, have both seen their political careers nipped in the bud in the aftermath of allegations of collaboration with the Stasi levelled against them. Christa Wolf, doyen of an older generation of critical literati in the GDR, and Sascha Anderson poet and pivotal figure in the Prenzlauer Berg Circle of young dissident writers, have seen in different ways and with varying degrees of injustice their reputations tarnished, perhaps irrevocably, in the wake of allegations justified in similar ways. The accusations have resulted in what one author aptly describes as 'prognoses of an end of GDR literature' and as endeavours to secure its 'removal from the domain of research on German Letters' (Eigler, 1993: p. 80). And could not the purge of institutions of higher education in the former GDR, conducted in the first instance by West German scholars who had often been involved in bitter controversies with their eastern counterparts, be read as an endeavour, altogether in the spirit of 'internal colonisation', to decapitate an indigenous culture?

Clearly, there does exist a climate of opinion in the FRG today which seeks not only to infer continuities between the Third Reich and the GDR, but to suggest that the criminality of the two regimes was comparable. Thus, while the revolution in the GDR has, in common parlance, been demoted to the stature merely of a *Wende*, a turning-point, a parallel for Germans' failure to resist Nazism is now proposed with GDR citizens' collaboration or passive compliance with the rule of the SED. Analyses more critical of the 'colonising' tendencies observable in some West German approaches to the population of the new *Länder* have suggested an altogether different kind of parallel. West German feelings of guilt at their society's failure radically to denazify are displaced as they insist on hunting down every last Stasi agent. At the least, perpetrators of this kind of 'colonisation' conveniently disregard the links developed, partly in secret, between the SED and the western CDU and the SPD as recently as 1988.

There is also a growing body of evidence that East Germans are coming, in increasing numbers, to regard *Wessis* as unwelcome intruders.

Perhaps there are even indications that it is really only now that a distinctive East German identity, which the SED had striven so hard and so fruitlessly to instil in the population, is emerging. East German shop stewards have threatened to cause a split in the trade union movement. The PDS has begun to re-establish itself in East German politics by campaigning, not indeed for a renewed division, but for an assertive regionalism founded on pride in the past of the GDR. 'Hold up your heads, not your hands', it told East Berliners, who responded by making it the largest party in most of the electoral districts of 'their' section of the city in local elections in 1992. 'Committees of Justice' spanning a spectrum from the PDS to a prominent CDU politician in Brandenburg similarly seek to ward off a perceived West German assault on the society and values of the former GDR. Even the CDU faction in the *Bundestag* has experienced strains, its members from the new *Länder* having crossed the floor in the crucial abortion laws voting in June 1993, established their own caucus and joined with other eastern parliamentarians in cross-party talks to promote a regional interest. And the popularity of Manfred Stolpe in Brandenburg owes much to the stridency with which he proclaims that, while his activities in the former GDR had fallen far short of heroism, he had managed to retain his integrity and to maintain contact with state organs, as had innumerable other citizens. In all these manifestations of a regionalist reaction from the five new *Länder*, an almost truculent quasi-nationalism is mingled with the accentuation of themes of social solidarity. This may owe less to any internalisation of Marxist propaganda by those at whom it was targeted, than to the development of a sense of community forged either in passive structural resistance to that propaganda, or at least in a sort of struggle to 'get by'. 'Anne', one of *Der Spiegel's* youthful neo-Nazi respondents, echoes the sentiment: 'Among us, and in contrast to the old *Bundesländer*, inter-personal relations were not and are not oriented toward money. In GDR times we all needed each other, were dependent on one another: there was a feeling of community.' The same sensibility informs the attitudes not least of CDU politicians from the East, who demand of their party a return to the spirit of its first programme, which had by no means been uniformly hostile to the ideas of socialism and had contained a marked commitment to the notion of constraining the operation of the market via the imposition of social obligations. It may thus be contended that a measure of egalitarianism is constitutive of an East German identity which has not merely survived the dismemberment of the GDR, but has paradoxically been strengthened by the experience of 'unification', however varied the forms of its expression.

However, three qualifications (if not objections) to the thesis of a resurgent and combative East German identity, founded on a struggle for regional and social rights, deserve consideration. First, in spite of the diminution in levels of satisfaction with Germany's 'unification' in the new *Länder*, satisfaction nevertheless remains the rule. Second, the new *Länder* exhibit not only marked differences in their perceptions of German politics and society, but no small degree of mutual hostility. Brandenburgers and Saxons, in particular, periodically give vent to prejudices regarding each other which reflect very different experiences of 'actually existing Socialism' and seem to belie the possibility of a single East German identity. Third, albeit with more honourable intent than West German 'colonisers', former dissidents have added fuel to the fires of a purge mentality. On one level, the *Literaturstreit* between Wolf and Anderson and their respective adherents was a generational and political conflict among East German cultural producers (Brockmann, 1993). And the political establishment of the Federal Republic has been accused of shielding tainted figures whenever it has found it expedient to do so. Leading figures of the civic movement and human rights activists have gone so far as to appeal to President von Weizsäcker to rein in a perceived Bonn conspiracy to rescue Manfred Stolpe, as the sole Social Democratic premier of an East German *Land*, from the tribulations of too close an examination of his political past (*Der Spiegel*, 12, 1993: pp. 26-7).

A measure of recognition of the particular interests of the new *Länder*, variously expressed through support for a shift in the balance of power from the *Bundestag* to the *Land* administrations or the incorporation of specific social rights, provided one theme in the 1993 debates about revision of the Federal Republic's Basic Law. However, the first significant amendments to the spirit of the Basic Law have come in relation to the foreign policy options of the FRG and to the strikingly liberal Article 16 which secured the right to political asylum. These revisions have been legitimated in similar ways, with appeals to the notion that Germany should now adopt the behaviour of a 'normal' nation. In September 1993, the CDU sought to tread a careful path. On the one hand, it denounced racist violence and extremist nationalism with a vehemence hitherto absent from its public pronouncements. On the other, it broke a post-war Federal Republican taboo by promoting 'patriotism' and 'healthy national consciousness'. Quite how the nationalism it denounces really differs from the 'healthy' national consciousness it seeks to instil in the German public remains unclear. Even as he attacked racist action, Helmut Kohl was presenting a new candidate for the presidency of the FRG to its citizens. Steffen Heitmann, on whom Kohl's choice fell, emerged from the relative obscurity of office in the

Saxon *Land* administration rapidly to gain notoriety for his repeated complaints that Germany was facing the danger of being *überfremdet* - over-run by foreigners (*Der Spiegel*, 36, 1993: pp. 20-21). The withdrawal of Heitmann's candidacy in December 1993, however, has rewarded the strenuous efforts of the broad interests that had coalesced to oppose him.

Certainly Germany has, since 1990, borne the brunt of the flow of refugees especially from Eastern Europe and the former Yugoslavia, accepting a total of 256,000 in 1991 alone. And equally clearly, many of these refugees, by virtue of the fact that they sought only temporary asylum, availed themselves of a law which was not designed to cope with their particular predicament. In the FRG, they 'joined' nearly six million foreign residents, their arrival exacerbating extant tensions (growing in tandem with a rise in unemployment) between Germans and so-called 'guest' workers. Dubbed, with racist implications, 'sham asylum seekers' by many Germans, and dispersed within Germany with little sensitivity either to their own needs or to the mood and concerns of local German populations, they were subject to sporadic violent attacks, largely more or less spontaneously carried out by skinheads and other youths flirting with what is commonly referred to as the far right 'scene', from the latter half of 1991 onward. A number of the most virulent outrages were committed in the new *Länder*. Yet the targets of violence throughout Germany have more often been members of 'guest' worker communities than *Asylanten* (asylum seekers).

The reaction of the Federal Republic has been twofold. While it has sought to outlaw and suppress neo-Nazi organisations, the government at first also, implicitly and explicitly, tended to offer apologias for racist violence in the course of its attempts at explanation. This trend was, in a sense, continued with the attempt to confine the right to asylum to those for whom the Federal Republic was the first port of call. While many supporters of the amendment to asylum rights, who included the bulk of the parliamentary SPD, attempted to justify their stance with the argument that a modest reform would take the rug from under the feet of the *Republikaner* and the racist youth gangs, their critics in the *Pro-Asyl* movement countered that a change to the Basic Law would rebound on its authors. Voicing the fear that reform would serve only to legitimate xenophobia and even encourage further violence, campaigners for liberal asylum rights viewed the major parties' response as a reaction to the symptoms rather than the causes of social tensions.

Serious endeavours to comprehend the phenomenon of racist violence in contemporary Germany have frequently been overly reliant on psychological examination of the roots of xenophobia and aggression, on broken homes and disturbed childhoods. Klinger's observations on the right-wing 'scene' in Eisenhüttenstadt, however, reveal that participation in this sub-culture of violence is not limited to the offspring of long-identified local social misfits and that a still evident prejudice against these has not prevented youth from 'respectable' backgrounds from participating equally in attacks on foreigners (Klinger, 1993: p. 155 ff).

Perhaps it is not so much broken homes as the demolition of civil society in the former GDR that has offered the racist 'scene' recruitment opportunities. The author Martin Walser has seen the behaviour of the so-called 'rowdies' (*Randalierer*) as expressing generational conflict, the outrage of a youth cohort facing poverty and unemployment and confronting the complacencies of their affluent elders. He reads the youths' strident nationalism as evidence of their profound lack of a real sense of identity and their adoption of the language and paraphernalia of Nazism as a calculated insult and challenge to a liberal German establishment, some of whose spokespersons had indeed gone even so far as to call into question Germany's right to unification in the light of the criminality of the Third Reich. Walser further asserts that the 'neglect of the national dimension' on the part of the FRG's 'opinion formers' has contributed to the emergence of a subterranean nationalism which, after 1945, remained alive only in 'samizdat' literature and in the sentiments of 'compatriots who would not or could not bear' the intellectuals' surrender of the concept of German nation-statehood. The existence of this nationalist undercurrent, he argues, helps explain the emergence of an extremist right 'in so short a time and without organisation' (*Der Spiegel*, 26, 1993: pp. 40-47). An alternative view, however, would focus rather on endeavours by political and intellectual elites historically to legitimate even aspects of Nazism (see Maier, 1988; Habermas, 1993: pp. 180ff).

In the scholarly debate, Erwin Faul's lines of reasoning reflect many of the themes indicated by Walser. Faul seeks to identify a veritable conspiracy mounted by multiculturalists within Germany, which purportedly aims at destroying German national identity. Faul contrasts a national identity (which he evidently considers to be natural and obvious) with multiculturalism (which he regards as a pernicious artificial construct). Positing, as a reaction to 'reunification', an 'hysterical intensification of multicultural missionary activity' he holds its proponents responsible in particular for seeking to place obstacles in the path of the social realisation of the unification of West and East Germany. Here, Faul even has some flattering things to say about the former GDR: by virtue of having altered 'hardly anything' in the ethnic composition of the population it had inherited. 'In this respect, [East Germany] contributed practically nothing to the burden of problems of the expanded Federal Republic which, from the outset, it was nevertheless expected to help carry.' He is on stronger ground where he highlights the paradoxical position multiculturalists find themselves in whenever they attempt to associate their position with 'constitutional patriotism' (see Oberndörfer, 1991). For the Basic Law accords the right to German citizenship on the basis not of a *ius soli*, but of a *ius sanguinis*. Only where he endeavours to enlist even Ernest Renan's *'Qu'est-ce qu'une nation'* in support of the ethnic definition of nationhood he is at pains to defend, does Faul stretch the internal logic of his case to the point of implausibility (Faul, 1993: pp. 408, 416, 417).

Of course, this is a nettle which proponents of multiculturalism are prepared to grasp, and indeed obliged to grasp given the grave difficulties, only marginally eased after a sequence of modest reforms, facing even guest-workers' children born and educated in Germany in their attempts to gain German citizenship. Extending into the parliamentary CDU, a broad spectrum of opinion favours the extension of civic rights, in particular opening the civil service, far more broadly defined and hence significant for employment opportunities in Germany than elsewhere in Western Europe, to guest workers. Their enfranchisement at least in local elections is as widely supported. Such reforms are often perceived as precursors to establishing the rights to full citizenship at least for German-born members of guest-worker families.

Furthermore, such redefinitions of German citizenship are frequently linked to criticisms of the right to 'return' accorded to members of 'German' communities living outside the FRG. The linguistic and cultural ties of such communities with contemporary Germany are generally tenuous, and their historical origins lie in migrations from Flanders, Holland and Switzerland as well as from the territories which comprise the modern German state (Bade, 1992).

The debate outlined above has become the peculiarly German version of a discussion of civil society. Multiculturalism, it should be emphasised, is the *reality* in Germany. Attempts to make it appear a construct, dredged up by '68 radicals in search of new paradigms since the disintegration of socialism, are invidious efforts to mask the fact that German society is at odds with its own ethnocentric understanding of citizenship (see Waever et al, 1993: p. 192). Social movements and advocates of multiculturalism and of the model of a 'Round Table' are ranged against neo-Bismarckian proponents of an integrative nationalism culminating in a strategy of 'negative integration' (that is, the endeavour to unify 'the' Germans by pointing up 'aliens' and 'alien' ideologies in their midst) and of the 'primacy of foreign policy'. Helmut Kohl, indeed, began to speak in undiluted Bismarckian tones, proclaiming for instance that 'Germany's fate is decided in its foreign and security policies' (*Der Spiegel*, 37, 1993: pp. 20-21). He would have done well to recall that, far more than Bismarck's flirtation with imperialism or his attacks on Social Democrats and Roman Catholics, it was his welfarist initiatives that made an enduring contribution to the national integration of Germany.

NOTE

1. Klubhaus der Werktätigen der VEB Leuna-Werke 'Walter Ulbricht' / FDGB *Kulturangebot '88*. My thanks are due to Professor Len Jones of the University of Wales, Aberystwyth for the loan of this document.

REFERENCES

Bade, Klaus J. (ed.) (1992), *Deutsche im Ausland, Fremde in Deutschland:Migration in Geschichte und Gegenwart*, Munich: C.H. Beck.

Brockmann, Stephen (1993), 'A Literary Civil War', *Germanic Review*, 48 (2).

Eigler, Friderike (1993), 'Die Mauer in den Köpfen: Mechanismen der Ausgrenzung und Abwehr am Beispiel der Christa-Wolf-Kontroverse', *German Life and Letters*, 46 (2).

Faul, Erwin (1992), 'Das vereinigte Deutschland, europäisch integrierte Nation oder diffuse "multikulturelle Gesellschaft?"', *Zeitschrift für Politik*, 39 (4).

Grote, Manfred and Kienbaum, Barbara (1991), 'East German Youth Policy', *East European Quarterly*, 24 (4).

Habermas, Jurgen (1993), *Vergangenheit als Zukunft. Das alte Deutschland im neuen Europa?*, Munich: R. Piper.

Klinger, Fred (1993), 'Sozialer Konflikt und offene Gewalt. Die Heraunforderungen des Transformationsprozesses in den neuen Bundesländern', *Deutschland Archiv*, 26 (2).

Maier, Charles S. (1988), *The Unmasterable Past. History, Holocaust, and German National Identity*, Cambridge, Massachusetts and London: Harvard University Press.

Naimark, Norman M. (1992), '"Ich will hier raus": Emigration and the Collapse of the German Democratic Republic', in Banac, I. (ed.), *Eastern Europe in Revolution*, Ithaca: Cornell.

Oberndörfer, Dieter (1991), *Die offene Republik. Zur Zukunft Deutschlands und Europas*, Freiburg: Herder.

Oberndörfer, Dieter (1993), *Der Wahn des Nationalen. Die Alternative der offenen Republik*, Freiburg: Herder.

Oeser, H. (1980/81), 'The Multi-Party System in the GDR, Its Character and Function', *GDR Monitor*, 6.

Philipsen, Dirk (1993), *We Were the People. Voices from East Germany's Revolutionary Autumn of 1989*, Durham and London: Duke University Press.

Rosenberg, Dorothy (1991), 'The Colonisation of East Germany', *Monthly Review*, 43.

Sylvia, Stephen J. (1993), 'Left Behind: The Social Democratic Party in Eastern Germany', *Western European Politics*, 16 (2).

Waever, Ole; Buzan, Barry; Kelstrup, Morten and Lemaitre, Pierre (1993), *Identity, Migration and the New Security Agenda in Europe*, London: Pinter.

Watson, Martin (1993), '"Flüstern & Schreien": Punks, Rock Music and the Revolution in the GDR', *German Life and Letters*, 66 (2).

5. From the Single European Act to Maastricht: the Creation of the European Union

Peter Holmes[1]

INTRODUCTION

Popular attitudes to European integration have gone through an astonishing series of swings in the last ten years. In 1981 the European Community (or Common Market as it was usually called) seemed moribund as a political entity, and a distant bureaucratic annoyance to ordinary people, the alleged architect of schemes to relabel ice cream as 'iced vegetable fat'. About 1988 Europessimism gave way to Europhoria, which in turn has gone sour, just as in the early 1990s the member states have created a European Union which came into formal existence on 1 November 1993.[2]

The present paper argues that what is now the European Union (EU) began life as an essentially interstate system designed both to promote peace between France and Germany and also to functionally promote economic benefits. But in order to achieve limited diplomatic and economic ends it has had to take on a much broader role which ends up directly affecting the lives and rights of citizens and economic actors. To create even free trade has meant radically transforming the relationship between states and citizens. This transformation has enhanced the rights that the citizens of the new Union have across Europe, and these can ultimately only be further strengthened if popular demand expresses itself. But for the time being, it is the member states that will be the moving force of the Union as a political and social entity.

The mythical date of '1992' has passed by in a cloud of Maastricht dust, but we should remember that the Single European Act (SEA) of 1986 was essentially an agreement to adhere to the original goals of the 1957 Rome Treaty, above all to a true Common Market, ingeniously renamed the 'single' or 'internal' market. The SEA was not a radical new plan; it barely modified the agenda, and institutional changes were mainly intended to iron out a number of divergences between rules and practice. Though itself the culmination of a thirty-year process, the SEA revived in a new form the political agenda of EC integration to which the Maastricht Treaty was intended to respond. On the political side, the Maastricht Treaty created a European Union with two new elements, a common foreign policy and a union citizenship. The nature of this citizenship is largely symbolic; it does confer some direct rights, for example to vote in local and European Parliament elections if one is resident in another Union member state. Ironically it provoked a negative reaction in both France and Denmark, where anti-Maastricht campaigners somewhat misleadingly argued that this risked diluting national citizenship. In addition, of course, the Maastricht Treaty proposed a scheme for monetary union, since called into question by events.[3]

Maastricht largely confirms the existing socioeconomic rights accorded by the Rome Treaty, such as freedom of movement embodied in the EEC Treaty, making only a tentative beginning in the area of basic political rights. But it is difficult to separate the different areas of 'rights'. The Rome Treaty has largely been about giving people freedom to engage in market activity without hindrance, but it has never been only about that. The market-opening provisions imply a 'level playing field' not merely a free one, and the anti-monopoly provisions went far beyond anything in the legislation of any member state except Germany. Even the market-related rights are embedded in the idea that markets must have a social framework. Most of the citizenship rights that have in practice been created in the European Community have in fact come from the European Court of Justice, using somewhat creative interpretations of the Rome Treaty to confer rights on individuals. Some of these enhanced people's ability to exercise freedom of choice in the market, some of which gave entitlement to social protection (for example, rules on equal pay for women). There is a sense in which the Rome Treaty is a form of liberal constitutional regime for the Community and the member states. This point should not be pushed too far however. The Community institutions are a framework for common action. In the absence of a common policy consensus, they will act largely as a restraining influence on states to inhibit them from engaging in mutually harmful acts. Where there is a consensus for common action, whether on education, labour laws or foreign policy, the EC system provides a ready-made system for collective decision-making.

The Maastricht Treaty does not go much further in this process. It establishes a 'European Union', which is really a framework for interstate cooperation outside the rules of the Rome Treaty (see Wyatt and Dashwood, 1993, ch. 23). New mechanisms provide for the formulation of a joint foreign and potentially defence policy if this is in fact wished for by the member states. For the time being these aspects are not governed by the same procedures as EC economic rules, though there is provision for amendment to the Treaty after 1996. Its advocates argue that the current disarray on the European scene increases rather than weakens the case for facilitating cooperation.

The process of EC integration has been led by elites developing a framework for state-to-state cooperation. The EC is literally the creature of the member states and is designed to facilitate their cooperation. From 1957 to 1990, until Maastricht it can be argued that this elite agenda had a counterpart at grass roots level. Popular opinion did not lead the integration process but in time it embraced it. The need to prevent war between France and Germany was more than an abstract idea, and over the years the Common Market, originally an instrument towards creating mutual economic interdependence, took on a real identification in people's lives. Frontiers opened physically and the rights to travel and to trade, freely conferred by European law, were of practical value to EC citizens. The European Community is by now an integral part of the structure of the states that make it up, not merely a set of external obligations.

The Maastricht Treaty seeks to extend the integration process by developing issues referred to only in terms of aspiration in the Rome Treaty. There is a continuing emphasis on a framework for interstate relations. These extend into areas that touch people's everyday life, for example, crime and justice, but the Maastricht Treaty was not seen as responding to an evident need. Perhaps one reason for the negative reaction against Maastricht has been that too much energy has been devoted to discussion of forms which policy cooperation should take rather than the substantive tasks of dealing with the real problems such as unemployment and assisting the peaceful transformation of Eastern Europe.

THE HISTORICAL BACKGROUND

The historians Paul Kennedy (1988) and Bernard Porter (1983) have suggested that Britain in the early nineteenth century was an abortive example of a state oriented around the principle of minimising military expenditure and seeking to profit by persuading its neighbours to keep their markets open by offers of trade rather than conquest. There were a remarkable series of proposals for free trade in nineteenth-century Europe, including the Anglo-French Commercial Treaty of 1860 and the plan for a common currency for the members of the Latin Monetary Union.[4] But in the end the cruder forces of political nationalism took over. Charles Kindleberger (1987a) has suggested that a key element had been missing from the moment that others had perceived the weakness of Britain's resources to act as a liberal hegemonic power. Even 'liberal' Britain was drawn into militarised competition with other European states. He argues that the economic and political crises of the 1930s were due to the US refusal to take responsibility for stabilising the world economy. He acknowledges that a more symmetrical rule-based alternative to domination on leadership by one power is in principle possible. This is what the EC (not yet the EU) attempted to offer in Western Europe.

After 1945 the United States at first assumed the role of an external actor threatening the European states with sanctions if they did not cooperate with each other (see also Kindleberger, 1987b). According to Richard Rosecrance, the post-war world has seen the 'Rise of the Trading State' (see Rosecrance, 1986). German and Japanese post-war experience call into question, he suggests, the evolutionary survival of state systems built on the conquest of territory and relying on their military power to survive. François Duchêne (1990) also argues that the imperative driving EC integration forward is the recognition that economic factors matter more than military ones in the world today. The process had to be driven by more than the prospect of economic gain if conflict could be minimised. Clearly the political elites of France and Germany shared a profound sense of the need to work together. And in this they were driven first by the carrot of military and economic assistance from the USA which favoured all forms of European cooperation in the 1940s, and second by the stick represented by the apparent Russian threat.

Despite the pressures to come together several schemes for European Union came to nothing, including the European Defence Community of the early 1950s. The British tried to prevent the emergence of anything beyond a free trade area. In 1951 the Treaty of Paris set up the European Coal and Steel Community. It provided for rather more supranational decision-making than the 1957 Treaty of Rome which still forms the political and economic constitution of the EC.

THE EC SYSTEM

From the start, the Rome Treaty contained three kinds of objectives; some are pious hopes, others are ambiguous obligations but a few are clear obligations with deadlines and instruments for implementation. The commitment to abolish all intra-EC tariffs by 1969 was unambiguous and all parties recognised that if it were not implemented to the letter the whole enterprise would be called into question. The subsequent evolution of the EC has seen the gradual transformation of looser longer-term aims into more concrete objectives. The early process of integration tended to stress 'negative integration', rules to prevent states taking harmful action, more than 'positive integration', the actual development of common policies.

In the European Community system, the supreme decision-making body is in almost all fields the Council of Ministers in which the states are directly represented. Decisions in the Council for the most part had to be unanimous under the Rome Treaty. In fact some articles provided for majority voting even in the early years. The EC Commission has a limited number of powers delegated to it in the Treaties and later legislation. The Commission's main role is to propose legislation to the Council and to implement agreed policies: its control of the agenda for decision-making gives it some additional control of events. The Commission was, exceptionally under Articles 85-94 of the Rome Treaty, given direct control of the Competition Policy (that is, anti-trust and anti-subsidy rules).

So the Community should not be seen as a new extra layer of government on top of the nation-states but essentially as a set of horizontal linkages, reflecting the realities of its growth. The division of responsibility between the Commission and the Council is a brake on the development of decision-making in Brussels. This is exacerbated by the fact that both institutions prefer to wait for a consensus to form rather than to act decisively when new policy initiatives are broached.

General de Gaulle played a curious role in EC history. His first act of economic policy in 1958 committed France to respecting the Treaty provisions creating the Common Market in its most basic sense. Ironically his authoritarian approach gave credibility to his commitment to intra-EC free trade, despite his scepticism about the wider aims of the Rome Treaty and its institutions. De Gaulle in effect narrowed down the elements of the Treaty which were considered truly binding. He also insisted with absolute firmness that power should remain with the Council of Ministers not the Commission, and that in the Council discussion should go on indefinitely on a proposal until unanimous consensus was reached if any member felt its vital national interests were at stake. This was the so-called Luxembourg Compromise which became part of the *de facto* constitution of the EC. Even now, though majority voting is used where the Treaties provide for it, there is an understandable fear by member state governments of forcing one of their number to accept something it considers vital to the interests of the nation or a sufficiently vocal section. Ironically this is seen by governments as displaying 'solidarity' towards the individual sensitivities of their partners.

On the other side, we must stress the role of the European Court of Justice which has succeeded in persuading national governments and national courts to accept a radical interpretation of the Rome Treaty under which Community law supersedes national law. The Court of Justice has read into the original Treaties a 'teleological' interpretation which interprets the wording in the light of what the Court thinks they must have meant when they signed the texts! National courts have been invested with the power to invoke EC rules as a basis to challenge national laws, a role which they have been keen to adopt. Governments have gradually accepted this in the knowledge that their partners do too.

SOVEREIGNTY AND THE CITIZEN

What makes the EC system unique is not so much that there are some provisions for majority voting in decision-making. Rather it is that once decisions are taken they are irrevocable because they can be enforced in the national courts by the community's citizens. The system confers rights, albeit mostly economic rights, on the nationals of the member states as the member state remains part of the EC. Withdrawal from the EC is a threat that a member state can make but it is hard to make credible given the interests tied up in membership. While one is a member, the core obligations and benefits have to be taken as a package and not sampled *à la carte*.

The Court of Justice has enunciated the doctrine of 'direct effect'. This means that where the Rome Treaty or legislation passed by the Council of Ministers is sufficiently precise, then an individual (or a firm) can enforce it in the national courts regardless of national law. National courts will declare national laws invalid if they go against EC legislation consistent with the Rome Treaty. EC law has been very effectively used by women to secure equal economic rights.[5] According to the UK's 1972 European Communities Act, the Rome Treaty and secondary EC legislation are indeed recognised as automatically binding, until or unless the 1972 Act is repealed and we leave the EC. EC law in other words is comparable to a written component of the constitution for the UK which parliament cannot override, and the national courts are bound to respect, and indeed they generally do so, so long as we stay in the EC. Other EC states have in effect recognised that EC law forms part of the constitution (Louis, 1990). The German Constitutional Court's acceptance of the Maastricht Treaty did put some limits on the extent to which the government could bind parliament through the Treaty alone.

In practice, tacit agreement among the member states led to many provisions of the Rome Treaty not being applied by many or even all member states. But in the late 1970s the Court of Justice began to indicate a taste for greater judicial activism.[6] and at the same time the politicians began to see the virtues of common respect for rules.

THE TURNING-POINT OF THE EARLY 1980s

By the early 1980s the EC had still failed to complete some of the targets of the Rome Treaty, including a full Common Market, and looked as if it would never achieve them. There was a widespread feeling of crisis, perhaps most acute in the UK, where the Labour opposition was committed to withdrawal from the EC and the government was hardly enthusiastic about the system. But the key anxiety lay in France. Diminishing German enthusiasm for the New Cold War was threatening to undermine the commitment to the alliance with France formed by a generation who had seen the cost of its absence. One could legitimately ask in the early 1980s what the EC actually existed to do. It operated a common external tariff, a common market which was no more common than that within EFTA, and it ran the costly CAP. This sense of crisis led to a perception of the need for make-or-break decisions to raise the stakes in the move to a European Union.

A conjuncture of external events rendered the existing 'low level equilibrium' of cooperation unstable. A perception arose in France and Germany that 'something had to be done'.   One can argue how far any of the actors actually foresaw the changing shape of the world scene, but it would be unwise to exclude a long-term strategic vision above all on the part of President Mitterrand. The stimuli to action included:

- growing UK reservations about the economic basis of the 'Common Market', undermining Britain's role as a counterweight for France *vis-à-vis* Germany;
- instability in relations with the USA, partly masked by the New Cold War;
- the perceived economic threat from Japan and the tendency of EC member states to respond with individual trade and industrial policies;
- the realisation that with Greece, Spain and Portugal as members, decision-making would be unsustainable if any one member state could veto any proposal;
- a French perception that national economic sovereignty was worth less than it had seemed in de Gaulle's time.

François Duchêne (1990) argues that the most important element was the fear of paralysis if Greece, Spain and Portugal all had vetoes over everything. In any event there was a sharp reversal of French policy in the early 1980s. In a sense it was a change of tactics more than strategy. De Gaulle had always been willing to sacrifice sovereignty if he thought there were clear benefits. In 1983 France decisively rejected the idea of opting out of EC rules to solve its economic crisis. France agreed with its partners that Jacques Delors would become President of the Commission in 1985 with a mandate to revive the Community. He offered the member states three plans:

- Monetary Union;
- Political Union;
- A revived European Defence Community.

None commanded universal support. The UK said: 'Why not just create a real Common Market?' This was seen by Mrs Thatcher as an alternative to loftier ambitions. But other states saw the completion of the Internal Market as an essential first step to monetary and political union, which the French and German governments in various ways favoured. They reasoned that any momentum that could unblock the way to the single market would almost certainly be able to go beyond that. A primary obstacle was the 'Luxembourg Compromise' whereby member states claimed an informal 'right' of veto even if the Treaty gave no grounds for this. The ECJ had confirmed that this had no legal basis in a 1982 case unwisely brought by the UK. But the acceptance of majority voting[7] required a change in political culture for member states to allow themselves to be outvoted. The incentive to agree to this is that others also agree to be bound by rules too. Once this is accepted the EC becomes a new form of organisation. Sovereignty is handed over voluntarily, but once handed over it cannot be reclaimed. The EC can be said to be a 'Cooperative Game' among members, because once promises are made they become binding and can be enforced in the courts.[8] Of course a member state can still exercise political pressure on its partners not to force matters to a vote. But since trade policy is a matter for majority voting, France's power to veto a GATT deal rests only on its ability to cajole threaten or bribe its partners into accepting its views.

It is worth recalling that despite the attacks by the British Conservatives on Jacques Delors no serious attempt has been made to remove him as Commission President, even though his mandate has had to be renewed every two years under Article 165 of the Rome Treaty. No other President since the first has served eight years and his extension until 1995 was quite unprecedented. Perhaps the British position can be interpreted as one of accepting what was seen as inevitable.

In the last five to six years the depth of the original commitment has been widely acknowledged. It is not to everyone's taste however. Cohen-Tanugi (1992) suggests that one factor in the disillusionment with the Maastricht Treaty was the realisation that there had been a kind of '*coup d'état* by the legal system'. France was finding itself being transformed into a rule-based regime in which both national and EC law would act as a restraint on the state. Many in the elite regarded this as a positive development but others saw it as a blow to popular sovereignty. The fact that the French Socialist Party embraced the European concept so enthusiastically along with the liberal Right meant there was no one apart from the National Front and the Communists taking up the cause of those who felt they were losing from the process of modernisation and economic integration, a group which became much larger as the 1990s recession stopped the modest boom that anticipation of the single market seems to have launched in 1988.

WHAT DID THE SINGLE EUROPEAN ACT REALLY DO?

The Single European Act (SEA) gave few new powers or domains of competence to the Community organs, but it was a highly visible commitment to the original Rome Treaty. The SEA contains various elements:

- it provided for more majority voting on matters relating to the internal market, the new Article 100a (but tax harmonisation still requires unanimity);
- it extended EC competence into new areas such as technology and social policy and the environment, with unanimity required before major steps could be taken;
- it formalised certain pre-existing practices such as meetings of heads of state/government in the European Council;
- it gave the EC system a role in foreign policy coordination, though 'European Political Cooperation' was set up as a separate pillar with a lesser role for the Commission;
- it enunciated further aspirations towards monetary and political union.

The accompanying declarations of ministers recognised that realising this agenda was not automatic and required further concrete commitments to be made. Since 1987 the member states have largely lived up to their promises in the SEA as far as the Single Market was concerned, with the important exception (to date) of the removal of all frontier controls for people![9] The SEA extended the domain of majority voting in the Council of Ministers and so symbolised acceptance of the principle. But for it to be actually implemented the informal rules of the game had to be altered too. The true significance of the SEA is the unwritten understanding that henceforward majority voting would actually be used when the rules said so. In July 1987 an apparently technical change was made to the rules of procedure for the Council of Ministers. This in effect allowed a member state or the Commission to demand that a vote be called if the majority were in favour of ending the discussion (see Louis, 1990, p. 36 and Official Journal L291 15 October 1987). There is simply no procedural room for a member state to demand an informal right of veto under the so-called 'Luxembourg Compromise'. Several authors (for example Moravcsik, 1991 and Taylor, 1991) have pointed out that there was no formal commitment to abandoning the Luxembourg Compromise. The national right of veto, where it is not written into the Treaties, rests on the unwillingness of member state governments, even if they are in a majority, to force one of their number into a corner.

FROM THE 'SEA' TO 'MAASTRICHT'

After 1989 there was no more 'Soviet threat' as an impetus to union. But the end of the year saw France accepting German reunification and Germany accepting the principle of monetary union. It was agreed to proceed faster along the existing course rather than re-think the strategy. In 1990 the member states agreed to amend the Treaties to move towards political and monetary union and during the course of 1991 ministers met behind closed doors in an 'intergovernmental conference'. While the SEA had been intended to realise an objective largely laid down and agreed in principle 30 years before, the ministerial meetings embraced with little modification a plan for monetary union drawn up in 1989 by Europe's central bankers (see the 'Delors Report' 1989), and seem to have concentrated their main energies on the short-term political expediencies of the moment, including accommodating British demands.

The monetary provisions of the Treaty would in fact transfer more sovereignty to the independent European Central Bank than the member states have been willing to transfer to the less than totally autonomous EC Commission. The political provisions essentially provided a pre-fabricated decision-making structure for policy cooperation in a variety of new spheres, notably foreign policy and police cooperation. The Treaty enshrines the principle of subsidiarity, namely that decisions should be taken at the lowest level possible, but this is really a political aspiration rather than a legal constraint, above all where member states are acting on the basis of a consensus.

The European Union was created, on 1 November 1993, embracing the European Community legal structure and also all the ancillary cooperation arrangements among its members, but this is far from any kind of federation. Union citizens are given the right to vote in municipal and in European Parliament elections in their country of residence on equal terms with nationals of that state. The individual will be the bearer of a form of dual nationality, citizens of the European Union as well as of their member state. Almost all benefits and duties for citizens will relate to the nation state. But some rights will derive from citizenship of the Union. So far these rights are few; in addition to the voting rights in municipal and European Parliament elections in any member state of the Union where they may reside, citizens have the right to consular protection outside the Union from diplomats of any member state if their own is not represented, and to make petitions to the European Parliament. The creation of the Union and its citizenship takes one step further the notion of rights conferred by the EC system.

The Maastricht Treaty proposes a variety of Union activities to be carried on an intergovernmental basis, with limited involvement by the existing institutions of the Community. From the point of view of citizens' rights the crucial question is whether actions taken can be appealed against under EC law in the national courts and ultimately the European Court of Justice. Until or unless the member states agree to further changes, most aspects of police and justice are to be considered purely intergovernmental decisions. This means that a citizen cannot appeal to the ECJ. The UK government, for one, particularly wishes to avoid an involvement of the ECJ in these areas.

Even the small extension of European Union rules into the domain of citizenship has provoked an intense debate. The recent Irish abortion case has illustrated the overlap between civil and economic rights and its aftermath has created complications for the Maastricht Treaty. Meanwhile the French Constitutional Council declared that the new citizenship provisions of the Maastricht Treaty required a modification of the French constitution before they could be ratified.

The SEA created an unfinished political agenda. Its effective functioning required closer political cooperation but no new institutions were created for this. Events have created the necessity for closer economic and political cooperation and the Maastricht Treaty provides mechanisms which can be used as long as this necessity is perceived. In terms of the ideas we have developed earlier the value of these arrangements does not lie in forcing a common interest where none exists, it is a way of making cooperation easier when the underlying will is there.

In fact the substantive impact of the political union clauses of Maastricht are very limited. They provide a framework that can be filled if the political will is there. The treaty provides for a further revision in 1996. At this point the EC will have to tackle some fundamental questions, ignored at Maastricht (and for this reason as well as space limits only touched on here). The EC will have to decide *inter alia* whether it wishes to pursue the same degree of integration for all members, current and future. Much is made in the Treaty of a commitment to subsidiarity, but this idea will be what politicians make of it.

CONCLUDING OBSERVATIONS

This chapter has therefore focused on the fact that at the heart of the European Union is a framework for relations between states. The states have on the whole respected their obligations to refrain from actions that would be harmful to their neighbours and a surprising degree of positive co-operation has occurred. It has made war between France and Germany unthinkable. A degree of legitimacy has arisen for the existing institutions. Rules have to some extent replaced naked power in relations between states and this affects everyday lives. The EC has largely been about state-to-state relations and the impact on individuals has largely been to enshrine legal rights in the market-place. But in spite of its very limited sphere of activities the European Community could not have fulfilled its original aim of facilitating cooperation between governments if it had not been allowed to develop into something much more than an intergovernmental forum. In order to achieve their original aims the member states have allowed Community institutions that go well beyond the remit of promoting free trade. The European Commission has been able to use its limited powers to set the agenda and influence events. It has sought to mobilise elite and broader opinion and has promoted debate and discussion on a scale disproportionate to its modest size. The EC has also created social, scientific, cultural and educational programmes, whose importance is not only symbolic. The European Community (or Union) actually touches many people's everyday lives. But the Commission is not a government; it can do almost nothing without the consent of the member states and to best secure this it needs popular backing. To say that the EC has been largely a legal and intergovernmental arrangement is not to condemn it, but to identify a need for a parallel growth of European civic consciousness.

Popular opinion responded to the '1992' initiative with enthusiasm but this faded with the recession. The Maastricht Treaty was agreed in haste behind closed doors and debated in parliaments after it had been signed. It did nothing to create a project that people could identify with. It contained little to inspire and much that was inappropriate. Monetary Union is a widely but not universally shared goal and the chosen route was economically flawed as well as politically contestable, requiring deflationary policies in a severe recession. Far from strengthening political unity, it has undermined popular support for it. There is no space to consider the Monetary Union plan here except to note that it has been subject to serious theoretical criticism and has run into difficulty almost at once!

On the political union side, the complaint is not so much that the politicians did the wrong things as that they have concentrated on form rather than substance, and above all that the public debate came *after* not before the signing. Future developments will have to create a constituency in public opinion for what is to be done, in the same way that opinion was mobilised between 1988 and 1993 for the single market idea. There will have to be a much more complex reflection on what rights and obligations the Community and its citizens owe to each other and to their neighbours. The European Union is going to have to agree rules acceptable to prospective future members and whose functioning would permit the emergence of a wider space of European cooperation. It will remain up to the citizens and electorates of these nations to demand of the political leaders a recognition of the extreme degree of mutual interdependence that affects the whole continent. A top priority is to make the governments answerable to public opinion for their European policy. The 'democratic deficit' does not exist because 'Brussels' imposes things on member governments. Rather, the member states find the Council of Ministers to be a convenient device to ignore their own parliaments. Until now the élites have been able to act first and convince public opinion afterwards. The speed with which the implications of the Maastricht Treaty provoked controversy contrasts with the slow dawning of what had been agreed in the Rome Treaty and the SEA. We must avoid a reversion to short-term nationalistic populism, but there is a need for much more openness and accountability about the way decisions are made in the Union.

The debate about subsidiarity is a bit of a red-herring: as it is currently envisaged, the issue amounts to little more than whether policies are to be decided by national governments acting collectively via the EC or individually. If there is to be a more imaginative approach to decentralisation, the solution must lie either in more effective *ex ante* control, but it will only come if citizens demand it, at first in existing political arenas.

Critics of the EC integration process have argued that it stresses individualism and liberalism (see Ferry and Thibaud, 1992). This is only partly true, but to the extent that it is true, it reflects political currents of recent years. A major criticism of the Maastricht Monetary Union plan is that it seeks to tie future generations to a monetarist fad of the mid-1980s, namely independent central banks dedicated solely to the control of inflation. But the system is likely to reflect the tide of general opinion rather than to dictate to it. A 'social Europe' will come about if voters elect politicians committed to this notion. Any European central bank will lose its independence if Keynesian thinking becomes predominant again. The priority to the fight against inflation has been chosen by politicians not forced on them. Ironically, the process of economic and political integration is easier in a conservative era. It is easier to agree on a rule of thumb of free trade than to decide what form a common industrial policy should take even if we agree there should be one. Positive integration must overcome political inertia, but this is surely a feature of any complex moderately democratic system.

It seems likely that for the foreseeable future the agents of such developments will be the political leaders of the nation-states. We should surely not underestimate the importance of the efforts to build institutions to avoid conflict in Western Europe. But we seem to face very different problems in the 1990s. A revision of the Treaties is scheduled for 1996. Public opinion must mobilise before, not after, the states meet, if the member states and the Union as a whole are to properly equip themselves to address the important issues raised elsewhere in this book.

NOTES

1. The research on which this paper is based is supported by the ESRC's European Initiative. The author is very grateful for many conversations with François Duchêne, Zdenek Kavan, Helen Wallace and Alan Cawson.
2. The main test of this paper was written before this date and on the whole refers to the European Community rather than the Union.
3. Space will not allow us to say much about the monetary side of the Maastricht Treaty. The apparent collapse of the existing ERM may conceivably be helpful in forcing a rethinking of where Europe is heading. As events have shown, even this agreement merely laid out a way the member states could form a union if the political and economic conditions had been satisfied.
4. The franc as the name of currency in France, Belgium and Switzerland is a relic of this plan.

5. The ECJ's role is not in fact to act as a final appeal court, its job is to interpret the law for all levels of court.
6. Notably in the Cassis de Dijon case (1978) where it struck down a German ban on a French drink, advocating mutual recognition of standards unless a government could make a valid case against this.
7. The original Rome Treaty provided for Qualified Majority Voting in a number of areas, which the SEA extended. Big states have more votes than small ones; a roughly two-third majority of votes is needed to pass legislation under QMV. Two large and one small states can form a legal blocking minority.
8. A French importer can go to a German court to claim his rights of free access, as happened in the famous Cassis de Dijon case.
9. This is being implemented by some of the EU member states in the form of the separate Schengen agreement, named after a small village at the meeting point of several frontiers.

REFERENCES

Cohen-Tanugi, L. (1992), *l'Europe en Danger,* Paris: Fayard.

Delors Report, on Economic and Monetary Union, 1989, Luxembourg: European Community Publications.

Duchêne, F. (1990), 'Less or more than Europe? European integration in retrospect' in Crouch, C. and Marquand, D. (eds), *The Politics of 1992,* Oxford: Blackwell, pp. 9-22

EC Commission (1985), *Completing the Internal Market,* Luxembourg: European Community Publications.

Ferry, J.-M. and Thibaud, P. (1992), *Discussion sur l'Europe,* Paris: Calmann-Levy.

Kennedy, P. (1988), *The Rise and Fall of the Great Powers,* London: Fontana.

Kindleberger, C. (1987a), *The International Economic Order,* London: Harvester

Kindleberger, C. (1987b), *Marshall Plan Days,* London: Allen & Unwin.

Lenoir, R. and Lesourne, J. (eds) (1992), *Où va l'Etat,* Paris: Le Monde-Editions.

Louis, J.-V. (1990), *The EC Legal Order,* Luxembourg: European Community Publications.

Moravcsik, A. (1991), 'Negotiating the SEA', *International Organization,* Vol. 45, No. 1, Winter.

Official Journal of the European Communities, L291 15 October 1987.

Porter, B. (1983), *Britain Europe and the World,* London: Allen & Unwin.

Rosecrance, R. (1986), *Rise of the Trading State,* New York: Basic Books

Taylor, P. (1991), 'British sovereignty and the EC', *Millenium* Vol. 20, No. 1. Spring, pp. 73-80.

Wyatt, D. and Dashwood, A. (1993), European Community Law, London: Sweet & Maxwell.

6. Gender and Citizenship in East Central Europe After the End of State Socialist Policies for Women's 'Emancipation'

Barbara Einhorn

Post-1989 dialogue between East and West is necessarily difficult because of the very different political paradigms dominant in Europe during the period 1945-89. These involved different and shifting conceptions of citizenship, specifically of the balance between the rights and duties of citizens: the extent of individual responsibilities *vis-à-vis* state provision of benefits. In the immediate aftermath of state socialism, reconstructed notions of citizenship are burdened with the felt need to curb the formerly intrusive public regulation of private lives. Hence emphasis is placed on individual responsibility. However, as this paper will argue, there is a blind spot concerning gender equality as an essential component in the construction of active citizenship.

I grew up in New Zealand as the daughter of German refugees from fascism in Europe. The clear New Zealand light was for me refracted through the lenses of cross-cultural difference and the resultant scope for both greater tolerance and misunderstanding. Sometimes misunderstanding was deliberate. Mrs Koppel, one of the few grandparent figures from that distant European past who presided over my childhood, used to withhold one essential ingredient from the versions of her cake recipes she passed on to admirers. This ensured that no competitor could ever emulate her baking skills. The newly opened dialogue between East and West offers similar scope for misunderstanding, as well as learning from cross-cultural difference. Successor governments to East Central European state socialist regimes claim to be applying Western recipes for citizenship and democracy. Yet in adopting liberal theory and practice, they are replicating the fundamental lacuna of Western market societies. In both cases, gender is the essential ingredient missing from the specifications of citizenship, without which there can be no truly democratic society.

GENDER AND DEFINITIONS OF CITIZENSHIP

Active citizenship and the revival of civil society was what the upheavals of 1989 seemed to promise for the former state socialist countries of East Central Europe. Yet in the time elapsed since then, women's rights appear to have been eroded. Women have been made redundant on a mass scale, and currently constitute the majority of the unemployed in most of Eastern and Central Europe (Einhorn, 1993a; Fong and Paul,1992 Table 4; Paukert, 1991 and 1993; UN, 1992). Levels of female political representation have fallen drastically (see Einhorn, 1993a; Klimenkova, 1993; Posadskaya, 1993; Šiklová, 1993; Šilovic, 1993; Timár, 1993; Watson, 1993). Laws guaranteeing the right to have one's job held open during maternity and extended childcare leave are being ignored.[1]   Reproductive rights are massively under attack, with moves in several countries to rescind the laws providing the right to free and legal abortions (see for example Clements, 1994; Einhorn, 1993a; Heinen and Matuchniak-Krasuska, 1992).

Gender issues are at the hub of potentially explosive processes of historical and social transformation. Newly emerging dominant discourses posit the family and the nation as central in the search for identity and for new ethical and moral values in the vacuum left by the demise of state socialism. Yet while market-oriented democratic theories stress individual autonomy, currently emerging forms of nationalist pressure subordinate women yet again to a collectivity which denies them participatory citizenship and democratic control. Nationalism appears, as for much of its history, to construct a definition of autonomy and citizenship which is male. Woman, even when represented as icon of the Nation, is in fact the quintessential Other of nationalist discourse. This construes women as passive beings who have not attained political majority, but are in their reproductive role nevertheless the crucible of the nation, for whose protection (male) citizens are prepared to lay down their lives.

Nationalism in the nineteenth century confined citizenship and suffrage to property-owning adult males. Women, confined to the private sphere, were excluded on the basis of gender. State socialism catapulted women into the public sphere of work and politics. But the fundamental contradiction for women in East Central Europe was that they did not gain emancipation as citizens in their own right, but as the reward for exercising their right to work. Even this conditional citizenship, however, was complicated by their dual role as workers *and* mothers. State benefits prioritised women's productive role, but highlighted their reproductive role in times of demographic crisis. Now, market pressures are retrenching women, sending them back to hearth and home, where nationalist ideology tells them that their primary responsibility is to 'produce babies for the nation'. This chapter contends that currently re-emerging nationalist ideologies, while they vary in content and force across the region, are helping to build a concept of citizenship in the former state socialist countries of East Central Europe which is both gendered, and more generally exclusionary. Exclusion on grounds of ethnic group or language defines a national identity which is profoundly undemocratic, and inherently dangerous. The omission of gender equity from notions of citizenship being developed in these countries has similarly negative potential for the development of a society of active citizens, not to mention a society based on social justice.

Neither state socialism nor the newly democratic societies of East Central Europe seem able, thus far, to provide an environment in which women can develop their full potential as equal citizens. In the past rights were given, from above, now they are taken away by the pressures of the market and 'new' traditionalist ideologies.

The patriarchal socialist state expanded women's workplace rights at the expense of 'citizen rights' (Chamberlayne, 1990, pp. 155-6). But there was no miraculous transformation after autumn 1989. Rather, there seems at one level to have been a simple reversal. Women now 'find themselves in the peculiar position of having gained a significant expansion of their [formal] civil rights at the expense of vital economic ones' (Rosenberg, 1991, p. 129). Socialist patriarchy cramped and confined the exercise of individual initiative and autonomy; unemployment and the traumas of social upheaval and economic insecurity do not empower women to become active, participatory citizens.

Theorists of nationalism and the nation-state have emphasised the fact that it confers, at least in theory, a unitary and egalitarian status as citizen. Citizenship was defined in terms of membership of the nation-state. In practice, as William Rogers Brubaker argues, in the model of the French Revolution 'the principle of unitary citizenship ... far outstripped revolutionary practice, to which distinctions of class and gender were crucial' (Brubaker, 1990). English history provides ample illustration of the fact that women were excluded from citizenship status on the basis of their lack of majority in the eyes of the law, based on their inability to own property. 'The classical status of citizen was explicitly defined so as to exclude women' (Lister, 1993, p. 3). Their access to citizenship rights was passive and secondary, mediated by their husbands who played an active role in the public spheres of work and politics.

Hence gender, while rarely encountered as a category in theories of nationalism and the nation-state, has in practice operated as an exclusionary mechanism, hindering female entitlement to the rights and duties of citizenship. Concluding their review of historical concepts of citizenship and past social practice, Vogel and Moran point out that concepts of both citizenship and of the nation-state are currently disputed and problematic, and that 'under pressure of economic and political crises, the frontiers of membership may contract' (Vogel and Moran, 1991). Tendencies in East Central as well as some of Western Europe to confine citizenship status to the members of one ethnic or linguistic community at the expense of another are examples of such a contraction. Relegating women to the private sphere in the name of the national interest, depriving them of the right to self-determination through active participation as citizens in the public sphere, is another.

A culture of active citizenship necessitates both state legislation and social infrastructure, and for people to have the political space for articulating demands and exerting pressure. An independent women's movement *and* a political climate responsive to women's needs are crucial ingredients in constructing democratic societies characterised by gender equality. Vogel (1991, p. 82) emphasises that both grassroots activism and the involvement of women at the level of state institutions are necessary for the realisation of gender equality and women's autonomy. And participatory citizenship needs to be non-gender-specific, she suggests, to be meaningful and effective for both men and women in a democratic society.

One of the problems with realising such a conception of citizenship is the general distaste felt across East Central Europe in the aftermath of all-intrusive state socialism for politics in general, and more specifically, for any form of state intervention whatsoever. Hungarian sociologist Júlia Szalai writes: 'there is a strong and broad opposition in our countries to everything that has the slightest flavour of "statism". It is a long process to get rid of the idea and practice of the totalitarian state and to define a state that is "ours", that is created and controlled by the democratic processes of the civil society' (Szalai, 1990, pp. 34-5).

Indeed the reaction against state intervention has been so violent as to preclude any careful examination of the state socialist record on women's behalf. There are numerous obstacles to sifting through the debris of state socialism's emancipatory model in order to discover whether there were any features worth building on in the future.

One such obstacle is that women tended not to perceive the benefits of state socialist 'emancipation' as gains. Their employment rights were seen as the outcome of a state-imposed obligation or material necessity, and not as associated with the right to work. And the social (welfare) rights such as childcare facilities which underwrote their labour force participation were so taken for granted as to be invisible. Since equal rights in employment and public childcare provision have historically been high on the list of demands made by Western women's movements, there is an immediate conceptual mismatch here which becomes painfully evident in dialogue between women in East Central Europe and Western feminists.

A further problem is that the perversion of language itself by the over-simplistic sloganising of the past makes differentiated critical analysis rare. Feminism is lumped together with socialism, and any '-ism' is regarded with the utmost suspicion. 'Wonderful concepts like equality, emancipation, solidarity, can no longer be used', maintains Anastasia Posadskaya, Director of the Moscow Gender Studies Centre. 'They were used to describe a reality which was quite their opposite ... but what language do we have? We have a real linguistic crisis, and this affects our ability to communicate' (Posadskaya, 1991, pp. 134-5).

Nor is it easy, in the aftermath of state socialism, to hypothesise alternatives. As Slavenka Drakulic noted:

> We may have survived communism, but we have not yet outlived it ... [because] what communism instilled in us was precisely this immobility, this absence of a future, the absence of a dream, of the possibility of imagining our lives differently. There was hardly a way to say to yourself: This is just temporary, it will pass, it must. On the contrary, we learned to think: This will go on forever, no matter what we do. We can't change it. (Drakulic, 1992; pp. xvii, 7)

Such a failure of imagination, overlaid with women's physical exhaustion which precludes resistance, opens the way for an idealised vision which unites woman, family and nation.

THE PUBLIC/PRIVATE DIVIDE FROM AN EASTERN PERSPECTIVE

The economic need to shed labour in the transition to new market conditions is being masked by a 'new' traditionalist ideology. This celebrates women as mothers, defining them as keepers of hearth and home and custodians of the spiritual and moral values of the ethnic or wider national group. Exhausted by their double burden as mothers and full-time workers under state socialism, many women are in the short term embracing with a sigh of relief the opportunity to fill just one of these roles. This makes them susceptible to the new ideology linking the maternal role with nationalist aspirations. In several countries, politicians have peppered their rhetoric with the notion of the 'family wage'. Reinventing this notion reveals the gap between rhetoric and reality inherent in this ideology, since to implement such a move would be realistic in the former state socialist countries from the point of view neither of the state, nor of the individual family.[2]

Electoral advertising in the 1990 Hungarian elections appeared to reinforce this primary identification of women with motherhood and the fate of the nation. In the last days of the election campaign, the Hungarian Democratic Forum (MDF), which emerged from the election as the strongest partner in the coalition which governed from 1990 to 1994, 'angled for the "women's vote" with a poster showing its ideal of new Hungarian womanhood, a heavily pregnant woman gazing at the sky. The MDF believes Hungary is in need of more babies if it is to be strong' (*The Guardian*, 7 June 1990). Quite apart from the dangerously xenophobic overtones of this kind of propaganda, such discourse effectively diminishes women's citizenship rights, implying their exclusion from participation in the public sphere of politics by confinement to primary responsibility for the private domain. It would seem as if in the short term at least, while the transition to democracy in East Central Europe may be associated with the formal conferral of democratic rights, in reality it means a loss of citizenship status for women.

Women's role in the family has been central in definitions of that institution both 'before' and 'after' the upheavals of 1989. Yet subtle shifts in both official and unofficial, public and private discourse about the family underline the actual loss of citizenship status implied by the current identification of women with motherhood and the family.

'Before' 1989, the family was officially designated in state socialist rhetoric as the basic unit in society, whose function it was to produce and rear the socialist citizens of the future. However, little attention was paid to the power relations within this unit. The family therefore continued to be characterised by gender inequalities, with the well-documented result that women remained responsible for the vast majority of domestic labour in addition to their full-time jobs outside the home. Indeed, the constitutions and other legislation of the state socialist countries inscribed this dual role in law, defining women as workers and mothers without any equivalent definition of men.[3]

Unofficially, however, the private sphere enjoyed an enhanced aura both as a haven from the long arm of the socialist state, and as a site of resistance to oppressive state power. Indeed 'a partial "rehabilitation" of the right for privacy' was explicitly granted to Hungarians by János Kádár from the early 1970s in return for compliance in the public sphere.[4] Slavenka Drakulic gives voice to the ambivalent feelings about, but fierce defence of, private spaces universally felt by the women she visited across East Central Europe during early 1990:

Apartments were for us mythical cult objects ... they were life prizes, and we still regard them as such. ... An apartment, however small, however crowded with people and things, kids and animals, is 'ours'. To survive, we had to divide the territory, to set a border between private and public. The state wants it all public, it can't see into our apartment, but it can tap our telephone, read our mail. We didn't give up: everything beyond the door was considered 'theirs'. They wanted to turn our apartments into public spaces, but we didn't buy that trick. What is public is of the enemy. So we hid in our pigeonholes, leaned on each other in spite of everything, and licked our wounds. (Drakulic, 1992, pp. 91-92).

Many people invested the family with meaning as the source of dignity and creativity in a society characterised by alienated labour processes. There was a tendency to idealise it, construing it as a harmonious collectivity, pitted against the difficulties and strife of coping with the shortcomings of daily life, in a unity of interests against the intrusive state and over-politicised public domain. Benefits dispensed by this same state in the form of affordable housing, subsidised transport, food and children's clothing, public childcare facilities, and extended maternity and childcare leave, were so utterly taken for granted that they did not figure in the calculation.

The family was also regarded as fostering solidarity in an atomised society. It united the 'we' of non-existent or embryo civil society against 'them' in state power. This explains why subjectively, women did not protest their unequal position within the family. Polish sociologist Mira Marody asserts that despite being 'objectively disadvantaged' in both their private and their public roles, women did and do not perceive their situation as involving 'socially determined gender inequalities'. Rather, they tend to accept their inferior status as biologically rather than socially determined, so that it is 'natural that women spend more time at home, and men [in] public activity'. This perception of 'natural' roles is in turn reinforced by the above-mentioned 'us' versus 'them' mentality, which Marody sees as embodying an '"authorities vs. society" dichotomy' (Marody, 1990, p. 268, and 1992, pp. 2, 3).

The microstructures of the private sphere were clearly mediated by the women at the centre of the family. In the GDR, women were situated, through their role as wives, mothers, sisters and friends, at the focal point of the highly valued 'niche' society, the term coined by Günther Gaus (1983) to describe the privatised world of family and friends. The centrality of this role, together with the gender-transcending solidarity of the private sphere, seems to have overridden any oppression suffered by women within it.

Women were prepared to maintain privacy and non-intrusion by the state in the name of individual autonomy, even if that autonomy were exclusively male.

By contrast, Western feminists wanted to validate women's subjective experience within the family. Using the slogan 'the personal is political', they carried this subjective reality into the public sphere and demanded a hearing for it there. Further, they sought to break through the rigid public/private divide which confined women to a lesser realm by demonstrating that both the state and the economy depend upon the family.[5] The argument that family life is in fact state-regulated is corroborated by legislation concerning marriage and a wife's tax status, sexuality and social welfare, which denies the liberal claim to the inviolable principle of privacy within the family.[6]

Western feminists have had considerable success in challenging the view that legal regulation stops at the garden gate. State institutions like the police and the judiciary have come to mediate and adjudicate in cases of domestic violence which previously remained confined within the jealously guarded privacy of the marital home. Rape within marriage can in Britain now be contested in court. In a contrary trend, far from 'exploding' the public/private split, state socialism in effect entrenched this divide. The private sphere was idealised, in unofficial perceptions, along classical nineteenth-century liberal lines as the only site of autonomy and privacy in an over-politicised regime. Within this haven, gender-neutral solidarity took precedence over any consciousness of gender inequalities within the family.

'After' 1989, the roles of public rhetoric and private perceptions have been reversed. Public discourse by nationalist politicians and Church dignitaries alike has glorified the role of the family as the basis of the ethnic and/or national grouping, and hallowed women's role within it as mothers, as bearers of moral and spiritual values and as keepers of the national cultural heritage. The search for a new identity untainted by the state socialist legacy has led people to leapfrog history backwards and to idealise a harmonious community of an earlier epoch pitted in a struggle for national independence and sovereignty. Janina Frentzel-Zagorska points out that long before 1989, Poles tended to identify first with family and friends, then with the nation, united 'against' the socialist state, leaving a vacuum in the intermediate space where the informal associations of civil society could not exist (Frentzel-Zagorska, 1993).

Hungarian historian István Rév feels there is an identity conflict in the face of state socialism's collapse. He describes the urge to rewrite history, to erase the unpleasant memory of most people's failure to oppose the former regime, of their daily accommodation and collaboration in the struggle for survival. Nationalism is the convenient legitimising factor in this, since it defines the former Soviet Union as the quintessential 'Other', and state socialism as a 'foreign' system imposed from outside. This enables East Central Europeans to define themselves 'by right of birth' as 'insiders', who can thus assert, simply on the basis of their national identity, that they 'had always been against it'. In this way, self-definition in terms of nationalism provides a convenient mode of collective forgetting, of repressing the recent past in order to evade confrontation with one's own personal shame. What he calls 'post-Communist national identity' has a constant need for the 'Other', the 'enemy' who can be held responsible for past and present hardships. Thus he views the present intolerant and exclusionary forms of nationalism in East Central Europe as the inevitable outcome of the immediate state socialist past, and of what he sees as perverted efforts to come to terms with it (Rév, 1993).

The family model which goes along with this reincarnation of an earlier epoch is one characterised by a strict gender-divided hierarchy of roles. Additionally, while the nationalist project may endow the family with value and enhance women's role as mothers within it, in practice, the family and the friendship networks of the private sphere, so crucial in an era where the informal associations of civil society were unable to operate, have lost status in favour of the (currently male-dominated) mainstream political institutions of the public domain.

What is striking is that women's relegation to the hearth is occurring precisely at the moment when the private sphere has lost the significance it inadvertently gained as a substitute for civil society. In other words, at the very moment when women are being once again assigned to the private sphere, it is the public sphere which is being revalued, at least for men. So, while former dissident men move out of grassroots anti-political activity into the glare of public life in the structures of mainstream politics, their female counterparts fade into oblivion. There is an echo here of the nineteenth-century public/private demarcation leading to a depreciation of the domestic sphere. And the ideological celebration of hearth and home may hamper recognition on women's part that a newly entrenched public/private split plus female economic dependence will ensure only male and not female autonomy.

ESSENTIALISM AND THE EQUALITY VERSUS DIFFERENCE DEBATE

The demise of state socialism in East Central Europe has been accompanied by a rejection of the egalitarian social model it espoused. In the search to establish new collective identities to replace earlier class-based identities, social and cultural differences are emphasised. This results not only in self-identification along the lines of national heritage or ethnic origin, but also suggests an acceptance (which is already showing signs of cracking) of fast-growing social inequalities in the name of liberal individualism and economic opportunity. What is seen as the false collectivism of the past is discarded; social solidarity has gone under in favour of individual enterprise and personal responsibility for one's fate and fortunes. When times are hard, nationalism offers a safe haven in which this new burden on the individual can be sloughed off and responsibility for present hardships placed on the faceless Other outside one's own ethnic or national group. In another context, Joan Scott speaks of the way 'discrimination was redefined as simply the recognition of "natural" difference' in a process which Naomi Shor claims 'essentializes difference and naturalizes social inequity' (Scott 1988, p. 171).

Scott goes on to argue that the 'equality-versus-difference' dichotomy is an 'intellectual trap' which is also politically inhibiting. This is evident in the case of East Central Europe, where despite 'difference' models based on ethnic origin or language, there is reluctance to include gender as a category and basis of difference, because this might 'demote women to a subset of society, with a stigmatized status like Slovaks or gypsies or Jews' (Snitow, 1993, p. 42). Yet this political reluctance coexists with an ideological highlighting of 'difference' between the sexes, with the newly demarcated private and public spheres ascribed to women and men respectively. Confining women to the private sphere and to the unitary role of mother as opposed to their former dual role of mother and worker, in a context where paid employment still counts (as it did in state socialism and does in most Western social policy models, although not in the more restricted definitions of citizenship of classical liberalism and current neo-liberalism) as the expression of citizenship duties and the basis of entitlement to citizenship rights, severely curtails their citizenship rights.

It is not mere exhaustion which leads women to collude with this sexual stereotyping without recognising the potential danger to their citizenship rights which it entails. Ann Snitow points out that 'essentialism, rather than seeming like a reductionist definition of a woman, is often equated with finally letting women flower as particular beings, with subjectivities, with private interests that cannot be defined by state interests' (Snitow, 1993, p. 42). Within the confines of the 'new' ideological discourse, the gender-neutral stereotype of 'socialist man' is rejected in favour of a rediscovery of differentiated masculinity and femininity. What was seen as the asexual and de-individualising configuration of citizens was underlined by their drab appearance for which the shortcomings of the consumer industry were responsible. Now, therefore, fashion and cosmetics, the notion of consumerism in a free market, are embraced as expressions of freedom and individuality.

However, this new ideological paradigm constrains and limits choices in the female role models available, since it comes packaged with old stereotypes of women as madonnas (asexual mothers in the traditional family model) or whores (with the prostitute cast by some commentators as pathbreaking entrepreneur in the market). Within the dominant discourse of the family as custodian of the cultural, spiritual and moral values of the nation, femininity tends to be equated with maternity, woman symbolically stands for the nation. As Scott (1988, p. 175) argues, 'to maintain that womanhood is motherhood is to obscure the differences that make choice possible'. In this essentialist paradigm, women are reduced to their reproductive role. This is exemplified in the attacks on reproductive choice which are visible in new laws undermining free access to abortion in Germany, Poland and Hungary. Taken to its extreme, this essentialist and masculine paradigm is expressed in the mass rapes and forced pregnancies which have resulted from the brutal alliance of ethnically-based nationalism and militarism in Bosnia.[8]

There is ongoing debate in feminist political theory on the appropriateness of a gender-neutral versus an 'affirmative action' approach in legislation and definitions of citizenship. Many scholars have stressed the inadequacy of a gender-neutral approach exemplified in the gender-blindness of, indeed the exclusion of women as a category from, liberal democratic universalistic concepts of citizenship (see Lister, 1993; Vogel, 1991; Anthias and Yuval-Davis, 1989). Others feel that the 'affirmative action' or 'difference' approach may be discredited as 'special pleading' for women and used to constrain their choices rather than being seen as necessary conditions to enable women to exert equivalent rights to subject status as citizens.[9] Ultimately, as Ruth Lister contends, 'the equality vs. difference debate can, if we are not careful, lead us into a theoretical cul-de-sac' (Lister, 1993, p. 13). What is needed is 'to transcend rather than be confined by the equality vs. difference dichotomy' (Scott, 1988 and Lister, 1993, ibid.). Lister's conclusion could be applied to East Central Europe:

> If women are to enter full citizenship, it is going to require radical changes in both the 'private' sphere *and* each of the public spheres [paid employment, social rights and the state, and the political sphere], *as well as* a challenge to the rigid separation between the two'. (Lister 1993, p.13)[10]

In the case of the former state socialist societies of East Central Europe, it has become *de rigueur* to emphasise the cultural and historical differences between them. Equally, the need to acknowledge differences between women has been frequently invoked (see, for example, Šiklová, 1993). Not only is the latter difficult in practical terms, since disaggregated empirical data do not, on the whole, yet exist. At a theoretical level too, the very fact of their shared history in living through the socialist experiment of women's 'emancipation' makes for common and hence comparable experiences (Snitow, 1993, p. 41; Einhorn, 1993a).

CONCLUSION

The recognition of cultural difference remains an important prerequisite for a constructive East-West dialogue. Such a dialogue could contribute creatively to a process of rethinking the concept of active, participatory citizenship in a way which includes gender equality. When studying developments in East Central Europe, it is therefore important for Western scholars not to succumb to the temptations of the 'colonialist gaze' adopted by Western businessmen and politicians, and so bitterly resented by people in East Central Europe (Bassnett, 1992).[11]

In her analysis of the cinematic *oeuvre* of Hungarian director Márta Mészáros, Catherine Portuges highlights the problems inherent in the approach of feminist film critics who claim as feminist Mészáros's films, on the basis that they all have female leads. Since the fall of state socialism in 1989, this tendency on the part of Western feminists has been hampering East-West dialogue on gender issues, both between scholars and grassroots activists. Portuges states on this subject:

> If we are truly to validate feminist claims that authenticate and honour subjectivity and difference, we must consider the vexing question of the critical appropriation of second world realities by first world formulations. ... Such colonizations, however unwitting, of the cultural products of a small, marginalized nation in the service of theorizing its discourse within the conceptualizations of a dominant Western discourse, oppositional though it may be in the context of its own mainstream, risks misreadings and misapprehensions'. (Portuges, 1993, p. 9; see also Snitow, 1993)

Creative East-West dialogue necessitates a constant awareness of and sensitivity to the enormous differences in life experience. It is likely that

Eastern European women's responses to their present situation will vary depending on their national culture and their more recent state socialist history. Their reactions will differ from country to country in East Central Europe, and will also diverge from the experience gained from the past twenty years of feminist struggles in the West. Their insights could help us to rethink our aspirations and demands, developing new approaches to ensure that gender is an integral focus of all debates on citizenship and democracy.

Former member of Charter 77 and gender studies pioneer Jirina Šiklová suggests that women in East Central Europe will get involved politically, but in a creative and new fashion which differs from that envisaged by Western feminists:

> Probably our women will not stress so much the importance of politics and will not consider a complete equality quota representation in all leading executive positions as the maximum point of their emancipation. ... I believe that our women who have had the experience of living under totalitarian regimes will not merely mimic men but that they will discover a new way of political participation and leadership with enough space for solidarity to uphold our traditional female qualities. (Šiklová, 1992, p. 17)

At the present time, women in East Central Europe do not perceive the return to hearth and home as necessarily a defeat or even a retreat. After all, in many of these cultures, traditionally women's role in the family was a strong one. In the nineteenth century of the idealised nation as now construed, in Poland for example, she protected the hearth and worked as sole provider for the family while her menfolk were fighting in insurrections to reclaim the nation, or exiled to Siberia, during the 150 years of partition. The dwindling self-esteem associated with motherhood by Western feminists may not be relevant. Indeed in the mid- to long-term, speculates Hungarian sociologist Júlia Szalai, women's experience in mediating the informal networks of the past, their adept ability to juggle and improvise using scarce resources, will stand them in good stead for creating the autonomous grassroots organisations of a future civil society (Szalai, 1991, p. 153). Again the developing country experience might suggest the notion of motherhood and responsibility for the family as a strong position from which politically effective activism can come, as in the case of the Chilean housewives banging their saucepans in Santiago, or the Mothers of the Disappeared in Argentina (see Fisher, 1993; Jacquette, 1989; Waylen, 1994).

Many women in East Central Europe stated in the immediate aftermath of 1989 that they had experienced their past working lives not as the expression of the right to work, but rather as a state-imposed obligation.

Yet oral and other evidence indicates that despite having no choice about whether or not to become economically active, and the burdens of their dual role, women gained more than relative economic independence from their past working lives.[12] More recently, survey and opinion poll evidence is emerging which underlines this, showing that a majority of women in Bulgaria, the Czech Republic, Hungary, the former GDR and the former Soviet Union would prefer to go out to work, even if they did not need to for material reasons (see Einhorn, 1993b and van den Heuvel, 1990).[13] It is likely, therefore, that in the medium term, women will defend their right to work. As Liba Paukert (1991) has commented, 'the professional activity of women has now become so much a part of the social norm in Czechoslovakia that a change might be difficult to accept'. The right to work and to the social amenities upon which the exercise of that right is predicated may well be the first citizenship rights which women in East Central Europe will want to defend. I would hypothesise that the right to adequate political representation of their needs and interests will follow (see Klimenkova, 1993 and Snitow, 1993). Already a myriad small informal, autonomous interest groups are being formed by women to defend lost social welfare rights or fight for the political rights which were previously granted them from above. The tradition of women's citizenship rights as being won by struggle is at this moment being born in East Central Europe. Ideally, the difficult but rewarding East-West dialogue could generate a new concept of active citizenship which celebrates choice, and institutionalises an equality of social opportunity which does not obliterate cultural difference, whether of sex, sexual preference, class, race or ethnicity.

NOTES

1. An example which stands for many is that of Poland, where Joanna Regulska points out that 'new legislation has omitted women as a category or introduced restrictions on previously attained rights' (Regulska, 1993, see also Klimenkova, 1993).
2. Ruth Lister (1993, p. 4) cites Pateman (1989) as noting that in British and other Western definitions of citizenship obligations, 'employment has replaced military service as the "key to citizenship"'. But the ideology of the family wage still lurking beneath this definition seriously undermines women's role as citizens. The same is true of East Central Europe, where social welfare rights were in the past linked to employment (Szalai, 1991, p. 153).
3. Section 3 of the GDR's 1977 revised Labour Code, for example, declared that:

   > The socialist state shall ensure that conditions are created everywhere which enable women increasingly to live up to their equal status at work and in vocational education and *to reconcile even more successfully their occupational activities with the duties they have to fulfil as mothers and within the family.* (Italics added)

4. For an elaboration of this 'innovation of Kádárism', see Szalai (1992, p. 42ff).

5. O'Donovan (1985, p. 160) points out that:

> the ideology of equality which nineteenth-century women relied on in their struggle against discriminatory laws and practices which denied them access to education and employment was formal equality. ... The interaction between private and public and the consequent restraints on freedom were ignored. Hidden behind the rhetoric of equality were issues of whether to recognize in the public sphere needs which arise out of the private. This continues today. The conflict reformers face between the values of individualism in the market-place and community in the family has been managed hitherto through reliance on the language of freedom of contract and formal equality.

Feminist scholars have also sought to explode the dichotomy behind the liberal concept of private and public defined as 'areas of activity and behaviour unregulated or regulated by law' (ibid. p. 3).
6. For an elaboration of a range of feminist critiques of the public/private divide, see Pateman (1989, pp. 118-41).
7. In the context of rural Poland, 'ideologically, the man is associated with the farm and productivity, the woman with the household and reproduction. ... Thus, male identity and prestige can be seen as linked to social and economic roles extending from farming and reaching beyond the family, while female identity and value revolve around the roles of wife and mother' (Pine, 1992, p. 63).

Ironically for societies in transition to the market, this traditional ideology resembles the gender-divided, household-based community (*Gemeinschaft*) which German sociologist Ferdinand Tönnies counterposed to the market-based, contractually regulated society (*Gesellschaft*). Households within the organic community were based, in Tönnies's view, on what he saw as a 'natural' division of labour, in which 'for women, the home and not the market, their own or a friend's dwelling and not the street, is the natural seat of their activity' (Tönnies' 1955, pp. 174-5, 186):

> In defending their common property the task of the woman consists in the protection of valued possessions; the man has to keep off the enemy. To obtain and provide the necessities of living is the field of the man, to conserve and prepare them that of the woman, as far as food is concerned. And when other work and the instruction of the younger therein is needed, we find that the masculine energy is directed towards the outside, fighting, and leading the sons. The woman, on the other hand, remains confined to the inner circle of home life and is attached to the female children. ... But such a division of labour may also be regarded as a relation between guidance and leadership, on the one hand, and compliance and obedience, on the other. It must be recognized that all these differentiations follow a pattern of nature. (Tönnies ibid. pp. 45-6)

8. For further discussion of women's reproductive rights and the impact of nationalism in undermining women's citizenship rights in East Central Europe, see Einhorn (1993a).
9. See, for example, Helsinki Watch (1992, p. 4) which argues that 'it is essential to realize that gender-specific laws have no place in a modern society and that even when meant as a protection, in effect they provide an opportunity for discrimination'.
10. For speculation on how an altered relationship between public and private spheres might look in East Central Europe, see Snitow (1993, p. 44).
11. See also Snitow (ibid., p. 41) who speaks of a 'healthy resistance to the colonial incursion of imported concepts'.
12. Jirina Šiklová (1993) does not 'believe in the often-mentioned idea that many of our women will leave the workforce for the proverbial "kitchen". Women have gained status, experience, qualifications and have found financial independence through their jobs. Many have also found their self-realisation and identify with their work'.
13. This survey and opinion poll data does not indicate whether differences between professional and non-professional occupations alter women's responses.

REFERENCES

Anthias, Flora and Nira Yuval-Davis (eds) (1989), *Woman-Nation-State*, Basingstoke: Macmillan.

Bassnett, Susan (1992), 'Crossing Cultural Boundaries or How I Became an Expert on East European Women Overnight', in: *Women's Studies International Forum*, vol. 15, no. 1, pp. 11-15.

Brubaker, William Rogers (1990), 'Immigration, Citizenship and the Nation-State in France and Germany: A Comparative Historical Analysis', in: *International Sociology*, vol. 5, no. 4, pp. 379-407.

Chamberlayne, Prue (1990), 'Neigbourhood and Tenant Participation in the GDR', in: Bob Deacon and Julia Szalai (eds), *Social Policy in the New Eastern Europe: What Future for Socialist Welfare?*, Aldershot: Avebury.

Clements, Elizabeth (1994), 'The Abortion Debate in Unified Germany', in: Elizabeth Boa and Janet Wharton (eds), *German Monitor, Women and the Wende: Social Effects and Cultural Reflections of the German Unification Process*, Amsterdam: Rodopi, pp.38-52.

Deacon, Bob and Júlia Szalai (eds) (1990), *Social Policy in the New Eastern Europe: What Future for Socialist Welfare?*, Aldershot: Avebury.

Deacon, Bob (ed.)(1992), *Social Policy, Social Justice and Citizenship in Eastern Europe*, Aldershot: Avebury.

Drakulic, Slavenka (1992), *How We Survived Communism and Even Laughed*, London: Hutchinson.

Einhorn, Barbara (1993a), *Cinderella Goes to Market: Citizenship, Gender and Women's Movements in East Central Europe*, London: Verso.

Einhorn, Barbara (1993b), 'The Impact of the Transition from Centrally Planned to Market Economies on Women's Employment in East Central Europe', Paper prepared for the Interdepartmental Project on Equality for Women in Employment, Geneva: ILO.

Fisher, Jo (1993), *Out of the Shadows: Women, Resistance and Politics in South America*, London: Latin American Bureau.

Fong, Monica S. and Paul, Gillian (1992), 'The Changing Role of Women in Employment in Eastern Eruope', World Bank, Europe and Central Asia Region, Population and Human Resources Division, Report no. 8213, February.

Frentzel-Zagorska, Janina (1993), 'Political Pluralism by Democratic Design (Poland, Hungary, Czech and Slovak Republics)', Paper given at the Conference 'Europe at La Trobe', Melbourne, 5-9 July.

Gaus, Günter (1983), *Wo Deutschland Liegt: Eine Ortsbestimmung*, Hamburg: Hoffman und Campe, und München: Deutscher Taschenbuchverlag.

Heinen, Jacqueline and Matuchniak-Krasuska, Anna (1992), *L'avortement en Pologne: La croix et la bannière*, Paris: L'Armattan.

Helsinki Watch (1992), 'Hidden Victims: Women in Post-Communist Poland', in: *News from Helsinki Watch*, vol. IV, issue 5, March 12.

Heuvel, Katrina van den (1990), 'Glasnost for Women?', in: *The Nation*, June 4, pp. 773-79.

Jaquette, Jane S. (ed.) (1989), *The Women's Movement in Latin America: Feminism and the Transition to Democracy*, Boston: Unwin Hyman.

Klimenkova, T.A. (1993), 'Problems and Strategies of the New Russian Women's Movement: Aren't We Involved in Politics?', Paper presented to the Conference on 'From Dictatorship to Democracy: Women in Mediterranean, Central and Eastern Europe', Barcelona, 16-18 September.

Lister, Ruth (1993), 'Tracing the Contours of Women's Citizenship', in: *Policy and Politics,* vol. 21, no. 1, pp. 3-16.

Marody, Mira (1990), 'Perception of Politics in Polish Society', in: *Social Research*, vol. 57, no. 2, Summer, pp.257-74.

Marody, Mira (1992), 'Why I Am Not a Feminist?', manuscript.

O'Donovan, Katherine (1985), *Sexual Divisions in Law,* London: Weidenfeld and Nicholson.

Pateman, Carol (1989), *The Disorder of Women,* Cambridge: Polity.

Paukert, Liba (1991), 'The Economic Status of Women in the Transition to a Market System: The Case of Czechoslovakia', in: *International Labour Review*, vol. 130 (5-6), pp. 613-33.

Paukert, Liba (1993), 'Women's Employment in East-Central European Countries During the Period of Transition to a Market Economy System', Geneva: ILO, Working Paper.

Pine, Frances (1992), 'Uneven Burdens: Women in Rural Poland', in: Shirin Rai, Hilary Pilkington and Annie Phizacklea (eds), *Women in the Face of Change: The Soviet Union, Eastern Europe and China,* London: Routledge, pp. 57-75.

Plakwicz, Jolanta (1992), 'Between Church and State: Polish Women's Experience', in: Chris Corrin (ed), *Superwomen and the Double Burden: Women's Experience of Change in Central and Eastern Europe and the Former Soviet Union,* London: Scarlet Press, pp. 75-96.

Portuges, Catherine (1993), *Screen Memories: The Hungarian Cinema of Márta Mészàros,* Bloomington: Indiana University Press.

Posadskaya, Anastasia (1991), Interview with Maxine Molyneux, in: *Shifting Territories: Feminism and Europe,* Special Issue no. 39 of *Feminist Review,* Winter, pp.130-40.

Posadskaya, Anatasia (1993), 'Women's Daily Life: Strategies and Development of New Identities', Paper given to the Colloquium on 'Women's Daily Life and Equal Opportunity Policies: Central and Easten European Societies in the Transition' held at the European University Institute, Florence, January 28-30.

Regulska, Joanna (1993), 'Citizenship in the Democratic State; Do Polish Women Have a Chance?', Paper presented at the Conference on 'From Dictatorship to Democracy: Women in Mediterranean, Central and Eastern Europe', Barcelona, 16-18 September.

Rév, István (1993), 'Post-Communist Identity', Public lecture to the School of European Studies, Sussex University, Brighton, England, 18 January.

Rosenberg, Dorothy (1991) 'Shock Therapy: GDR Women in Transition from a Socialist Welfare State to a Social Market Economy', in: *Signs*, vol. 17, no. 1, Autumn, pp.129-51.

Rosenberg, Dorothy (1993), 'The New Home Economics: Women in the United Germany, in: *Debatte: Review of Contemporary German Affairs,* vol. 1, no. 1, pp. 111-34.

Scott, Joan Wallach (1988), 'The Sears Case', in: Scott, *Gender and the Politics of History,* New York: Columbia University Press, pp. 167-78.

Šiklová, Jirina, (1992), 'Women in Leadership, Women in Power', Paper prepared for conference at Harvard.

Šiklová, Jirina (1993), 'Basic Information about Women in the Czech Republic', Paper presented to the Conference on 'From Dictatorship to Democracy: Women in Mediterranean, Central and Eastern Europe', Barcelona, 16-18 September.

Silovic, Dasha Sasic (1993), 'The Status of Women in Eastern and Central Europe', Paper for the Project on 'Transitions to Democracy in World Perspective', Center for Social Studies, City University of New York Graduate Center, June.

Snitow, Ann (1993), 'Feminist Futures in the Former East Bloc', in: *Peace and Democracy News*, vol. VII, no. 1, Summer, pp. 1, 40-44.

Stašná, Jaroslava (1993), 'Czechoslovak Women Yesterday, Today and Tomorrow', Paper given to the Colloquium on 'Women's Daily Life and Equal Opportunity Policies: Central and Eastern European Societies in the Transition' held at the European University Institute, Florence, January 28-30.

Szalai, Júlia (1990), in: Bob Deacon and Júlia Szalai (eds), *Social Policy in the New Eastern Europe: What Future for Socialist Welfare?*, Aldershot: Avebury.

Szalai, Júlia (1991), 'Some Aspects of the Changing Situation of Women in Hungary', in: *Signs*, vol. 17, no. 1, Autumn, pp. 152-70.

Szalai, Júlia (1992), 'Social Participation in Hungary in the Context of Restructuring and Liberalization', in: Bob Deacon, (ed.), *Social Policy, Social Justice and Citizenship in Eastern Europe*, Aldershot: Avebury.

The Guardian, 7 June 1990.

Timár, Júdit (1993), 'The Changing Rights and Conditions of Women in Hungary', Paper presented to the Conference on 'From Dictatorship to Democracy: Women in Mediterranean, Central and Eastern Europe', Barcelona, 16-18 September.

Tönnies, Ferdinand (1955), *Community and Association* (English translation of *Gemeinschaft und Gesellschaft*, by Charles Loomis), London: Routledge & Kegan Paul, reprinted 1974.

UN (1992), *The Impact of Economic and Political Reform on the Status of Women in Eastern Europe*, Proceedings of a UN Regional Seminar, 8-12 April 1991 in Vienna, ST-CSDHA-19-UN, New York: UN.

Vogel, Ursula (1991), 'Is Citizenship Gender-Specific?', in: Ursula Vogel and Michael Moran (eds) (1991), *The Frontiers of Citizenship*, Basingstoke: Macmillan.

Vogel, Ursula and Moran, Michael (eds) (1991), *The Frontiers of Citizenship*, Basingstoke: Macmillan.

Watson, Peggy (1993), 'The Rise of Masculinism in Eastern Europe', in: *New Left Review*, no. 198, March-April, pp. 71-82.

Waylen, Georgina (1994), 'Women and Democratization: Conceptualizing Gender Relations in Transition Politics', in *World Politics*, Vol. 46, no. 3, April, pp. 327-55.

PART II

7. Marketisation and Nationalism: a Critical Interface in the Process of Transformation

David A. Dyker

INTRODUCTION

As civil war rages in Yugoslavia, as Czechoslovakia prepares for dissolution into its constituent ethnic parts, and the CIS sinks to the level of little more than a football team at the European championships, this seems a grimly appropriate time to seek to reassess our ideas about the relationship between decommunisation and the movement towards a market economy, and renascent nationalism in Eastern Europe. So much has been happening simultaneously in Eastern Europe that we will, in the course of the investigation, come repeatedly up against the problem of direction of causality. But let us begin by looking critically at the underlying generalisation implicit in the formulation of the theme, that the new wave of nationalism in Eastern Europe is closely tied in with marketisation, whichever way the causation runs. It is, indeed, not difficult to find particular case studies which support the underlying generalisation. We pick out the Baltic region of the former Soviet Union and Slovenia, formerly part of Yugoslavia.

THE CASE FOR THE SIMPLE CORRELATION MODEL

The Baltic republics (Estonia, Latvia and Lithuania) of the former Soviet Union had been forcibly incorporated into that Union by Stalin in 1940, pursuant on the Nazi-Soviet Pact of 1939. Political repression did not stop them emerging in the post-war period as the most successful of the Soviet republics from an economic point of view, with a clear-cut specialisation in the fields of agriculture and light industry, though also with a very significant defence industry presence. It was no doubt partly on account of this comparatively strong economic record that the Baltic republics were picked out, even in the time of Brezhnev, as suitable proving-grounds for what passed at the time for radical economic experiments, along with their southerly Slav neighbour, Belorussia (now Belarus) (Dyker, 1991, pp. 138-9; 1983, pp. 77 and 87).

But it was in the early phase of Gorbachev's *perestroika* (1985-89) that the Baltic republics began to emerge as a critical focal point of the new, powerfully dynamic forces that were being unleashed in Soviet society. In formulating his concept of republican *khozraschet*, that is, republic-level business and financial autonomy in the context of hard budget constraints *vis-à-vis* the centre, the last Soviet president sought to make a crucial step forwards in his campaign to combine the logic and discipline of the market with a reinvigorated central planning. But the 'Estonia/Latvia/Lithuania plc' model backfired on Gorbachev. The governments and peoples of the Baltic republics welcomed their increased economic autonomy, but before long started to ask why this autonomy should be restricted to the economic sphere, and indeed why autonomy should not be extended into independence. The result was the development, from 1989 onwards, of increasingly vocal national independence movements, which the Soviet government sought to counter through a policy of economic pressure, intimidation and minor police violence. The efforts of the independence movements were finally rewarded when the separate, sovereign statehood of the three republics was recognised by the Soviet government after the *putsch* of August 1991. As independent states, all three republics are now vigorously implementing radical marketisation and privatisation programmes.

A similar story has unfolded in Slovenia, the most northerly of the republics of the former Yugoslavia. Always the most economically developed of the Yugoslav regions, Slovenia was able, during the difficult decades of the 1970s and 1980s, to maintain a degree of impetus in exporting to hard-currency markets. The late 1980s witnessed a deep political crisis in the little Alpine republic, with the League of Communists suffering an almost total loss of credibility (Dyker, 1990, p. 172) and the position of the Yugoslav army within the republic giving rise to extreme tension. In 1988 it was revealed that the army had a contingency plan for taking over in Slovenia in the event of Party authority collapsing altogether (Dyker, 1990, p. 183). These developments were accompanied by a big swing in popular preferences (as documented by public opinion surveys) towards political pluralism, private enterprise and hard budget constraints (Dyker, 1990, pp. 176-7 and 180).

The great watershed came in April 1990, with the holding of the first democratic election in Slovenia since the Second World War, in the wake of the wave of democratisation which had enveloped Eastern Europe from late 1989 onwards. The election gave the League of Communists only 17 per cent of the total vote, and a number of right-of-centre nationalist parties were able to come together and form a government under the collective name of DEMOS. The new government was quick to adopt a separatist stance, though cautious in moving towards an outright break with Yugoslavia. A referendum of December 1990 produced an overwhelming vote in favour of independence, but the government then decided it should give itself a six-month 'cooling-off' period before making any concrete moves. When the six months was up, however, Slovenia proceeded to secede formally from Yugoslavia. It was at this point that the Yugoslav army finally tried to implement something like its contingency plan of 1988, with a destructive, but ultimately unsuccessful, military campaign in Slovenia during June and July of 1991. On the subsequent withdrawal of the army from the northern republic, Slovenia attained *de facto* independence. The EC recognised that independence in early 1992. Since mid-1991 the Slovenian government has pursued wide-ranging policies of liberalisation and privatisation.

The Baltic states and Slovenia seem, then, to represent perfect illustrations of a process hereby relatively prosperous bits of the old communist world break off and join the world economic system, with national consciousness, pluralistic political attitudes and a market-oriented mind-set developing more or less simultaneously, feeding on each other and reinforcing one another.

THE CASE AGAINST

But yet we have to be careful not to try to squeeze too much mileage out of the Baltic and Slovenian cases. The latter case does, indeed, present one enormous methodological problem. Since Yugoslavia was practising a form of market socialism from as early as 1953, did the economic dimension of the revolution of 1990 represent anything more than a reconversion to the cause of private, as opposed to socialised, property and should that revolution not therefore be viewed as something essentially political in nature, with strictly subsidiary economic features? There are, certainly, no complications of that nature in the Baltic case, where the pre-independence economic system never moved very far from the principles of classic central planning. Rather the problem here is whether we can identify the Baltic case as typically Soviet. For just as the manner in which the Baltic region was absorbed into the Soviet Union was *sui generis*, so we find that the pattern of emergent nationalism is very different from the Baltic pattern in other non-Russian areas of the old union. In Transcaucasia, for example, the resurfacing of belligerent nationalism among Georgians, Armenians and Azerbaidzhanis alike seems to have been a purely ethno-political phenomenon, focusing largely on disputes about national territory (Nagorny Karabakh, Southern Ossetia and so on), with no specific economico-systemic dimension whatsoever. In Ukraine, by far the most important of the ex-Soviet republics after Russia from the point of view of both industry and agriculture, the increasingly strident assertion of national identity from 1990 onwards has been coupled, at the level of official pronouncements, with a programme of marketisation and privatisation on the economic dimension. At the level of implementation, however, Ukraine has scarcely forced the pace, and at the time of writing, critical issues relating to privatisation, agriculture and the budget had hardly begun to be addressed (Barabash and Vasilik, 1992).

Any attempt to portray the relationship between nationalism and marketisation in terms of a universal, simple, direct correlation is, therefore, doomed to failure. Yet that is surely not the end of the story. Are there not other factors involved here which tie in with both the nationalism and marketisation variables, and which can help us to identify a more complex pattern of interaction? My own view is that there may be many such factors. The one I want to concentrate on is the nomenklatura factor.

FROM *APPARATCHIK* TO NOMENKLATURA NATIONALIST: THE EVOLUTION OF A RULING GROUP

The professional apparatus of the Soviet Communist Party, and of its clones in Eastern Europe, was always organised on a territorial basis. From the early Stalin period onwards, the key actors were the professional Party secretaries at province and city level, who tended to dominate Communist Party Central Committees. These *apparatchiki* played a crucial role as trouble-shooters, oiling the wheels of creaky centrally planned systems, and generally making a system that was on paper unworkable, (just about) workable. This gave them great effective power, *vis-à-vis* centre and local populations alike. It was as systems became increasingly corrupt, from the 1970s onwards, that the system of territorial Party organisation degenerated into the pattern of *feudal-bureaucratic power and privilege* so characteristic of the last years of Soviet and East European communism.

This helps us to understand why Gorbachev, a genuine enough reformer, came up with the (to Western eyes) rather bizarre idea of Estonia/Latvia/Lithuania plc as he sought to reform the communist system without doing away with it altogether. Just as the *apparatchik* mind instinctively views administration in territorial terms, so equally instinctively, however illogically, it tends to see the decentralisation of administration in territorial terms. It is significant in this context that the first major economic reform in Soviet economic history, Khrushchev's *sovnarkhoz* reform of 1957, which signalled a strikingly early recognition that all was not well in the Soviet socialist economy, was based on the creation of a network of regional economic councils territorially identical with existing provincial/city/republican units, that is, identical with the territorial profile of the top Party elite. That Khrushchev's *sovnarkhoz* reform was a complete failure from the economic point of view was largely a function of the fact that it did nothing whatsoever to strengthen the market principle within the Soviet economic system, and that in enhancing the role of local political elites it merely exacerbated perennial weaknesses of that system, notably the tendency to organisational autarky (taking, under the *sovnarkhoz* reform, an explicitly territorial form). Gorbachev had by 1987 got as far as recognising that there can be no effective decentralisation without a dominant place for the market principle, but seems to have failed to recognise that in the Western international economy the spatial identity of large business organisations is nearly always defined in terms of lines of communication, rather than in terms of a well-defined, compact territory. He was not, however, alone in that failure, and many of his like-minded apparatus colleagues were still in power at the time of writing, most notably President Leonid Kravchuk of Ukraine.

The history of Yugoslavia offers a somewhat different, but equally fascinating story of interaction between nomenklatura politics, nationalism and the market. The uniqueness of the Yugoslav case derives from the fact that the Tito regime had, indeed, already introduced a form of market socialism at a time when economic Stalinism still reigned in the rest of Eastern Europe, and from the genuine federalism of the Yugoslav state that emerged from the confrontation with Stalin. Both the market and nationalism were already in the open in Yugoslavia by the 1950s, and there can be no doubt that Tito saw this 'liberalism' as, *inter alia*, a way of taking the heat out a situation that was fraught with ethnic and economico-territorial tensions deriving from the bloody intercommunal strife of the war years and the extreme regional inequalities of the Yugoslav area.

But the compromises of the 1950s, while providing a perfectly serviceable base for rapid economic growth, did not offer a permanent, stable solution to the underlying problems. By the early 1960s it was clear that economic growth would only continue if the free play of market forces was extended into the two areas that had hitherto been kept largely under state control, foreign trade and investment. The result was a series of reforms, 1961-65, which sought, in the realm of investment finance, to replace state capitalism with an active banking system, and tried to set out a pathway that would eventually take Yugoslavia to a liberal external trading regime.

At this point things began to go wrong. While the partial marketisation of the 1950s had generated a functional, though fragile consensus, the more full-blooded version of market socialism introduced in the early to mid-1960s soon gave birth to critical new political tensions

The main focus of the trouble was Croatia. Against the background of a rising wave of Croatian cultural nationalism, resentment mounted against what were perceived as anti-Croatian elements in the economic reform. The view from Zagreb can be summarised as follows. The economic reform had marketised banking capital which had previously been state capital, raised from general taxation, therefore more than proportionately from the better-off republics, including Croatia. But the big investment funds-turned-banks still had their offices in Belgrade, and that meant that they operated as essentially Serbian banks. The increasingly frantic Croatian press showed itself adept at finding cases where these banks were setting up exploitative financial relations with Croatian business organisations. Similar stories about the now autonomous, but still privileged, import-export houses abounded.

It is not our purpose here to pass judgement on the point at issue between Belgrade and Zagreb in this period. No doubt the Croats exaggerated, but no doubt also some real systemic problem areas were opened up by the attempt to implement a more consistent form of market socialism. For our theme, however, the important thing is the way that Tito tried to solve the problem, once he had decided, at the end of 1971, that with the unity of Yugoslavia threatened, enough was enough.

The initial reaction was a classically Leninis one. The Croatian League of Communists was drastically purged, to rid it of nationalist elements. But the purge was not confined to the problem republic, and in Serbia for instance, there were mass expulsions of 'liberal' elements. At the same time, however, the Yugoslav president sought to provide a new safety-valve for nationalist pressures by allowing the formal structure of the Yugoslav state to move further in the direction of federative polity. Indeed the new constitution of 1974 in some respects converted Yugoslavia into a confederation, with republics devolving powers to the federation rather than the other way round. What Tito was counting on was that a re-Leninised League of Communists, purged throughout Yugoslavia of unreliable elements, would provide the cement to hold the new system together, and ensure that republican governments used their new powers to advance the national interests of Yugoslavia, rather than just regional or sectional interests.

Tito's compromise of 1972-74 was a short-term triumph but a medium-term disaster.

> The new key to political legitimacy was, and remains to this day, the special national interests of the Yugoslav peoples, as represented and defended by the republican power elites. Yugoslav communism, which after the successful resistance to the pressures of the Cominform had become 'national communism' ... now became 'communist nationalism' ... The regime adopted nationalism as a key part of its own identity, a part which would later become the whole ... [For] it is possible to instrumentalise nationalism only in the short term. (Teokarevic, 1991, pp. 50-52)

At a more mundane level, communist cadres at republican level seized the opportunity to reassert their political dominance, but did so through the establishment of regional webs of nepotism, corruption and economic privilege. Politicians used their power over key appointments to turn republican banks into paymasters to the Party, and their veto power in the counsels of the Yugoslav Federation to block any attempts to implement the principle of the 'unity of the Yugoslav market'. In this way they were able to 'deliver' monopoly positions to big regional firms, often under the rubric of the 'planning agreements' which the 1974 constitution sought to develop as an 'associationist' alternative way of settling the investment questions which had become so fraught in the late 1960s. With the National Bank now virtually powerless to protect the national balance of payments, the republics, especially the poorer ones, went on an international borrowing spree which paved the way for the external debt-service crisis of 1982-83.

The first confirmed sighting of the genus 'nomenklatura nationalist' was probably not in Yugoslavia, but rather in the late 1950s in the Central Asian region of the Soviet Union. There, the political compromises of the Khrushchev reforms combined with a local ethnic pattern that made each *sovnarkhoz* identical with a national group ruled by a local nomenklatura composed largely of members of that same national group. The result was a level of autarkism which can hardly be explained purely in terms of the operational weaknesses of central planning (Dyker, 1983, especially chapter 2). But this had nothing to do with marketisation, and indeed when the post-Khrushchev government decided in 1965 to press on cautiously with marketisation (it subsequently changed its mind), it simultaneously abolished the *sovnarkhozy*. But it was unable to reverse the trend back towards a more traditional political economy which had established itself in the *sovnarkhoz* years in Central Asia. The 1970s were a decade of increasing political corruption in the region, and this was strongly correlated with vigorous growth in the second economy, that is, a kind of *sub rosa* privatisation (Lubin, 1984, especially chapter 6).

All of this happened, then, within the context of what remained a centrally planned economy. In the Yugoslav case, by contrast, it was the semi-market economy of the associationist system which provided the backdrop for the emergence of the nomenklatura nationalist as, for the first time, the dominant element in a notionally communist political system. A more fully-fledged version of the market economy would almost certainly have blown these nomenklatura nationalists away, since it would have deprived them of the basis for trading-in-favours. But as had become clear through the crisis of the late 1960s and early 1970s the alternative, in the Yugoslav case, was probably national break-up.

SYNTHESIS: A PRELIMINARY PROPOSAL

A more detailed persusal of the modalities of the Yugoslav pattern do, then, provide an explanation for the apparent paradoxes of the Slovenian case, as documented earlier. The Slovenian economy of the late 1980s was *not* a market economy. Rather it was an inefficient, associationist economy, run by a corrupt and ineffectual group of nomenklatura nationalist(s). On this reading, the 'revolution' of the late 1980s and early 1990s should be seen as representing a two-fold protest, against a bad economic system which had brought the country close to ruin, and against a bad political system which had made itself worse by trying to accommodate nationalism.

Having, as it were, 'saved' the Slovenian case as a classic example of close correlation between marketisation and separatist nationalism, we can use the foregoing material as a basis for advancing another hypothesis, that nationalism in Eastern Europe is by its very nature ambivalent:

> Nationalism is the last phase of communism. It represents the final attempt by the old ideology to find support within society for dictatorship ... At the same time, it is an expression of opposition to communism. (Michnik, 1990, p. 13)

It is precisely for this reason that we need to break down nationalism into its diverse forms. Clearly nomenklatura nationalism is essentially a phenomenon of communism-in-degeneracy, the last stage of the old dispensation rather than the first of the new. On that basis we might expect to find nomenklatura nationalist regimes generally implementing rather weak and inconsistent economic transformation packages, and the 'purer' nationalist regimes showing much greater punch and direction in their attempts to build modern, market economies. We have already picked out two examples from the former Soviet Union which seem to fit the hypothesis, the Baltic republics, with governments generally uncompromised by the past and muscular transformation policies, and Ukraine, with a classic nomenklatura nationalist in the presidency and a weak economic policy posture. But what about the countries of Eastern Europe?

It is certainly easy enough to find confirmation of the thesis that nomenklatura nationalist regimes are incapable of delivering robust transformation policies. Let us start with the cases of Serbia and Croatia (bearing in mind that President Franjo Tudjman of Croatia, though less transparent a nomenklatura nationalist than President Slobodan Milosevic of Serbia, was an army general and a close associate of Tito before going into dissidence in the 1970s). There, government privatisation policies have tended effectively to the nationalisation rather than the privatisation of commercial and industrial property formerly socially-owned under the self-management system. In both cases the principle has been established that the proceeds of privatisation should go largely into republican development or restructuring funds, and that companies not privatised by a certain date should automatically become the property of restructuring agencies (Kalodjera, 1991; Bogdanovic and Lakicevic 1991; Petrovic, 1992; Dumezic, 1992). These policies are consistent with an interpretation of which places primary stress on the drive on the part of the old elites to replace the informal, feudal-bureaucratic ownership rights enjoyed by them under communism-in-degeneracy with formalised (state) ownership rights, and at the same time to secure key industrial assets for the national patrimony in the context of threatened or actual inter-ethnic war.

But while Serbia and Croatia demonstrate the one half of the hypothesis clearly enough, it is less easy to find emphatic confirmation in Eastern Europe of the other half, namely that the 'purer' nationalist regimes are pursuing palpably more energetic transformation policies. In the case of Slovenia, for instance, the policy posture of the government has been criticised by local economists on precisely the same grounds that we have criticised the policies of the Serbian and Croatian governments, for seeking to concentrate control, and ultimately effective ownership over assets, in a Development Fund operating as a holding company (Grlickov, 1992; 'Koncept ...', 1992). Of course, it is possible to argue than Milan Kucan, president of Slovenia, is, after all, an ex-communist just like Milosevic and Tudjman, and that therefore the Slovenian pattern does actually fit in perfectly well with the general hypothesis. My own feeling is that this would be to strain the nomenklatura nationalism theory too far. But it is certainly a good reason to look beyond Yugoslavia to areas of Eastern Europe where the break with the political past has been that much cleaner.

I pass over the case of Czechoslovakia, which is dealt with in the chapter by Z. Kavan, to look now at that of Poland. While nomenklatura capitalism has been an important element in the Polish transformation process, the nature of the Polish revolution of 1989-90 virtually excluded the old nomenklatura from political power. Thus nomenklatura nationalism as such has been excluded almost by definition in the Polish case. It was, indeed, because the Mazowiecki/Balcerowicz government of 1989-91 was a genuinely 'new broom' that it was able to implement classic 'shock-therapy' policies with remarkable success in its first year or so in power, reestablishing balance in the state budget, getting the money supply under control and the balance of payments into surplus.

It is all the more striking that by 1992 Poland found itself, in relation to the key issue of privatisation, in a similar situation to the Yugoslav successor states. The pace of change was very slow, and it seemed likely that effective ownership of the greater part of Polish industry would pass, in the medium term, to holding companies similar to the development and restructuring funds of Slovenia, Croatia and Serbia (Schaffer, 1992). Now if Poland is to pass into a stage of state capitalism, it will clearly not be nomenklatura state capitalism. That suggests that there must be other very powerful factors conditioning the tendency towards state capitalism which have nothing to do with political survivals from the communist past.

It is surely significant that in Germany, which represents a unique case in the annals of Central and East European transformations in the sense that the old East German regime was totally cleaned out and the former communist state wholly integrated with an advanced capitalist state almost immediately, the holding company has been the key institution of transformation policy. It is to the *Treuhandanstalt* that the German government has entrusted the task of privatising the former East German economy, in the expectation that the undertaking will be a long-term one, and that therefore the *Treuhand* will remain a dominant actor in the old East German economy for many years to come. Since the German case, with all its difficulties and complications, remains the best hope for effective restructuring in East-Central Europe, it is hardly surprising if other countries follow the German model. The difference between Germany and the others is that while the *Treuhandanstalt* has realistic prospects of selling off substantial volumes of assets, restructured or restructurable into viable companies,[1] the other East European countries are faced with the stark truth that the great bulk of the large-scale industrial assets at their disposal are simply not saleable in the short-to-medium term. Thus while the *Treuhand* can, perhaps, still be seen as an institution of (long-drawn-out) transition, the holding companies and development funds of Poland and the Yugoslav successor states look like turning into grimly permanent features of the post-communist landscape.

CONCLUSION

We have identifed, then, nomenklatura nationalism as an essentially backward-looking political development, which mouths the slogans of the market economy, but is unlikely to deliver on genuine economic transformation. There is, however, a 'purer' form of nationalism which has come to the fore, as Michnik suggests, as the focal point of opposition to communism, in concrete terms opposition to Russian domination. To date, this 'purer' form of nationalism has, on the whole, delivered more sensible and more muscular economic policies than its nomenklatura cousin (though we should bear in mind that ex-President Gamsakhurdia of Georgia represents one of the purest strains of 'pure' nationalism). It cannot simply be assumed that this advantage will be maintained in the future. While the nomenklatura nationalist government of Ukraine seems hardly to know what shock therapy means, the moderately but 'clean' nationalist government of Hungary is now finding it extremely difficult to maintain any momentum in its economic transformation policies. Poland, on the other hand, despite privatisation problems and despite a certain slippage in relation to budgetary and macroeconomic balance, reflecting understandable pressures from the patriotic working class for better living standards *without* massive redundancies and also the break-up of the broadly populist working-class/Catholic/nationalist alliance which Solidarity represented, has actually managed to get industrial output growing again, a unique feat in Eastern Europe-in-transformation. While territorial autarkism is quite rightly diagnosed as a particular feature of the *apparatchik* mentality, it is no monopoly of the old nomenklatura. It is certainly significant that the three 'purest' regimes of East-Central Europe, Poland, Czechoslovakia and Hungary, have already signed association agreements with the EC, and that the three Baltic republics, Estonia, Latvia and Lithuania, have already entered into a number of free-trade agreements with Nordic countries. But these developments have been as much a consequence of initiatives emanating from Brussels and from the Scandinavian capitals as from any special policy impetus coming from the six countries involved - after all, even Milosevic of Serbia would no doubt jump at the offer of associate membership of the EC, and any of the Slav successor states to the Soviet Union would be cock-a-hoop at the idea of a free-trade deal with Sweden.

It is perhaps particularly significant that the 'purer' nationalist regimes have shown themselves no more ready than their more compromised counterparts to address the critical problem of breakdown in intra-regional trading patterns within Eastern Europe. If there is one safe critical generalisation that we can make about Eastern Europe and the former Soviet Union, it is that all incumbent governments overstress the importance of trading with America and the EC and underestimate the importance of trading with each other. If we remind ourselves that it is by trading with our neighbours that we in Western Europe have grown prosperous over the past few decades, and that this trend has been in great part the consequence of a political strategy to defuse nationalism as a destabilising political force, we may ponder over a future scenario for Eastern Europe that would be dominated by governments rich in rationalisations for trade policies that undermine the natural division of labour within the region, and that nurture the fantasy that ethnic identity is in some sense a geographical fact, on a par with the Atlantic Ocean or the Himalayas. It is a sombre scenario, and Eastern Europe has been there before. We all remember what happened last time.

NOTE

1. By July 1992 nearly 8,000 out of the 12,000 enterprises originally committed to the *Treuhandanstalt* for privatisation had been sold off. It is claimed that this has secured 1.17 million jobs and promises of collateral investment worth DM140 billion, of which DM40 billion has already been invested. While the 8,000 enterprises successfully privatised clearly account for considerably less than half the pre-reunification aggregate turnover of the total 12,000, the achievement is nevertheless a striking one. See *Frankfurter Allgemeiner Zeitung*, 17 June 1992, p. 15; *The Independent*, 3 July 1992, p. 8.

REFERENCES

Barabash, A. and Vasilik O. (1992), 'Byudzhet pod mikroskopom', *Golos Ukrainy*, 20 May, pp. 6 and 8.

Bogdanovic, S. and Lakicevic, M. (1991), 'Drzava odumire jacajuci', *Ekonomska Politika*, 15 April, pp. 10-11

Dumezic, T. (1992), 'Kovaci laznih deonica', *Ekonomska Politika*, 15 June, pp.1 7-18.

Dyker, D.A. (1983), *The Process of Investment in the Soviet Union*, Cambridge, Cambridge University Press.

Dyker, D.A. (1990), *Yugoslavia: Socialism, Development and Debt*, London, Routledge.

Dyker, D.A. (1991), *Restructuring the Soviet Economy*, London, Routledge.

Grlickov, V. (1992), 'Zamke svojinskih promena', *Ekonomska Politika*, 14 October, pp. 20-21.

Kalodjera, D. (1991), 'Nedopustiva avantura', *Ekonomska Politika*, 15 April, pp. 12-13.

'Koncept Korze-Mencinger-Simoneti' (1992), *Ekonomska Politika*, 16 March, pp. 24-5.

Lubin, N. (1984), *Labour and Nationality in Soviet Central Asia*, London, Macmillan, in association with St Antony's College, Oxford.

Michnik A. (1990), 'Natsionalizm: chudovishche probudzhaetsya', *Vek XX i Mir* (Moscow), No. 10.

Petrovic, S. (1992), 'Institucionalno vlasnistvo, stara logika', *Ekonomska Politika*, 6 April, pp. 31-2.

Schaffer, M. (1992), 'Poland', in Dyker, D.A. (ed.), *The National Economies of Europe*, London, Longman.

Teokarevic, J. (1991), 'Jugoslavia i Istocna Evropa', in Nakarada, R., Basta-Posavec, L. and Samardzic, S. (eds), *Raspad Jugoslavije. Produzetak ili Kraj Agonije*, Belgrade, Institut za evropske studije.

8. Privatisation and Economic Democracy in Hungary

Yudit Kiss

In the euphoric chaos that accompanied the collapse of the state-socialist systems in Eastern Europe in 1989-1990, people's expectations were expressed in certain keywords that became the mobilising platform of the popular movements: democracy, pluralism, market economy. Market economy was supposed to bring welfare and sustained economic growth, if possible, overnight, and the road leading to it was privatisation. Privatisation was also envisaged as a crucial component of political democracy, since it contributes to the diversification of the economic agents and undermines the state's ubiquitous power.

The social backing for the general idea of privatisation was so overwhelming that the first democratically elected government of Hungary since the Second World War could bypass a public discussion on the main goals, methods and techniques of privatisation. The new Cabinet and its experts had a virtual free hand to elaborate and introduce policies that would shape the development of the country, for generations to come. But since the desired results were to enforce democracy and prosperity, at the beginning there was hardly any concern that such a major social transformation was introduced in such an anti-democratic way. Sadly enough this ambiguous overture became fairly representative of the way privatisation has been pursued in Hungary.

This chapter argues that instead of widening democracy and fostering social welfare, the process of privatisation has gradually become an instrument of the state, used to cement its power and recreate a new form of clientelist economy in Hungary. Despite the fact that the importance of the private sector has considerably grown, the state's intervention in the economy has remained decisive. Instead of fostering democracy, privatisation became an exclusive process, contributing to an increasingly uneven distribution of both economic and political assets. This conclusion calls into question the democratic credentials of the whole transformation and endangers its 'purely economic' outcome as well.

The first part of the chapter describes the simultaneously unfolding, different privatisation processes that have been taking place in Hungary in the last three years. The second part presents how these processes and the emerging new ownership structures influence the development of a genuine democracy in Hungary.

I. THE MAIN TRACKS OF PRIVATISATION

In April 1990, when the new Hungarian coalition government, led by the MDF, the Hungarian Democratic Forum, came to power, there were already several forms of privatisation going on (although hardly anybody dared to describe them as such). There were joint ventures and some foreign companies, there were plenty of small and medium-scale private or quasi-private firms on the fringes of the economy and there was the fairly controversial process of the so-called 'spontaneous privatisation' that dated back to 1988-89.[1]

One of the main priorities of the Democratic Forum-led new government was to regulate spontaneous ownership transformations and accelerate and widen the whole privatisation process. After the necessary personal reshuffle, the new MDF government delegated its power to the State Property Agency, created by the outgoing HSWP[2] in March 1990, to regulate and carry out ownership transformations. Since then this state organisation has been in charge of defining the targets, determining the general conditions and managing the bulk of privatisation in Hungary.

The proposed main form of ownership changes was the sale of assets, on a case-by-case basis, with the participation and supervision of the SPA or its representatives. Free distribution of property in different forms of mass-privatisation has been discarded (both by the government and its opposition) in order to demonstrate the 'purely market-oriented' nature of the whole process, and, more importantly, because one of the main initial goals was to create revenues for the state budget.[3]

Privatisation launched by government agencies seemed to be reasonable at the beginning, since the whole institutional system of a market economy (functioning factor markets, an extensive, multi-layered bank system, stock-exchange, investment funds, and so on) that could have facilitated the process, was still largely missing. This starting condition however became a fixed characteristic of the whole Hungarian privatisation process. Unlike in Poland or the Czech Republic, where local authorities and private agents have been entitled to participate at least in some phases of the privatisation management, in Hungary the state maintained its almost exclusive role.

There have been different tracks of privatisation in Hungary, which are presented here by the decreasing degree of state (SPA) control.

1.   Large-scale SPA Privatisation Projects

These spectacular 'shop-window' privatisation projects were launched by the Agency soon after the elections. 'Packages' of enterprises were offered for sale, mostly targeted at foreign investors, with the aim of generating quick privatisation revenues, experimenting with different techniques and giving an initial boost to privatisation. Virtually each element of the process from the selection of the companies through choosing the potential buyer and the conditions of the sale is controlled by the SPA.

Despite the significant initial interest in the programme, only a handful of enterprises have been eventually privatised, and by the end of 1992 even the SPA admitted the failure of these projects.

2.   Controlled Enterprise Transformations

The creation of the SPA did not stop spontaneous enterprise transformation, (that is, the commercialisation of state-owned enterprises) only adjusted them to the new requirements. They were renamed 'enterprise-initiated privatisations', suggesting that the companies can initiate their own transformation, but the SPA maintains its right to set the conditions and control the process. While the 'spontaneous privatisations' could be considered as uncontrolled intentions to get rid of the weakened and already not too rewarding state protection, in the enterprise transformations the managers of the state-owned enterprises return to the previous practice of individual bargaining with the state bureaucrats. In the old-style command economy the stake of the bargain was the plan, later the various economic regulations, now it is the conditions, methods and main parameters of the transformation, and eventually privatisation process.

According to a 1992 government decision all still state-owned enterprises were obliged to convert into business corporations by 30 June 1993. Companies that failed to meet the deadline of 30 June 1993, were put under direct state, that is SPA, control. This step in theory might have meant the acceleration of the privatisation process, but in reality it forced hasty formal changes, instead of genuine restructuring and opened space for a renewed centralised control over the enterprises' internal decision-making process.

At present enterprise transformations represent the dominant form of ownership changes in Hungary. In reality fairly few of them led to genuine privatisation; their main result is a complex cross-ownership system between mostly state-owned enterprises, banks and other government institutions.[4] These transformations have also made possible the economic survival of some of the former state managerial class: those who were quick and flexible enough to adjust to the dramatically changed political conditions. Under centralised state ownership the state managers enjoy considerable informal freedom, since the supervising institutions seem to be unable (and most likely unwilling) to extend their control on questions of actual management. This formal dependence, coupled with the absence of real owner's responsibility, both on the side of the state and the managers, leads to the cultivation of survival tactics, rather than efficient economic management.

3. Pre-Privatisation

Pre-privatisation was one of the State Property Agency's first large-scale privatisation projects. More than 10,529 small shops, service and catering units were to be sold on open auctions exclusively to Hungarian citizens. Owing to the grinding, bureaucratic SPA procedure, inconsistencies of legal regulations and the lack of available credits to facilitate the purchase of the announced units, the process started very slowly. Only after several SPA decisions to simplify the process, mainly the radical improvement of a specific credit scheme available for pre-privatisation, could the programme take off. By the end of February 1993, 7,637 units were privatised, although only in 30 per cent of cases was the property actually sold; the remaining 70 per cent were privately rented.[5]

In theory pre-privatisation is an open and democratic process, since property is offered to anyone at open auctions. In reality each deal had to be approved by the State Property Agency and there were other, more subtle forms of direct state control as well, like arbitrary restrictions defining the scope of concerned units or regulation of access, through shaping the conditions of related credit schemes.

4. Self-privatisation

In October 1992, after the evident collapse of its show-case projects, increasing criticism and the creation of a rival state-asset management company, (the SPM Ltd.), the State Property Agency launched the self-privatisation programme. Several hundred, carefully selected small and medium-size state-owned enterprises were given the opportunity to initiate and carry out their privatisation through a simplified procedure. The SPA delegated its managing power to 84 (in a later round 44) consultancy firms, but it retained the right to choose the participating enterprises (mainly from the service sector) and the consultants, to define the conditions and give individual authorisation to each deal.

The main advantage of self-privatisation is that since the enterprises and the consultant firms are relatively independent, they can try to shortcut administrative obstacles and concentrate on finding a quick and favourable solution of the firm's situation. There were 563 companies that participated in the programme, of which 207 signed a sale contract, the remainder expected to finish privatisation by the end of 1993, when the whole project was due to end, despite its relative success. (The 57 firms which did not even begin transformation negotiations, were transferred to the SPA.)[6]

5. Hidden privatisation

This formally independent track is another version of enterprise transformations, with the important difference that the transfer of state assets to private firms takes place without any visible, legal change. It is a fairly widespread phenomenon, occurring on different levels, from simple stealing of the SOE's (State Owed Enterprises) materials, machinery or other mobilisable goods, to creating 'Foundations for public use' with state capital.[7]

6. Foreign Direct Investment

Foreign direct investment, as well as organic privatisation described below, are not privatisations in the narrow sense, since they do not necessarily mean de-etatization. Their importance is manifested not so much in the dismantling of the state property but in creating an alternative economic space, partly by reallocating resources formerly used by the state sector, representing (hopefully) a different, new entrepreneurial mentality.

Between 1990 and 1992 the State Property Agency's activity focused on attracting potential foreign investors to the state-regulated privatisation process. Foreign investors were actively encouraged, because FDI was seen as the quickest way of transplanting a functioning market economy to the fertile Hungarian soil. In addition, hard currency privatisation revenues were used to service the heavy foreign debt burden of the country.

Although in some cases privatisation with foreign participation brought the expected benefits, as a whole it reinforced the strongly monopolistic nature of the economy. The policy of the foreign firms is to buy up the local market, by purchasing the crucial Hungarian firms. In some industries, for example in insurance, cement, sugar, paper, road construction, printing and food-processing one to three large TNC's (Transnational Corporations) dominate the market, usually the same ones which already control similar industries in the neighbouring Eastern European countries.[8]

7. Organic Privatisation

Organic privatisation is the creation of new Hungarian private enterprises. In the last three years the Hungarian private sector has demonstrated an undoubtedly spectacular growth,[9] but caution is necessary when looking at statistics. Many of the new private enterprises are created to avoid heavy tax or customs duties, to make access possible to preferential credits reserved for new enterprises, to provide additional income or to escape unemployment. The increase of the number of the new private enterprises is accompanied by a relatively high number of failures or only nominally functioning companies.

The major problem with most of these new private ownership forms is that in order to survive, they inevitably tend to adjust to the existing environment, in which the state succeeded in preserving its decisive role not only in shaping privatisation, but in influencing other, wider economic conditions as well. In the crisis-stricken, amorphous and disintegrated Hungarian economy there is a fierce struggle for limited resources (investment capital, loans, foreign assistance, information) and there seems to be no other institution able to replace the state and act as a mediator, arbitrator and redistributor. This explains why the new, even genuinely private firms feel it necessary to accommodate themselves to the requirements of the state sector and state administration and instead of creating horizontal professional networks, they tend to be engaged in hierarchical relation-building, via private bargaining with representatives of the political power.

8. The Non-Privatisation Track

The development of privatisation in Hungary has to be considered together with an increasingly important re-etatization process that has been evolving simultaneously. After lengthy discussions about its size, precise functions and personnel, a second large-scale state asset managing holding, the State Property Management Ltd. (SPM Ltd.) was set up in October 1992. Its main role is to supervise, reorganise and eventually privatise approximately 163 SOEs, among them all major raw material, energy, transport and communication firms, several significant industrial and commercial firms and the commercial banks. The SPM Ltd. controls about 35 per cent of the state's assets and it is entitled to take all decisions concerning the enterprises under its supervision, including their eventual sale or change of management.

At the beginning the quick, profitable sale of as many as possible state-owned enterprises was one of the declared goals of the government. By mid-1992, however, there was a significant change in privatisation goals and related techniques. The emphasis shifted towards restructuring of the still state-owned enterprises and banks, prior to privatisation. The SPM played a leading role in this change, among others, by pushing for its own project to reorganise the major SOEs, clear the balance sheet and recapitalise the main state banks. It was, however, not specified how this programme would be financed, how efficiency criteria would be established or how the competent managers, able to carry out the necessary structural readjustments, would be selected.[10]

In late 1992 the government announced its project of 'credit-consolidation', to clear the state enterprises and banks of bad credits by way of transferring the burdens to another, recently set-up state-owned institution, the Hungarian Investment Foundation. Another large-scale 'rescue-operation' was the selection of the 'dirty 13', 13 large-scale SOEs, whose saving, according to the official explanation, was indispensable for the general restructuring of the whole Hungarian economy.[11] This project is likely to develop into a wider 'debtor-consolidation' programme, aiming to revive 'worthwhile' enterprises.[12] In early 1993 the regulations of the bankruptcy law were softened.

All these steps suggest that despite the privatisation rhetoric, the government takes specific measures to rescue and consolidate the state sector. This in itself is necessary, since it is clear that a significant amount of national assets will remain in state property for some time to come. However, the way enterprises are selected and state help is pledged, suggests that instead of introducing a more efficient, productive management, a new protection system is in the making for the 'chosen' enterprises.

These methods awkwardly resemble those of the previous political system, where economic aspects were clearly subordinated to political considerations. They seem to lead to similarly wasteful and inefficient management as well. While the number of enterprises under direct control of the two large state property management funds is growing, a recent State Audit Office Report points out fundamental legal and economic shortcomings in their activity. The state's 'entrepreneurial wealth' is not even registered properly. Even according to Mr Csepi, managing director of the SPA, between 1991 and 1992 the purely state-owned assets lost approximately 20 per cent of their value.[13]

II. PRIVATISATION AND DEMOCRACY

Although the state's 'omnipotence' is certainly undermined, it manages to preserve considerable economic and political power, partly as a result of the process of privatisation. The state itself at the same time is difficult to define, since it lacks a consistent ideology and solid social background. In the last three years major strategic decisions were shaped by the temporary results of a permanent power struggle between different parties and factions within the governing coalition and against the parliamentary opposition. The most representative example is the law on compensation, which was accepted, against the expressed will of the social majority, only to satisfy the Smallholders' Party, a small coalition party.

The most stable and rewarding principle in this fairly amorphous political system seems to be personal loyalty. While in the state-socialist system political fidelity was acknowledged mostly by informal services and goods transfers, in the new nationalist clientelist system loyalty is often paid in more marketable goods, in cash, capital transfers or highly remunerative economic positions. However undefined the state's economic policy is in general, it is clear that it uses both the would-be privatised and the remaining state assets as if they were its private property.

As far as privatisation management on a macro-economic level is concerned, for more then two years the only valid privatisation legislation was the often amended Property Policy Guidelines, still inherited from the previous system. Although in summer 1992 laws on privatisation and state-asset managing were passed, the Property Policy Guidelines that regulate actual privatisation management are regularly elaborated and accepted after a long delay. In the absence of clear and systematic regulation, momentary political constellations and subjective criteria play a significant role in decision-making.[14]

When the whole transformation began, 'market privatisation' was assumed to be democratic by its very nature. Although this itself is questionable, the way it was put into practice turned out to be far from democratic. In theory following the principle of 'neutral market', equal chances should be guaranteed to any buyer. In reality, however, the government and its worldly representative, the SPA, have been using special preferences in their decision-making process. These preferences have been hidden from the public and tend to change with the shifts of economic policy. In the first two years the SPA gave preference to foreign buyers; since early 1993 Hungarian citizens have advantage over their foreign competitors. In some cases, buyers promising to keep employees, in others, those who are able to offer the highest price or pay immediately in cash, are likely to win the tenders.[15]

One of the major requirements of democratic management is transparency. Ordinary citizens, as well as those involved should be provided with detailed and up-to-date information about the state agencies' evaluation criteria and privatisation strategies, the real state of the enterprises and the conditions of deals, for example prices and employment implications. These data however are rarely published, and often even the concerned parties are kept uninformed.[16] The lack of systematic and reliable information was one of the main factors that undermined the initial social backing for privatisation. As a consequence now even clear and undoubtedly honest deals are under scrutiny and whenever a new privatisation scandal becomes public, it is automatically interpreted as the mere tip of the iceberg.[17]

The next requirement of a democratic privatisation would be easy and equal access to the process. The government's first crucial decision about 'market' privatisation was evidently of exclusive nature, since it made participation possible only for those who possessed mobile capital. This meant foreigners, members of the old nomenklatura and economic elite, the cream of the former grey or black economy entrepreneurs, adventurers, Mafiosi and 'accidental businessmen'.[18] Since the decades of state-socialism did not favour capital accumulation, and at the beginning of the privatisation process there were few opportunities to receive preferential credits to compensate for this lack, the bulk of the population was excluded from the new redistribution of the economic assets.

Another, more subtle form of exclusion is the limited access to information concerning privatisation regulations, the situation of enterprises, special credits and other forms of hidden subsidies or advantageous privatisation opportunities. In the chaotic and insecure conditions of social transformation 'information capital' becomes extremely valued and, since it is mostly available for those close to political decision-making centres, in contrast to the (above mentioned) mostly economic exclusion, it accomplishes a primarily political selection.

At the beginning the rather exclusive nature of the Hungarian privatisation process did not seem to be an obstacle. Later, however, the best enterprises having been sold, the initial social backing eroded and the whole process visibly slowed down, it became inevitable to take steps to facilitate access. Techniques that were marginalised at the beginning, for example employee or manager buy-outs, recently have been officially promoted, together with new methods like privatisation leasing, preferential credits (new constructions and improved conditions for the existing ones) and privatisation paid in instalments.

The most spectacular change however is a mass privatisation project, announced by the government earlier this year. Preserving the facade of 'market-privatisation', no free coupons or vouchers would be distributed to the Hungarian citizens, who register themselves for a nominal fee, but state-backed, low interest, long-term loans are offered for the shares of SOEs floated to the stock exchange. The plans envisage the offer to the public of some Ft30bn worth assets, created from a portfolio of enterprises belonging to the SPM Ltd. (70-80 per cent) and the SPA (20-30 per cent).

The problem with all these forms is that they create many weak, dispersed owners, while on the other side there is an increasing concentration of capital, both state and private. The plan for mass-privatisation even prescribes this as a necessary precondition for an efficient privatisation: small-scale future share-owners could only hold a minority, up to 10-20 per cent of the concerning enterprise's shares, while the majority stakes would be offered to solid professional investors.

Another aspect of a democratic privatisation management would be a wide and efficient social control over the decision-making process. Originally the SPA was created as a small expert organisation, responsible to Parliament and its decisions could be vetoed in legal forums. During the last three years the Agency's originally independent experts have been replaced by loyal government administrators, who are directly responsible to the government; the Director and the members of the Managing Board are nominated by the Prime Minister and its decisions cannot be contested anymore.

The SPM Ltd. is an independent holding, which is directly accountable to the government with only a formal duty of reporting to Parliament and it is not subject to any other outside form of social control. It functions as a one-person shareholder's company, in which the owner, the state, is represented by Mr Tamas Szabo, Minister of Privatisation. The 11 members of the Managing Board and the five representatives of the Committee of Control are all assigned by the Prime Minister.

Since both access to and control over privatisation are fairly limited, to date there have been two ways to influence government policy on privatisation: the critique from within the government coalition and the silent threat of the growing social dissent. There have been sharply critical currents both within the Democratic Forum and among its minor allies, specifically the Christian Democrat Popular Party, accusing the government of selling out the country at a rock-bottom price, excluding Hungarians and letting corruption dominate privatisation deals. As a result, several

Supervising Committees were created within government, which assure access to privatisation for those groups in the new political elite who had hitherto been excluded from it due to their critical attitudes.[19]

The popular confidence and support given to the government at the beginning of the transformation has eroded quickly, in the face of some spectacular failures and the generally ambivalent results of privatisation. The increasing public disenchantment and often open animosity seems to be the only efficient popular means to influence, in an indirect way, the government's privatisation policy, as the hasty measures to introduce 'Hungarian privatisation' or mass privatisation show.

Even if the very process of privatisation is anti-democratic, if its results seem to enhance efficiency and a just society, at least in the medium or long run, society might still be ready to pay the price for it. Looking at the actual results from the aspect of future democratisation, unfortunately the picture is not too promising either.

In quantitative terms, from the starting SPA portfolio of 2,060 companies with an aggregated value of approximately Ft2,000-2,200bn, some were transferred to the SPM Ltd., some to local authorities, 200 became private, 550-600 enterprises are still entirely state-owned and another 500-550 are mixed property. The present value of SPA assets is about Ft8-900bn. In Mr. Csepi's interpretation this means that half the national wealth has already been privatised.[20]

The incomes created from privatisation are channelled to finance other government projects. The 1992 revenues, for example, were used to service the country's foreign debt, the creation of the SPM Ltd. and the Hungarian Investment Foundation which provide urgent financial infusions to bankrupt small banks and some large-scale SOEs, and to capitalise the Foundation for the World Exposition and some insurance companies. In 1993 privatisation incomes are largely used to finance the threateningly growing deficit of the state budget.[21]

Economic development in the last three years has been fairly lop-sided. The lingering uncertainty concerning property rights has had dramatic consequences in some sectors, for example in agriculture, which was a former success story of the Hungarian economy. The excessive 'concentration' on privatisation had diverted government attention from other equally important questions, for example the reform of a state budget system, of the large-scale welfare systems, industrial policy, or the question of investment, R&D, anti-monopolist regulations and the like. The 'privatisation agony' has actually prevented many enterprises from dealing with economic restructuring and is certainly one of the major reasons for the sharp fall in output, investments and productivity in the last three years.

Even if privatisation is introduced in a non-democratic way, there has been an assumption that economic growth sooner or later will 'trickle down' and the whole society will benefit from it. This has not been the case. This is partly because there has not been any growth to share, but also because the economic and social structure that has been emerging, seems to reproduce the previous, unhealthy structure of the economy: domination of strong - both state and private - monopolies, centralised and hierarchical methods of decision-making, the lack of a flexible and efficient background economy created by horizontal networks of independent, flexible, small and medium-size region-based companies.

The 'new' society is marked by unprecedented social differentiation, a rapid and dramatic process of massive impoverishment and marginalisation, with an increasing tendency of exclusion. The most vulnerable groups are the long-term unemployed, retired people, first-time job-seekers, the Roma population and women. Basic social problems such as healthcare, education, culture and care for the elderly remain unaddressed, since the state was quick to roll back welfare functions and there are only a handful of alternative, functioning welfare institutions to fill the gap even though it is so reluctant to withdraw from direct economic intervention.

The new Hungarian entrepreneurial class is a rare symbiosis of state and private, newcomers and old-style managers. Its structure is rather imbalanced, with large inequalities of opportunities for those who are at the bottom and who are at the top of the pyramid. At the 'lower end' there is a numerous, but dispersed and harassed group of private entrepreneurs, running mostly new, small and medium-scale enterprises, struggling for survival, under extremely unfavourable tax and credit conditions.

On the top a strong, large-scale Hungarian entrepreneurial elite is emerging, representing both private and influential state managers. Their position is incomparably better than the former group owing to their economic power which provides multiple advantages in a monopolistic economic structure and to their political influence, exercised both in formal and informal ways.[22]

It was probably naive to expect privatisation to create social justice and democracy. It should, however, have led to a more efficient economy and the creation of an institutional system based on fairness. It is a real historical loss that Hungary, despite its relatively advantageous starting conditions, could not accomplish even that.

NOTES

1. Thanks to a set of new laws facilitating the creation of new, non-state ownership forms, some SOE managers transferred the state enterprises' assets into quasi-independent business corporations. In the majority of cases no actual property transfer has been taking place beyond the change of legal form.
2. Hungarian Socialist Workers Party, the governing Party of the previous system.
3. There were some exceptions, for example the compensation of those whose property was confiscated after the communist takeover, the reprivatisation of the property of the historical Churches and the transfer of assets to the social welfare system and local municipalities.
4. In April 1993 the distribution of the asssets of the newly established (commercialised) enterprises was as follows: 73 per cent SPA, 22 per cent other, 3 per cent foreigners and 2 per cent local authorities, *Népszabadság,*16, April 1993.
5. Originally 50,000 units were destined for pre-privatisation.
6. *Népszabadság*, 2 September 1993
7. Matolcsy (1991); Voszka (1993a).
8. Vissy (1992); *Népszabadság*, 1 September 1993.
9. In Mid-1993 there were 170,000 economic associations and more than 600,000 private entrepreneurs in Hungary (*Népszabadság*, 6 October 1993).
10. According to news available in September 1993 the SPM Ltd. was about to borrow $100mn from a syndicate of foreign banks to finance its reorganisation project (*Figyelö*, 23 September 1993).
11. The closer analysis of the selection shows that instead of future growth and market opportunities, national, strategic and employment criteria were dominant in the decision-making (Karsai, 1993).
12. Interview with Tibor Pongracz, State Secretary, President of the SPA, *Figyelö*, 8 July 1993.
13. Csepi interview, *Heit Világgazdaság*, 26 June 1993; *Figyelö*, 1 April 1993.
14. Both the SPA and SPM Ltd are supervised by Mr Tamas Szabo, Minister without Portfolio, in charge of privatisation, who in a recent interview said 'If it is possible, it is good to keep politics far away from privatisation. In Hungary, it seems, it was impossible' (*Tallozo*, 1 July 1993).
15. See for example: 'We have to admit that in the first stage of privatisation a Hungarian entrepreneur had no chance against a foreign firm, but this is about to change in the SPA's present practice ... according to the new Property Policy Guidelines in the case of two similar offers we have to favor the Hungarian one'. Interview with Mr Erno Racz, Deputy Director of the SPA *(Népszabadság,* 8 March 1993).
16. In October 1993 the SPA published the prices of some enterprises for the first time. The results of the tenders, though, were only made public after signing the contracts (*Népszabadság*, 4 October 1993; *Figyelö,*16 September 1993).
17. The latest scandal about the SPA paying Ft28mn to Istvan Cskurka, an extremist nationalist, at the time vice-president of the governing MDF, to write the scripts for a film aimed to popularise privatisation, only became public, because Csurka was excluded from the Party, so the SPA ventured to mention that the work has never been done (*Heti Világgazdaság*, 11 September 1993).
18. A small group of people, mostly intellectuals, became rich overnight thanks to the unexpectedly opened business alternatives. Making use of the instant import liberalisation, they began to import computers, photocopy machines or cars and they set up the first leasing companies and the first private travel agencies.
19. 'Outsiders', like opposition parties or expert groups do not seem to have a major impact on decision-making. Even the reports of the State Audit Office are often dismissed on formal grounds.
20. *Heti Világgazdaság*, 26 June 1993. Other, even SPA, officials have different data, for example Mr Racz, deputy director, claims that in value terms only 18 per cent of the assets has been privatised (*Népszabadság*, 9 June 1993).
21. *Népszabadság*, 28 January 1993; Csepi interview, *Heti Világgazdaság*, 26 June 1993.

22. The large-scale entrepreneurs have already three well-articulated and fairly influential professional associations and two political parties to represent their specific interests.

REFERENCES*

Economic Commission for Europe (1992), 'On property rights and privatisation in the transition economies', *Economic Survey of Europe in 1991-1992*, Chapter 6, UN, New York.

Economic Commission for Europe (1993), 'Progress in privatisation, 1990-1992' in: *Economic Survey of Europe in 1992-1993*, UN, Geneva.

Grosfeld, Irene (1991), 'Privatisation of state enterprises in Eastern Europe: The Search for a market environment', *Eastern European Politics and Societies*, Vol. 5, No. 1.

Grosfeld, Irene and Hare, Paul (1991), 'Privatisation in Hungary, Poland and Czechoslovakia', CEFR Discussion Paper No. 544, London.

Inzelt, Annamaria (1992), 'Privatizacio es innovacio' (Privatisation and innovation), *Kulgazdasag*, No. 10.

Karsai, Gabor (1992), 'Politika pedig vagyon' (There is politics), *Figyelö*, 29 October.

Karsai, Judit (1992), 'True entrepreneurs or just clinging to power. Management buy-outs in Hungary', Manuscript, Research Institute of Industrial Economics of the Hungarian Academy of Science.

Karsai, Judit (1993), 'Fedoneve: reorganizacio' (Pseudonym: reorganisation), *Közgazdasági szemle*, Vol. XL, No. 9.

Kiss, Yudit (1992), 'Privatisation in Hungary - Two years later', *Soviet Studies*, Vol. 44, No. 6.

Kiss, Yudit (1993), 'Privatisation paradoxes in East Central Europe', *Eastern European Politics and Societies* (Forthcoming.)

Kocsis, Gyorgyi (1992a), 'Kezratetel' (Hands on), *Heti Világgazdaság*, 27 June.

Kocsis, Gyorgyi (1992b), 'A rejtelmes sziget' (Mystery island), *Heti Világgazdaság*, 9 May.

Laki, Mihaly (1993), 'A posztszocialista allam a vallalatok piacan' (The post-socialist state on the enterprise market), *Közgazdasági szemle*, Vol. XL, No. 5.

Matolcsy, Gyorgy (ed.) (1991), *Labadozasunk evei. A magyar privatizacio. Tenyek, trendek, privatizacios peldak* (Our years of convalescence. Hungarian privatisation. Trends, tendencies, facts), Tulajdon Alapitvany-Privatizacios Kutatointezet, Budapest.

Mellar, Tamas, (ed.) (1992), *Labadozasunk evei. 2. A privatizacio tapasztalatai Magyarorszagon* (Our years of convalescances 2. The Hungarian privatisation experience), Tulajdon Alapitvany-Privatizacios Kutatointezet, Budapest.

Mihalyi, Peter (1992), 'Fosztogatas-osztogatas-fosztogatas. Az allami tulajdon tundoklese es bukasa' (Plunder-squander-plunder. The state ownership's splendor and demise), *Közgazdasági szemle*, Vol. XXXIX No. 11.

Mora, Maria (1991), 'Az allami vallalatok (al)privatizacioja' (The pseudo-privatisation of the state owned enterprises), *Közgazdasági szemle*, No. 6. Budapest.

Sarakozi, Tamas (1993), 'Jogi abszurdok az allami szuperholdingrol' (Legal absurdities about the state superholding), *Népszabadság*, 29 May.

Stark, David (1990), 'Privatisation in Hungary: From plan to market or from plan to clan?', *Eastern European Politics and Societies*, Vol. 4, No. 3.

Stark, David (1992), 'Path dependence and privatisation strategies in East Central Europe', *Eastern European politics and Societies*, Vol. 6, No. 1.

Szalai, Erzsebet (1991), 'A hatalom metamorfozisa?' (Metamorphosis of power?), *Valosag*, No. 6, Budapest.

Vissy, Ferenc (1992), 'Verseny es privatizacio a magyar Gazdasagi Versenyhivatal szemszogebol' (Privatisation and competition from the perspective of the Hungarian Office of Competition), Paper presented at the Conference: Competition and Privatisation. Budapest, 12 November 1992.

Voszka, Eva (1992), 'Az ellenkezoje sem igaz: a kozpontositas es a decentralizacio szinevaltozasai' (The contrary is untrue as well: changes of centralisation and decentralisation), *Kulgazdasag*, Vol. XXXVl, No. 6.

Voszka, Eva (1993a), 'Allami tarsasagok - a "spontan privatizacio" es a kenyszeratalakulasok szulottei' (State corporations, born from "spontaneous privatisation" and compulsory transformations), *Közgazdasági szemle*, Vol. XL, No. 1.

Voszka, Eva (1993b), 'Escaping from the state, escaping to the state', in: L. Somogyi (ed.) *The Political Economy of the Transition Process in Eastern Europe*, Edward Elgar, Aldershot/Vermont.

Zsubori, Ervin (1993), 'Az ismeretlen birodalom' (The imperium of the unknown), *Figyelö*, 1 April.

* References to short news in newspapers and current periodicals are in the main text.

9. International Business: Global Political Economy and Eastern Europe

Sonia El Kahal

The dramatic events of Central and Eastern Europe and the consequent so-called 'problems of transitions' have produced Western responses by academics, business journals and state policy-makers which have generally focused on interests, actions and policy making in separate state units. The general assumption is that Central and Eastern European States, the former USSR and the Council of Mutual Economic Assistance are in some important sense outside of the global political economy and the prevailing system of international trade, thus needing to be brought *into* it. These events, constructed as spectacular, chaotic, disorderly and dangerous, have been articulated both as potential sources of regional and global instability, insecurity, and simultaneously as progressive and providing new positive opportunities. A positive outcome is expected to depend upon the kinds of economic and political choices made by local decision-makers.

All this together represents, in my view, a narrow and reductionist tendency. If we wish to understand what is going on in Eastern Europe, we need to link these apparently 'local' or 'domestic' events with changes occurring at the level of the global political economy. Of particular importance is the global trend towards privatisation and deregulation, and more specifically, the recent application of private sector management, budgetary and accounting models and techniques to public international organisations such as the World Health Organization (WHO), the International Labour Organization (ILO), the International Monetary Fund (IMF), the International Bank for Reconstruction and Development (IBRD), the United Nations and The United Nations Educational, Scientific and Cultural Organisation (UNESCO) in particular.

The central issue addressed in this chapter is whether Central and Eastern European States are outside the global political economy and thus adjusting their internal political and economic systems in order to 'join'; or whether they are facing the problems that they do *because* of the nature of their already subordinated integration within the global political economy. It is argued here that analysis of the relations between domestic, or national events and conditions, and the prevailing conditions of the global political economy is central to answering this question. In order to deal with this problematic, I will first review the current actions and reactions to the problems of 'transition' in Eastern and Central Europe from a centrally planned to a free-market economy. I will then show the limitation of the explanations so far presented by economists, politicians, business leaders and academics by relating those particular events to the recent trends towards global privatisation and to the global political economy. I will then present a brief illustration of this current international movement towards the imposition of global business ethics more concretely by taking an international public organisation such as UNESCO as an empirical case study and finally conclude by offering some comments about the relations between the changes in Eastern and Central Europe which are constructed as problems of 'transition' and those changes which are characteristic of the international political economy.

ACTIONS AND REACTIONS

The dramatic political and economic changes that have occurred in Eastern and Central Europe have attracted the attention of politicians, economists, state policy-makers, business leaders and academics. Their current response to the problems of transition, however, provides in my view an unsatisfactory account of the causal mechanisms at work in this process.

Central and Eastern European countries have been experiencing a 'seemingly' dramatic transition from centrally planned systems to free-market economies. According to Czechoslovakia's Minister of Economics, Vladimir Dlouhy 'For Eastern Europe to have a market economy, the government must get out of the way'. (Donlon, 1991). In a roundtable discussion with US Chief Executive Officers about creating a market economy, Bella Kadar, Hungarian Minister of International Economics, asserted strongly that 'if Central European countries wish to be *integrated into the world economy*, they must adjust to the international rules of the game' (Donlon, 1991). The important implications of this argument are first that the range of choices available to individual actors is already partly determined by the existing structures of the global political economy and second that these units are in some discernible sense *outside* of the global political economy.

Economic reforms and market-oriented policies introduced since 1990 particularly in Czechoslovakia, Hungary and Poland, to facilitate this process of liberalisation include privatisation programmes; full price liberalisation, the removal of trade restrictions and the total liberalisation for foreign trade; restrictive monetary policy, the restructuring of the banking systems, insurance services, and bankruptcy laws; the devaluation and internal convertibility of the domestic currency and the establishment of stock markets (Frydman et, al., 1993; Earle et,al., 1993; Ettlie, 1993).[1]

All of these reforms have given rise to a widespread belief in the West that the potential exists for a 'Capitalist Renaissance' in Eastern and Central Europe once property is privatised, prices are set free, the currency is stabilised and regulated competitive markets are introduced (Kregel and Matzner, 1992).

In the aftermath of the 1989 revolutions, international businesses were attracted towards untapping this vast new potential market of approximately 393 million consumers, who have been deprived of most Western consumer products for forty-five years (Siren and Shaw, 1991; Korabi and Grieve, 1990; de Bendern, 1990). The Bush Administration actively encouraged US companies to expand trade of non-strategic goods, such as health-care products, with Eastern European Countries.

Johnson and Johnson, Dow Chemicals, Du Pont, Pfizer and Eli Lilly International are among the US Health Care Companies to have opened offices in Poland, and are looking for further opportunities in Hungary, Czechoslovakia and Yugoslavia (Reihn, 1991). US hoteliers have also been competing for deals and properties in the area. Groups such as Marriott, Hyatt International Group, Sheraton and Hilton are all establishing hotels in that region (Pesmen, 1990; Niemeyer, 1990). The food and retail industry achieved considerable headway in Eastern Europe too, with MacDonald's and Pizza Hut opening up their first restaurants in Moscow in 1990 (Hume 1990; Foster, 1991; Ryan, 1992). In Russia alone, in the computer industry, the installed base of personal computers is expected to grow from its current 400,000 to 28 million during the next ten years (Crumney,1991).[2] With respect to the automobile market, most of the direct investment comes from the US and West European manufacturers. General Motors, Ford, Volkswagen, Audi, Fiat, Renault, Mercedes, Citroen and Peugeot all now have manufacturing operations in the region, and Rover is at present considering assembling a facility in Bulgaria (Weston, 1993). Some investment banks and foreign trade banks are also starting to set up their own financial companies to deal with the newly established East European banks (Quartermaine, 1993). Credit Suisse First Boston, for example, is one of the first to have expanded its business in Central Europe (Central European CEE, 1993).

Furthermore, programmes sponsored by the US Commerce Department to 'help US companies do business in Russia and the Newly Independent States constitute now key elements in President Clinton's overall economic plan to promote economic revival in the region and to assure democracy there (*Business America*, 1993). On 5 March 1993, Secretary of Commerce Ronald H. Brown announced that four organisations will receive $400,000 grants under the Consortia of American Businesses in the NIS, known as CABNIS.[3]   Additionally the Commerce Department is now establishing American Business Centers in Russia and the Newly Independent States under the Freedom Support Act of 1992 (*Business America*, 1993).

But the euphoria that followed the dramatic changes since 1989 towards the establishment of a free-market economy, is now slowly dying down, and we are beginning to see the challenges that lie ahead in the reconstruction of the Eastern European market economies. Since 1992, Foreign Direct Investment did not increase as much as expected,[4] mainly taking place in the hotel, restaurant and retail trade, where it displaces indigenous enterprises, especially supply chains. After excessive optimism in the winter of 1989-1990, the reform of Europe in centrally planned economies into Western-style market economies has proved much more difficult in practice. All countries are now suffering from the aftermath of the negative external shocks of the collapse of trade within the former Council for Mutual Economic Assistance (Oldersma and Van Bergeijk, 1992; Wood, 1992). The greatest obstacle resulting from the liberalisation of trade and privatisation lies within the factories themselves, which are now left to operate on a self-accounting basis and able to negotiate commercial contracts directly with Western firms without approval from Moscow ministries. This dramatic transition has caused, and still is causing, serious problems in adopting democratic and Western business practices. Up until the recent movements towards privatisation over 90 per cent of all orders to factories were placed, priced and distributed by the state. The state also chose suppliers and determined prices and wage levels (de Bendern, 1990). The situation is summed up as follows:

The East European countries who are now embracing the politics of the free market, have been used to central planning for the past 4 to 5 decades. In a planned economy, state enterprises are used to receiving allotments of raw materials and funds, and have to produce enough goods to fulfil the plan that is imposed by a State Planning Committee. If they fall short of the plan, state subsidies are increased to help boost the output. If they surpass the plan, the surplus is reabsorbed by the state. Concepts such as profit, loss, cost accounting and marketing play no role in the functioning of the state enterprise. Whatever the end year results, the status quo within the enterprise remains the same. (de Bendern, 1990)

Consequently Soviet managers have no concept of competitive markets, quality control or workers' participation in decision-making.[5] Gorbachev's chief economist, Abel Aganbegyan summed up the problems facing Soviet managers :

> The current structure of the economy is backward and conservative. Within it mining and agriculture occupy exaggerated positions, and in contrast manufacturing industry and the processing of raw materials are insufficiently developed. Even worse developed is the so-called tertiary sector, the service sector. In the same way the quality, efficiency and competitiveness of goods produced is universally low. There is a high proportion of obsolete production. The range of goods and services available substantially diverges from effective demand and does not satisfy real social needs. Both the branches providing for consumption and for what one might call welfare services have seriously fallen behind, as has the whole social sector. (Lindsay, 1989, p. 8)

Management training in Western business practices has as a result become an urgent priority for the former USSR. Soviet and Eastern European managers are now seeking practical solutions to the problems facing them as they struggle towards a free market (Storm, 1991). Some of the problems faced by these companies include overmanning, technical backwardness, management shortages, lack of capital and debt. Eastern European firms need technical advice on how to restructure their internal organisation, how to create new departments such as Procurement, Finance, Personnel and Marketing and how to introduce New Technology.[6] Universities, colleges and management consultancies from all over the world have developed considerable plans to offer management and marketing education in the countries of Central and Eastern Europe based on the general belief that without Western knowledgeable practices, market economies and democratic regimes in Eastern and Central Europe can neither be successfully introduced nor developed (Brademas, 1991; Nelson-Horchler, 1991). Management Schools as a result have been springing up throughout Eastern Europe with the establishment for example of the Moscow International Business Management School, the Sofia School of International Management (signed with Cranfield School of Management) and most recently the US Business School in Prague (Staudohar, 1990; Aurichio, 1991; Silver, 1991) and the MBA Enterprise.[7] This particular focus on the mechanics of introducing privatisation by simply concentrating on the techniques and tools needed for a successful implementation of privatisation has neglected to consider whether the infrastructures do in fact exist for privatisation to succeed in Central and Eastern Europe, for example the lack of capital, money-markets, technology, 'know-how' and so on. As a result, the adoption of Western business ethics and business models in Central and Eastern Europe, contrary to the general expectation and experience of the workforce, has so far failed to improve the local economy while neo-liberal fiscal and monetary policy is causing disastrous economic and social consequences at a tremendous human cost in growing unemployment and increased poverty (Ringen and Wallace, 1993; Hank, 1993; Wood, 1992; Kapl et al. 1991; Euromoney, 1990). The rate of increase in unemployment has often been underestimated, and there are no indications that this rising trend of unemployment is close to an end (Boeri, 1993, p. 21; Kabaj, 1992). For example, in Poland in December 1990 there were 1,126,000 registered unemployed and by December 1991 there were already 2,155,000. In February 1992 this number reached 2,260,000 with an estimated rise to 3.5 million by the end of 1993 (Danecki, 1993, p.51). The proportions of people living below the poverty line is also alarming. While in the 1960s and 1970s it oscillated between 15 and 20 per cent, in 1983 it rose to 27.2 per cent, and to 37.4 per cent in 1991 (Danecki, 1993, p. 49). The Bulgarian situation is also quite illustrative. In 1991, 45.2 per cent lived at or under the subsistence level versus 24 per cent in 1990, and 64.6 per cent of those who lived at or under the social minimum level versus 43.4 per cent in 1990 (Chavdarova, 1993, p.163). Unemployment is particularly serious in countries where full employment has been taken for granted and where social benefits were often provided by enterprises.

Despite these disturbing and alarming figures a scarcely questioned belief still remains in Eastern Europe that the free market, namely privatisation and deregulation, will improve the domestic economy and benefits will ultimately trickle down to the poor. What is interesting and intellectually puzzling here is first, what explains this tacit public acceptance of privatisation, economic liberalisation and deregulation despite the detrimental effect it has on the poor ['*Social Limits to Growth*' (Hirsch, 1977)]. Second, in spite of the huge differentiation between Eastern and Central European states in terms of economic development, education, culture and political history, what explains the simultaneous convergence of state decision-makers around the norms of privatisation, marketisation and trade liberalisation?

There are, of course, domestic factors which have to be taken into account when explaining these trends. First the most successful privatisation has been the so-called small privatisation that is, shops, restaurants, plumbers and mechanics. This is popular both because many individuals value the opportunity to engage in independent economic initiative and because life is much smoother if you can ring up a local plumber, go to a friendly restaurant and so on. Second, many believe that privatisation is necessary for democracy. Formerly the state controlled everything. It is very difficult to be critical of the state if there are no independent sources of income . Third, many people, it is claimed, have benefited from the changes for example the middle class, especially the new economic elite, who prefer higher prices and availability of Western consumer goods to hours spent queueing. Finally, privatisation and liberalisation represent the negation of what went before. However, it is not clear whether these reasons for privatisation and liberalisation are widely shared, whether they are favoured beyond a narrow elite. Nor is it clear whether the adoption of the new positions was really an autonomous choice although explicitly and intentionally chosen, or whether the choices made arise because of their already subordinated integration within the global political economy and its attendant structures and discourses.

PRIVATISATION, INTERNATIONAL BUSINESS AND THE GLOBAL POLITICAL ECONOMY

Part of the answer may be found by relating the recent trends towards global privatisation to current changes in the global political economy, for example the transnationalisation of the economy, hegemony and order in the international system, and the global articulation of a dominant business ethic and its mediation through public international organisations such as the IMF, the World Bank, WHO, the International Telecommunications Union (ITU) and more recently UNESCO, as well as through state formations.

Part of what explains the emergence of privatisation and the extent of its globalisation, particularly in Central and Eastern Europe, relates to the powerful internationalisation of its content. This has been made possible through its transfer from the subjective domain it originally occupied, that is as the value-based policy or decisions taken by policy-makers, into the objective domain it now dominates as a technical, rational, value-free, expert knowledge of economics and offered as being objectively in the interests of all. This powerful objectification of 'privatisation' and consequently its globalisation as an impartial, technical instrumental knowledge is connected to the dominant liberal ideology and its separation of economics from politics into rational economics (objective) and non-rational politics (evaluative), and the acceptance or general belief that economic issues are resolvable on the basis of rational economic knowledge and resolutions of technical problems (MacLean, 1981; 1984 and 1988b).

In the literature, 'privatisation' so far has been narrowly defined in terms of actors' interests, actions and outcomes, and in a context of separate units (Peacock, 1984, p. 4).[8] On this view privatisation is seen as occupying a level of behaviour, and thus analysis, below that of the global political economy, and involves simply the rolling back of the activities of the state and its replacement by the market.   All of the definitions of privatisation share a set of common assumptions: first, that privatisation is principally a technical economic concept and thus in itself is apolitical; second, that it can be located and understood in wholly empirical terms; and third, that globalisation means its transfer to other territorial locations, located still at the level of actors and policy-making. A review of the literature dealing with 'privatisation', as presented so far by academics, business analysts, political scientists and economists, reinforces the general prevailing shared assumption that the case for privatisation rests upon supposed deficiencies of the various forms of state intervention, and on the ability of some form of privatised system to remedy them. Many countries, it is claimed, whose public sectors expanded in recent decades, now find themselves confronted by rising debt and strong resistance to higher taxes. The privatisation of state-owned firms, it is claimed, promises to bring some permanent relief particularly where the treasury has been heavily subsidising unprofitable enterprises. Privatisation is thus offered as a remedy to cut social expenditure and boost revenues by converting debt to equity, and to improve the overall financial structure of the economy. Privatisation is also expected automatically to increase efficiency.[9] The idea that the public sector will prosper and become efficient when run on business criteria runs through many statements made by politicians.[10] Only privatisation, it is affirmed, can take the public sector into the purely economic world and thereby increase efficiency by taking away their status as political entities and transforming them into economic ones (Pirie, 1988 p. 52). 'Once they are free of the State', Pirie argues, 'most of the decisions made about them will become economic ones' (ibid. p. 53). Thus it is assumed, once freed from their political influence, most of these decisions will become rational, technical/expert and thus apolitical. A very good illustrative example here is the recent appointment of Jeffrey Sachs of Harvard Business School as an advisor to Boris Yeltsin (Hank, 1993). Sachs also assisted Home Deputy Minister Leszek Balcerowicz in introducing deep economic reforms in Poland during the transition period between 1989-91 (Hunter, 1992). Accordingly, privatisation then becomes primarily a technical and administrative problem-solving concern consisting of first any shift of activities or functions from the state to the private sector and second, more specifically, any shift from the public to the private sector of the production of goods and services.

This conventional separation of politics from economics can be traced historically to the eighteenth and nineteenth centuries, a period which produced a conceptual separation between state (political society) and civil society (in the Western sense) (MacLean, 1988a; Tooze, 1984). The separation broadly corresponds to two distinct spheres of human activity, to 'an emergent society of individuals based on contract and market relations which replaced a status society, on the one hand, and a state with functions limited to maintaining internal peace, external defence and the requisite conditions for markets, on the other' (Cox, 1981, p. 126). Theoretically the justification for such a separation is based on the assumption that social reality, like physical reality must be broken down into variable pieces if it is to be studied (Gilpin, 1987, p. 5). Economics is therefore concerned with the use of scarce resources for unlimited wants, in other words what is the most efficient allocation of resources. This obviously involves a set of related questions about how markets behave, which government policies are best and how different parts of the economic system function (Strange, 1988, p. 5). Politics, on the other hand, is about providing public order and public goods. It is mostly concerned with what sort of order is best and how it is to be achieved and maintained (ibid., p. 14). The consequence of such a separation, argues Strange, is that each discipline tends to take the other for granted. Markets are studied in economics on the assumption that they are not going to be disrupted by war, revolution or other civil disorders; and politics assumes that the economy will continue to function reasonably smoothly 'whether it is a command economy run according to the decision of any other bureaucrats, or a market reflecting the multiple decisions taken by prudent and profit-maximizing producers' (Strange, 1988, p. 16).

Such a rigid separation between economics and politics, the private and public, business and government, fails to provide us with a general understanding of the totality of political and economic reality, and its historical development. Consider, for example, recent economic events in the international economic system, such as the claimed failure of the Bretton Woods System, the debt problems of the Less Developed Countries, global interdependence and transnational relations such as the internationalisation of financial institutions, production and information technology, or, more recently, the changes occurring in Central and Eastern Europe where economic reforms are being introduced to facilitate, it is claimed, the process of liberalisation and transition to democracy. These 'transition' problems have dramatically shown that 'governments will not survive long if they have not somehow made sure that the national economy is able to earn or borrow enough foreign exchange to pay for the imports of capital goods, or raw material and of technology necessary to maintain economic growth and higher material standards of living' (Strange, 1988,

p. 16) . 'Firms like states', affirms Strange, 'play a role in markets and technological development and can restrict, or enlarge the range of options open to policy-makers in governments and in other firms'. The state in fact profoundly influences the outcome of market activities by determining the material and distribution of property rights, as well as the rules governing economic behaviour. The market itself is, on the other hand, a source of power that influences political outcomes (Strange, 1991).

This separation of economics from politics, private and public, states and firms, national and international, is also reproduced and reinforced by the traditional discipline separation of International Relations and International Business, or 'mutual neglect' as I call it. International Business studies have focused mainly on the provision of empirical, practical knowledge of the Eastern European environment, and how to operate successfully within it. While not denying the practical value of such normative knowledge, given the recent changes in the international system, for example the internationalisation of production, distribution and consumption, or the role of new information technology and international communications, such an approach, by concentrating only on the normative and prescriptive nature of the discipline, has neglected the issues and factors which underlie the growing tendency towards 'internationalisation' and globalization (El Kahal, 1992, 1994). International Relations has, in its own way, denied the role of international business in that it has traditionally focused almost exclusively on what is seen as political, and has rarely focused upon the role and awareness of international business and its increasing internationalism. Both disciplines in their methodological and theoretical content, by focusing only on the empirical and observable action of states, firms and international organisations, have failed to theorise adequately the 'global'. The latter remains an empirical concept which assumes that certain practices are spread from the domestic to the international level. Consequently the particular focus on Eastern European business development, problems and prospects, as developed so far by business studies and also to a certain extent by the discipline of International Relations, simply assumes that Eastern European business operations can be abstracted from the global political economy as a whole, and explained in terms of separated units. This approach provides too narrow a framework for dealing with global political and economic changes and their implications for Eastern Europe. By ignoring the underlying social structures and causal mechanisms that produce the internationalisation of business operations, and of privatisation in the case of Eastern Europe, such an approach provides us with a reductionist notion of the causal mechanisms involved in the increasing internationalisation of the world. It is, as John MacLean pointed out, 'mistaken to suppose that the world appears wholly external and objective to us, as a universe of raw data, events or movements, one whose relations and connections can be grasped fully from the events and movements' (MacLean, 1988a and 1984).

Analysis of the problems of transition in Central and Eastern Europe, from centrally planned economies to free market systems, needs to be related more explicitly to the current changes in the global political economy rather than being restricted to the regional and domestic level. Business activities can no longer be evaluated and understood in terms of economics only, or international finance, but increasingly need to be related to the way in which the world is politically organised, for example the nature of capital, problematic relations between states and markets, and the underlying structures and dynamics of information technology. Considerable socioeconomic and political relations operating at the global level are increasingly influencing international business relations even at the regional and domestic level. Some of the practical and substantive issues that have contributed to these developments can be seen in the recent full internationalisation of business operations due to new Information Technology, the International Communications Networks and European Integration (RACE, ESPRIT), and in the increasing management of the international system by international organisations, such as the International Chamber of Commerce known more widely as the World Business Organization (WBO), WHO, ITU, INTELSAT (Crockett, 1991), and UNESCO, which are at present very active, together with the ITU, in mediating privatisation and deregulation in the field of telecommunications and satellite technology, in the internationalisation of private sector management and budgetary practices, and in the establishment of a global business ethic.

This current trend towards the internationalisation of business practices and the movement towards privatisation is therefore not just a characteristic of Eastern Europe seen as a simple consequence of political events, a sudden choice by decision-makers to shift their economy through some form of demonstration effect to a more free open market. The international system itself has already provided the structure for these developments to occur. Privatisation is now becoming one of the core policies of the IMF and the World Bank.[11]

INTERNATIONAL BUSINESS, PRIVATISATION AND INTERNATIONAL ORGANISATIONS

This movement towards the global articulation of a dominant business ethic, and the international application of private sector management, is largely the result of the pressure from the already established and existing conditions of the global political economy which are being mediated not only by international lending institutions, but also by international organisations. The prevailing and dominant view is that privatisation is the solution to the claimed inefficiency, corruption, mismanagement, bureaucracy and increasing politicisation of international public organisations, the UN specialized agencies in particular.

The United Nations Economic Scientific and Cultural Organization (UNESCO) provides a good illustration here. In the past few years many international organisations have been criticised for their claimed inefficiency, corruption and 'politicisation'. As a result the Reagan Administration in the early 1980s instructed a systematic review of all of the UN specialised agencies and a reassessment of their objectives and operations. The stated purpose of such a review was to initiate the process of restructuring the UN system so as to make it more fully capable of dealing with problems of international economic cooperation and development in a comprehensive and effective manner (General Assembly Resolution 3362), with the underlying belief that international public organisations can be reformed through the introduction of new private sector management techniques. Of all the UN organisations, UNESCO has been more severely criticised for its deviation from its supposed apolitical character as a neutral, technical organisation mandated to promote education, science, culture and communication, into a highly 'politicised' forum for the propagation of radical Third World and Soviet positions, and for having the most irresponsible and unrestrained budgetary expansion in the UN system (GAP Report, 1984). Since his election in November 1987, Federico Mayor, the new Director of UNESCO, spent his first two years in office planning and restructuring the organisation. In December 1988, an International Commission chaired by Doug Hammarskjold was set up, with the task of submitting recommendations for improving efficiency and staff management (24C/INF.11 Rev. p. 13). The recommendations of this Commission were that private sector management practices would provide the best tools to cure the organisation of its claimed politicisation, mismanagement and budgetary deficiency (Hammarskjold Report, 1989). A system of Management By Objectives (MBO) (DG/Note, 1990), bottom-up decision-making process (129 EX/INF.13 p. 4), Quality Circles (DG/Note,

1990, p. 3), Zero Base Budgeting (130 EX/PP14 Recom No.5, p.10) and a new management matrix chart (DG address to staff December 1988 p. 6) have been introduced. Armed with these tools, which were assumed to be neutral, non-cultural and apolitical and therefore universally applicable, UNESCO's Director General, it was believed, should be able to restore the organisation's efficiency and efficacy, and eliminate its claimed politicisation.

CONCLUSION

Bringing these considerations back to the changes in Central and Eastern Europe and the problems of transition, raises several questions, which need further investigation. The choices that are actually being made in Eastern Europe and the way in which the problem is being characterised and articulated in the West, are both partly located in the already established existing conditions of the global political economy. Consequently, we cannot say that these changes in Eastern Europe constructed as problems of 'transition' are merely or only direct reflections of structures and developments at the global levels; it is also clear that we cannot make full sense of these without analysing them in relation to the global political economy from the outset. These problems then no longer seem particular or peculiar to Eastern Europe, although clearly the actual behavioural form of them may well be 'Eastern European', but can be seen rather as a part of a long history of maintaining and establishing the identity of Western Europe as 'self' and Eastern Europe as the 'other'. Finally there seems to be a massive correspondence of choices being made in Eastern Europe with what is being agreed upon at the global level. Those choices, as I have shown above, should not be seen as chaotic and at all surprising, but as indications of the way in which the international global political economy is developing. This calls into question the centrality of concepts like sovereignty, freedom, participation and so on in relation to the assumed impartiality, non-ideological and technical nature of the economic and business discourses seen as providing 'solutions' to the problems of transition.

NOTES

1. See also Ash (1991); Tomarchio (1991); Alperowicz (1991); Newbury (1991); Nut (1991); and Adam (1992).
2. Lotus Development Corporation, for example, now has 45 dealers in 25 cities throughout Russia. In the first three months of the Lotus 1-2-3 availability in Russia, Lotus sold more than 1,000 copies of it. Crumney (1991), p. 25.

3. This new NIS Consortia programme is funded by the Agency of International Development and administered by the Commerce Department.

4. Direct foreign investment:

Disbursements in $ US millions	1991	1992
Bulgaria	56	42
Czechoslovakia	592	1054
Hungary	1,459	1,471
Poland	117	185*
Romania	37	73**
Former Soviet Union	200	

*Jan-Sep; **Jan-Nov

Source: Economic Survey of Europe in 1992-1993, United Nations Economic Commission for Europe.

5. A recent USSR-based study demonstrated that 35 per cent of managers questioned had no knowledge of world standards, and 52 per cent only had a minimal knowledge. The third of executives polled 'thought' their products were competitive with world standards, but few knew of international market standards. Quoted in N. Hibbert (1991), 'Training Soviet Mangers', Coventry University, Pioneering courses, European Agency.

6. For detailed case studies see Sir John Harvey-Jones's business trip to Eastern Europe in April/May 1991, BBC Documentary, 'Troubleshooter in Eastern Europe', 1991.

7. The MBA Enterprise Corps was formed in 1990 by a 16-school consortium headed by the University of Carolina's Kenan-Flagler Business School.

8. See, for example Peacock, A. (1984), Asher, K. (1987), Heald, D. (1983), and Swan, D. (1988),

9. Evidence in support of this comes from the record of public and private municipal services. For example, see Davies, D.G. (1971).

10. John Moore declared in his 1983 speech, for example, that privatisation 'will help provide a remedy for some ills that have beset the UK industrial performance', *'Why privatise?'* Conservative Political Centre, London, 1983.

11. The reform programme launched in February 1991 in Bulgaria was approved by the International Monetary Fund which conditionally provided a standby loan for one year. See Frydman et al. (1993), p. 3. Also in February 1992 the IMF signed a three-year agreement with Hungary. The agreement provided for around 1.6 billion US dollars in new lending, 68 million dollars of which was available for borrowing in 1991. The IMF also approved a second tranche of the Credit Programme in March 1992, quoted in Frydman et al. (1993), p. 96.

REFERENCES

Adam, J. (1992), 'The possible new role of market and planning in Poland and Hungary', in Anders, Aslund (1992) (ed.), *Market Socialism on the Restoration of Capitalism*, Cambridge: Cambridge University Press, p. 55.

Alperowicz, Natasha (1991), 'Czechoslovakia: Big changes, emerging opportunities', *Chemical Week,* Vol, 148, Issue 27, 24 July.

Ash, Nigel (1990), 'The Privatization Dilemma', *Euromoney,* September, pp. 145-148.

Ash, Nigel (1991), 'Czechoslovakia: Fulfilling the New State Plan', *Euromoney,* pp. 511-514.

Asher, K. (1987), *The Politics of Privatization,* London: Macmillan.

Aurichio, Kenneth (1991), 'Western Accounting Principles head East', *Management Accounting,* Vol. 74, Issue 2, August, pp. 54-56.

Beesley, M. and Littlechild, S. (1983), 'Privatization: Principles, Problems and Priorities', *Lloyds Bank Review*, No. 149.

de Bendern, Samantha (1990), 'Eastern Europe towards the Millenium. Economic miracle or Weimar year 2000?', *Economic Situation Report*, Vol. 21, No.3, Summer, pp. 26-30.

Boeri, Tito (1993), 'Unemployment in Central and Eastern Europe: Transient or Persistent?', in Ringen and Wallace (1993), pp. 13-28.

Brademas, J. (1991), 'A moment to seize: Management Training and Market Economic Education in Central and Eastern Europe', *Vital Speeches*, Vol. 57, Issue 14, 1 May, pp. 432-435.

Business America (1993), Author anonymous, 'Building business ties with Russia', NIS / Eastern Europe, Vol. 114, Issue 6, 22 March, pp. 2-7.

Central European CEE (1993), Author anonymous, 'Central European Awards 1992-1993: CS FB's private pursuit', Issue 21, April, pp. 40-41.

Chavdarova, Tanya (1993), 'Irregular Economic Activities: The Bulgarian Case of Hidden Privatization', in Ringen and Wallace (1993), pp. 163-173.

Cox, R.W. (1981), 'Social Forces, States and World Order: Beyond International Relations Theory', *Millenium Journal of International Relations*, Vol. 10, No.2, p. 126.

Crockett, Barton (1991), 'Darkening Skies. Intelsat faces threat to dominance', *Network World,* Vol. 6, Issue 35, 2 September.

Crumney, Steve (1991), 'Adventure in the Soviet market place', *Computer World*, Vol. 25, Issue 18, 6 May, p. 25.

Danecki, Jan (1993), 'Social costs of System Transformation in Poland', in Ringen and Wallace (1993) pp. 47-60.

Davies, D.G. (1971), 'The Efficiency of Public versus Private Firms: The Case of Australia's two airlines', *Journal of Law and Economics*, Vol. 12, April.

Donlon, J. (1991), 'The hard work begins', *Chief Executive*, Issue 6, July/August, pp. 60-76.

Earle, John, S., Frydman, Roman and Rapaczyunski, Andrezej (eds) (1993), *Privatization in the transition to a Market economy. Studies of preconditions and policies in Eastern Europe,* London: Pinter Publishers.

El Kahal, S. (1992), 'International Business and International Relations : A case of mutual neglect', *British Academy of Management* Newsletter, 13 July.

El Kahal, S. (1994), *Introduction to International Business,* McGraw-Hill, Preface xvii.

Ettlie, John, E. (1993), 'The emergence of manufacturing in Hungary', *Production,* Vol. 105, Issue 8, August, p. 34.

Euromoney (1990), Author anonymous, 'Yugoslavia Supplement. Pains and Pleasures of Reform', pp. 13-16.

Foster, P.(1991), 'McDonald's excellent Soviet Venture', *Canadian Business ,* Vol. 64, Issue 5, May.

Frydman, Roman, Rapaczynski, Andrzej, Earle, John S. (1993), *The Privatization Process in Central Europe,* London, Central European Press.

Gilpin, R. (1987), *The Political Economy of International Relations,* p. 5, Princeton: Princeton University Press.

Hank, Steve (1993), 'The high cost of Jeffrey Sachs', *Forbes,* Vol. 151, Issue 13, 21 June, p. 52.

Harvey-Jones, Sir John (1991), 'Troubleshooter in Eastern Europe', BBC Documentary.

Heald, D. (1983), *Public Expenditure: Its defence and reform,* Oxford: Martin Robertson.

Hirsch, F. (1977), *Social Limits to Growth,* London: Routledge & Kegan.

Hume, Scott (1990), 'How Big Mac made it to Moscow', *Advertising Age,* Vol. 61, Issue 4, 22 January, pp. 16-51.

Hunter, Richard (1992), 'The Polish Experiment in Democracy and a Free Market: Its importance for Eastern and Central Europe', *Mid-Atlantic Journal of International Business,* Vol. 28, Issue 3, December, pp. 231-234.

Jones, Colin (1991), 'Hungary: Everything for sale', *Bankers,* Vol. 141, Issue 785, July, pp. 34-39.

Kabaj, M. (1992), 'Selected elements of the Programme to combat unemployment in Poland (1992-1995)', Paper presented at the IP, SS-IAB Friedrich Ebert Stiftung Conference, Warsaw, 2-4 April.

Kapl, Martin, Sojka, Milan and Tepper, Tomas (1992), 'Unemployment and Market Oriented Reform in Czechslovakia', *International Labour Review,* Vol. 130, Issue 2, pp. 199-210.

Korabi, Tarif and Grieve, David G. (1990), 'Doing business in Eastern Europe: A survival guide', Canadian Business Review, Vol. 17, Issue 2, Summer, pp. 23-25.

Kregel, J.A. and Matzner, E. (1992), 'Agenda for the Reconstruction of Central and Eastern Europe', *Challenge,* Vol. 35, Issue 5, September/October pp. 33-40.

Lindsay, Margie (1989), *International Business in Gorbachev's Soviet Union,* London: Pinter Publishers.

MacLean, John (1981), 'Political Theory, International Theory and Ideology', *Millenium, Journal of International Relations*, Vol. 10, No. 2, Summer.

MacLean, John (1984), 'Interdependence: An ideological intervention in International Relations', in Jones, R. and Willets, B. *Interdependence on Trial,* London: Pitman.

MacLean, John (1988), 'International Relations and Marxism: A Strange Case of Mutual Neglect', *Millenium, Journal of International Relations,* Vol. 17, No. 2, Summer.

MacLean, John (1988), 'Belief Systems and Ideology in International Relations: A critical approach', in Little, R. and Smith, S. (eds), *Belief Systems and International Relations,* London: Blackwell.

Newberry, D. (1992), 'The Netherlands', *European Economic Review*, Vol. 35, Issue 2, 3, April pp. 571 - 580.

Nelson-Horchler, J. (1991), 'Desperately seeking Yankee know-how', *Industry Week,* Vol. 240, Issue 5, 4 March, pp. 52-56.

Niemeyer, E. (1990), 'Hotels chase travellers to Eastern Europe', *New England Business,* Vol. 12, Issue 11, November pp. 72-74.

Nuti, Mario, (1991), 'Privatization of Socialist Economies: General Issues and the Polish Case', in Bloommestein, H. and Marrese, M. (eds) (1991), *Transformation of Planned Economies: Prosperity, Rights, Reform and Microeconomic Stability,* Organization for Economic Cooperation and Development, p. 62.

Oldersma, Harry, and Van Bergeijk, Peter (1992), 'The potential for an export-oriented growth strategy in Central Europe', *Journal of World Trade*, Vol. 26, Issue 4, August pp. 47-63.

Peacock, A. (1984), 'Privatisation in Perspective', *Three Banks Review,* No. 149.

Pesmen, Sandra (1990), 'US Hotels invade Eastern Europe or strengthen their service and reputations', *Business Marketing,* Vol. 15, Issue 10, October pp. 46-47.

Pirie, M. (1988), *Privatization,* Wilwood House, Aldershot.

Quartermaine, Andrew (1993), 'Trade Finance in Transition', *Central European (CEE),* Issue 22, May, pp. 28-30.

Reihn, R. (1991), 'Bright Prognosis for the Health Care Industry in Eastern Europe', *Journal of European Business,* Vol. 2, Issue 4, March/April pp. 47-51.

Ringen, Stein and Wallace, Clare (1993), *Societies in Transition: East-Central Europe Today,* Prague Papers on Social Responses to Transformation, Vol. 1, Prague: Central University Publ.

Ryan, N. (1992), 'Cooking! How Sara Lee plans to make it big in Eastern Europe', *World Trade,* Vol. 5, Issue 7, August/September, pp. 44-48.

Silver, Julia Flynn (1991), 'Adam Smith goes to Czechoslovakia', *Business Week,* Issue 3213, 13 May, pp. 78-79.

Siren, Michelle and Shaw, Des (1991), 'Assessing the market and the opportunities', *Directors and Boards,* Vol. 15, Issue 2, Winter, pp. 30-33.

Staudohar, Caras H.S. (1990), 'Welcome to business 101, Comrades. Seizing up the Soviet System', *Personnel Journal,* Vol. 69, Issue 12, December, pp. 36-43.

Storm, Rachel (1991), 'New dreams for old', *International Management,* Vol. 46, Issue 4, pp. 40-43.

Strange, S. (1988), *States and Markets,* London: Pinter Publishers.

Strange, S. (1991), 'An Eclectic Approach', in Murphy, Craig N. and Tooze, Roger (eds), *The New International Political Economy,* Lynne Rienner Publishers, pp. 12-33.

Swan, D. (1988), *The Retreat of the State: Deregulation and Privatization in the UK and US,* London: Harvester Wheatsheaf.

Tomarchio, J.T. (1991), 'Joint Venture Law in Eastern Europe', *Journal of European Business,* Vol. 2, No. 5, May/June, pp. 12-18.

Tomes, Igor (1993), 'Social Policy and protection in Czechoslovakia since 1989', in Ringen and Wallace (1993), pp. 137-147.

Tooze, R. (1984), 'Perspectives and Theory. A Consumer Guide', in Strange, S. (ed.), *Paths to International Economy,* London: George Allen and Unwin.

Weston, Peter (1993), 'Cars: Eastern markets pick up speed', *Central European* (CEE), Issue 24, July/August, pp. 54-57.

Wood, Barry (1992), 'The Eastern Bloc: Two years later', *Central European (CEE),* Issue 314, March, pp. 12-13.

UNESCO Archives

General Assembly Resolution 3362 S - VII, Section VII, Para 1.

GAP Report. Improvements needed in UNESCO's Management. 30 November,1984. 24C/INF.11 Rev.

Commission Hammarskjold, December 1989. Report Modes de Gestion et performance. Partie III Rapport de la Commission independente presidee par Mr. Hammarskjold.

DG/Note/90/4. 28 February, 1990. Objet: Mode de Gestion et efficacité p. 4. Items 12 and 18 p. 3. See also DG/Note/90 /4 Item 19 , p. 5.

129 EX/INF.13 p. 4.

130 EX/PP 14 Recom. No. 5 p. 10.

DG address to Staff of UNESCO Secretariat. 5 December 1988, pp. 5-6.

10. A Europe of the Citizen. A Europe of Solidarity? Social Policy in the European Union

Crescy Cannan

INTRODUCTION

All welfare states are undergoing change and retrenchment, debating means of meeting social needs in the context of rising unemployment, a higher proportion of dependent to working population, and changes in family structures. Criticism of the classic welfare state has come not just from neo-liberals who have portrayed it as promoting dependence and as too costly but from user groups and new social movements seeking to create new, democratised relations of welfare and calling for social rights based on membership of society rather than on employment records, family membership or nationality. These questions, debated across the political spectrum, in capitalist and former state socialist societies, have raised fundamental questions about the basis of citizenship, which in turn raise questions of nationality, immigration, poverty, and discrimination (Taylor, 1991/92).

This chapter will consider these questions by looking at the idea and ideals of Social Europe with its origins in postwar reconstruction and the promotion of peace and social integration. This vision seems of great importance today, not just because of the resurgence of nationalism, racism and xenophobia, but because, while the policies of the European Community (as the forerunner of the European Union) have strengthened some rights of its citizens, other groups are seeing a rapid deterioration in their social and political rights (notably refugees and asylum seekers, Gypsies and travellers, and Third World and other non-EU nationals who are workers or their dependents in the EU). I shall argue that there is a danger of a drift in the EU from a vision of solidarity based on social justice and a widening of opportunities for (formal and informal) political participation to a more performance-related Bismarckian welfare state which heightens social divisions in a context of a strong exclusion of outsiders, a heavily policed solidarity that runs counter to the original aims of European union.

SOCIAL EUROPE: THE VISION

There have been many statements of the values of 'Europe' such as this from a document on the European Community and Human Rights:

> The construction of Europe is not solely a matter of economics. Beyond the pragmatism of the Community's common policies - the fruits of history, necessity and will - human rights and fundamental freedoms are part of the common heritage of Europeans. With other concerns, such as education or culture they can stimulate our vision of the place of Europe in the world and the European model of society: a society in which individuals can thrive while being conscious of their obligations towards others - a unique model which we must all enrich and fulfil. (Commission of the EC, 1989a: p. 10)

The vision of Social Europe has its origins in debates on the nature and future of Western European nations in the aftermath of the Second World War. Some argued that a European social policy was crucial to promote economic development, to minimise the inevitable costs of restructuring, and to embody values of social justice, peace and democracy.

The foundation of the EU lies in the Treaty of Rome which, in 1957, established a common market with the goals of customs union and the elimination of tariff barriers between six European countries (France, West Germany, Italy and the Benelux countries). The Treaty spelt out its narrow objective of customs union, but included in its preamble a statement in which the social objectives 'appear ... as absolutely predominant, like the lighthouse guiding the efforts of the economic and political union' (Rifflet, 1985: p. 19).

These objectives included 'an ever closer union among the peoples of Europe', economic and social progress by common action, and the constant improvement of living and working conditions. The aim of customs union had emerged out of hopes which many Europeans held after the war for a framework for political cooperation, for a United States of Europe which would counterbalance the dangers of nationalism, and for common coal and steel production as a foundation for the preservation of peace (Rifflet, 1985).

The 'European movement' led to the establishment of the Council of Europe in 1949 to which 15 nations were affiliated, and which was to be important in developing concepts of human and social rights. In 1950, The European Convention on Human Rights and Fundamental Freedoms was drawn up, with contracting states' adherence to these rights to be supervised by the European Court of Human Rights. The Convention sought to free citizens from state interference and required respect for privacy (a stance understandable in the aftermath of fascism) (Hillestad Thune, 1987).

The Council of Europe's European Social Charter of 1961 was to introduce a more positive notion of rights and to broaden the field to social, economic and cultural rights. Here rights are conceived not in negative terms as freedoms from state interference but as a set of reciprocal obligations between citizen and state. It gives a clear statement of the right to work, to form a trade union, to vocational training, to health care, to social security and to social assistance. Furthermore, children and young persons and the family have the right to social protection. The right of migrant workers and their families to protection and assistance is stated.

Contracting states did not have to sign all the articles, but the force of the Charter lay in the new attitudes it enshrined: an emphasis on human dignity and decency, and a stress that persons receiving social and medical assistance should not suffer from a diminution of political and social rights. The new post-war welfare states should not reduce those who could not support themselves to the status of second-class citizens as had been the case in the days of charity and the Poor Law. Assistance was a right, and not just a subjective right but an obligation on the part of contracting parties including the state to provide such assistance. It echoed the universalism of the Beveridge Report, but also anticipated new ways of tackling social problems in the fulfilment of social objectives (Mayer-Fabian, 1987: pp. 27-33).

Jacques Delors, as President of the Commission of the European Community since 1984, has been preeminent in furthering the progressive vision. In his preface to the Cecchini Report (1988), which he entitled 'A Common Objective', he said that

> [The EC] has a social as well as an economic dimension, and must lead to a more unified Community. The twelve Member States have rightly decided that it should be accompanied by policies that will lead to greater unity as well as more prosperity. (In Cecchini Report, 1988: p. xi)

The concern with social cohesion and solidarity is central to this 'nation-building' process. Thus, Delors has argued that the social dimension is essential to the deepening of the internal market and

> consists of, in its three forms: solidarity, pure and simple, the defence of the moral and material interests of the workers and a minimum of agreement and participation in decision-making. (Delors, 1985: pp. xvii-iii)

The Single European Act of 1986, which completed the Treaty of Rome and committed member states to economic union by the start of 1993, mentioned in its Preamble both the European Convention on Human Rights and the European Social Charter. Again, these are described as the cornerstone for the construction of Europe; the Act incorporates a commitment to social protection and social cohesion.

THE RISE AND FALL OF EU SOCIAL POLICY?

The late 1980s were a watershed in EC social policy. The EC institutions, pushed by a working group of Members of the European Parliament, embarked on the single market project in earnest, stressing the social dimension of union. The Community Charter of Fundamental Social Rights of Workers (the 'Social Charter'; Commission of the EC, 1990), the Action Programme to implement it, and the Social Chapter of the Maastricht Treaty of Union of 1991 seemed to express with vigour and confidence the vision of Social Europe. Yet, disagreement, led by the British government at Maastricht over the social objectives, means that social policy has become an arena of conflict in the path to European union (Butt Philip, 1992), with much more restrictive policies now appearing to be on the ascendant.

Early EC social policies were restricted to legalistic measures to increase labour mobility within the Common Market, modest health and safety and equal opportunities measures, initiatives on youth and the establishment of the Social Fund (Brewster and Teague, 1989). From the mid-seventies however, the combined effects of the oil crisis, growing unemployment, and monetary upheavals were to put welfare issues on the agenda, and the social costs of the move to the single market continue to be a major factor in the social initiatives of the EU. Awareness of growing poverty, and a call for a human face to the EC from leaders such as Willi Brandt (also concerned at the costs for the Third World), meant that an Irish proposal for poverty programmes, which will be discussed below, was initiated in the late seventies (Dennett et al., 1982).

During the eighties the social aspect became an essential element of the 'big' aim of European union. Jacques Delors provided much of the vision, strongly reflecting French policy under President Mitterrand, during this period of determination to make union more than just a free trade zone. He promoted the concept of *l'espace* sociale in which the single market would be accompanied by a framework of partnership between employers and trade unions whose dialogue he hoped would create the broad ideas for EC policies. This social framework (the 'level playing field') was seen as necessary to control 'social dumping', the competitive devaluation of wages and deregulation of employment conditions in order to keep or attract capital. So we see a shift from the harmonisation of provision and laws, to a negotiation of broad principles and minimum conditions which would be implemented in accordance with the subsidiarity principle in ways that suited individual member states. At the same time European citizenship, identity and culture, and social measures to prevent exclusion, to provide safety nets of social protection, were promoted.

This phase saw considerable action in the field of equal opportunities. The action was designed to prevent labour market segregation of women and disabled people. The Medium Term Action Programme on Equal Opportunities for Women of 1986-90, and the Commission Report in 1986 on the Employment of Disabled People produced schemes such as HORIZON and HELIOS for disabled people and NOW and IRIS for women. These were designed to promote social integration by improving vocational training, and by providing complementary measures such as childcare for women and adaptations to the workplace for disabled people. Social integration in this approach meant extending access to and skills for employment.

The poverty programmes have been an EC response to the social costs of the single market in declining industries and regions. They have emphasised both a labour market approach to social integration and the possibility of a broader basis than employment for social rights. The second poverty programme (1986-89) was directed at 'the fourth world', the 'new' poor (single parent families, elderly people, workers in declining or precarious industries), as much as at those in 'traditional' (that is low wage, large family) poverty (Room et al., 1993). Unemployment and the poverty of those in precarious employment has risen alarmingly in member states: with 38 million in poverty in 1975, the figure had risen to over 44 million in 1985 (Room, 1989).

In declaring its clear involvement in the fight against poverty, the Commission reiterated that

> The persistence of poverty or even of a precarious work situation is incompatible with several key objectives of the European Treaties ... A people's Europe should be a Europe of solidarity, especially as regards the most underprivileged. (Commission of the EC, 1987)

The third poverty programme (1990-94) develops the second programme's approach of participative community development, emphasising the aim of reinforcing social and economic cohesion in the Community and of finding innovative sociocultural methods of so doing. The programme finances 39 projects which are expected to identify participative strategies of economic and social integration (insertion) of less favoured groups. The philosophy is that the poor need the means to overcome their precariousness, means which include good housing, good health and food, medical care, education, urban renewal, and a healthy environment. Only when these are tackled together will the cycles of marginalisation be broken (Benington, 1991).

This approach to social policy draws much from French socialist government initiatives during the eighties (for example) Commission of the EC, 1989b). The French 9th Plan (1984-88) emphasised the social and economic development of neighbourhoods, and locally coordinated action aimed at groups rather than individuals, for instance in the struggle against drug abuse, youth crime, measures in favour of immigrants, social integration of young people and the support of families, especially the socially isolated (Cannan et al., 1992; King, 1988; Thevenet and Desigaux, 1985). The importance of this approach is that it is an attempt to extend social rights to those marginalised by insecure positions in the labour force, to try to break the divide between insured, protected workers and their dependents and those unprotected who fall on to social assistance: there is a widening of the shared risk pool, and broadening of solidarity beyond membership of occupational groups and their insurance schemes (Chamberlayne, 1991/92).

The most recent phase of EU social policy has been one of doubt and dissension against the background of the great transitions occurring in Eastern and Central Europe, the reemergence of nationalism, and rising unemployment. There has been growing conflict between the majority of the member states who wished to see a Community committed to economic and political union alongside the social objectives and the British Conservative government which views labour regulation and social protection as socialist and corporatist horrors from which Margaret Thatcher had rescued Britain (and Eastern and Central Europe). In 1990 this conflict centred on the Social Charter; reflecting their abhorrence of its principles and claiming it would be too expensive for employers, the British government, alone of the twelve member states, refused to sign it.

The Social Charter, in accordance with the subsidiarity principle, places a responsibility on member states to guarantee rights which include protection for part-time and temporary workers, for pregnant women, health and safety measures, rights to 'decent' wages and 'minimum incomes', worker participation in company management, and states the necessity for measures to combat discrimination of every form. Its associated Action Programme consisted of 50 proposals, 30 of which have been agreed. The others, however, have been resisted and are bogged down or being watered down, notably the directives on rights for temporary and part-time workers, on employment rights for pregnant women, and the 48-hour maximum working week (from which the UK government negotiated a ten-year opt-out).

The Maastricht Treaty of Union reaffirmed the goal of 'the ever closer union among the peoples of Europe' and the social objectives of the Single European Act. With the Single European Act's abolition of internal frontier controls then planned for 1 January 1993, the Treaty decreed that citizens of member states automatically hold European Union citizenship and have rights and obligations under the Union, mainly economic rights but also basic political rights. The Social Chapter proposes no specific measures but is an enabling measure in replacing unanimous with qualified majority voting for directives covering health and safety, working conditions, worker consultation, equal opportunities between the sexes, protection of pensioners and the unemployed (the combating of social exclusion), and the work environment. The Social Chapter then is a broad statement of social policy objectives, enshrining the commitment of member states to the Social Charter by giving the Commission clearer powers to impose social legislation, and providing for (with unanimous voting) directives on social security, redundancy, collective representation, employment conditions for non-EU migrant workers and job creation schemes.

The EU role and interests in social policy are now widely drawn, especially when put alongside the role in education and culture. These fields can broadly be seen as positive forms of policy, setting minimum standards, promoting services that develop the European identity and protect the (worker) citizen. But the Maastricht Treaty, in creating the European Union, added two pillars to this first pillar of the supranational authority of the Treaty of Rome and its EC institutions. These consist of new intergovermental bodies. The second pillar coordinates the community's foreign and security policies, and the third coordinates policing and immigration control. This third pillar is of increasing interest to social policy. It is to that area we now turn - because it raises the issue of who belongs (and who does not) to the people's Europe and it shows another face than that of Social Europe, and one which the UK government has been active in shaping: a different, negative, social policy of a solidarity and identity based on discipline and exclusion.

FORTRESS EUROPE, CITIZENS AND NON-CITIZENS

We joined Europe to have free movement of goods ... I did not join Europe to have free movement of terrorists, criminals, drugs, plant and animal diseases, and illegal immigrants... (Margaret Thatcher, interview in the *Daily Mail,* 18 May 1989, quoted in Gordon, 1991: p. 8).

There are two sides to 'Europe': a progressive vision based on social justice and an authoritarian, 'other' Europe (Bunyan, 1991).

The initiatives for women, disabled people and those aimed at young people and the long-term unemployed, are designed to benefit EU nationals. What is happening to the 15 million (estimates vary from 12-17 million) non-EU nationals resident in the EU? What of these groups who, effectively, form the 13th member state? (Gordon, 1989; Paul, 1991). Here the British government has been keen to cooperate with other member states and to develop the policies and practices of the third pillar, of Fortress Europe.

From 1985 the Commission of the EC began advocating greater coordination of national policies on visas to complement the easing of internal frontier controls. Its 1985 Action Programme to achieve the single market by the end of 1992 included measures to ease internal frontier controls and to coordinate states' rules and policies on asylum seekers and refugees, visas and third country immigration (Gordon, 1989). By 1989/90 member states' ministers responsible for immigration were reaching agreement on asylum policies and measures to combat clandestine immigration, the creation of a special police force in customs control, the harmonisation of laws on aliens and the creation of a common visa policy to create a strong external frontier.

The mechanisms of this other Europe include the Trevi Group (now known as K4) and the Ad Hoc Group on Immigration which construct immigration as a law and order issue, associating black people, refugees and asylum seekers with drugs, crime, terrorism and disease (Bunyan, 1991: p. 19). The Trevi Group consists of member states' justice and interior ministers and representatives of security services, and was set up at the suggestion of Harold Wilson in 1975 (Gordon, 1991: p. 10). It has met as a secret group, but has gradually created its own secretariat and become an influential but unaccountable EU police institution in embryo. The Group has increased and 'harmonised' the list of countries (over 50) in Africa, Asia and South America whose nationals need visas to enter any EU state (while relaxing visa requirements for Japanese, Australian, and North American nationals). Third country immigrants will have, like asylum seekers and refugees, limited right of entry to the EU, no appeal, no rights of free movement within the EU, social protection or to family reunion.

The Ad Hoc Group on Immigration, comprising immigration ministers, was established in 1986, again at the prompting of the UK government, in order to coordinate the easing of frontier controls and the strengthening of external frontiers (Gordon, 1991). It has achieved its aims of preventing 'abuses' of the asylum process by making airlines liable if they carry passengers without entry documents, and of stopping asylum seekers moving to another EU country if rejected on first entry attempt. In 1993, under pressure from the new conservative French government, the Group agreed to toughen its policy of imposing an obligation on member states to detect and expel anyone who breaches immigration rules. The policy envisages more checks on people's residence permits, on people re-united with family, students, and people on resident or work permits gained as a result of marriage to an EU national, legitimating greater police powers both of intelligence-gathering and of general identity checks (*The Guardian*, 26 May, 1993).

Cooperation between EU police forces will increase the monitoring and checks on these groups. It is estimated that there are now 20 (16 concerned with immigration) intelligence-gathering and sharing organisations in Europe including the Trevi Group, Interpol, and the Schengen Information Service. The Schengen Accord of 1990 grew from an intergovernment agreement made in 1985 between Germany, France, Belgium, the Netherlands and Luxembourg; it included all EU member states except Britain, Ireland and Denmark. The aims were to harmonise and coordinate policing, visa policies, crime prevention and searching in connection with drugs and arms, and to exchange information on new asylum seekers, their groups and organisations and on undesirables (Bunyan, 1991: p. 23). Currently France is attempting to stall on the open borders proposed under Schengen for mid-1993: the 'free movement of persons' is becoming seen as a disadvantage, especially given the more tolerant policing of drug users in the Netherlands which has meant a growth in drug tourism affecting Germany, France, and Belgium (Doyle, 1993). The free movement is also seen to benefit organised crime, and this has been used to argue for stronger internal and border policing, whether or not internal frontiers eventually disappear.

Tougher criteria for granting refugee status have meant that the rate of acceptance in the EU as a whole fell from 65 per cent to 10 per cent between 1980 and 1990 (Webber, 1991: p. 15). The UK 1988 Immigration Act removed the right of settled Commonwealth citizens to be joined by their families, part of a gradual abandonment by the UK of its 'special relationship' with its former colonies by creating two-tier citizenship: only the full British citizen now enjoys freedom of movement in the EU and full social and political rights. It is becoming much more difficult to acquire British nationality: the numbers of successful applications fell by 28 per cent in 1992 to the lowest level for ten years, reflecting the final implementation of the 1981 British Nationality Act which sharply restricted entitlement to claim citizenship. Entry to the UK is toughened by the use of imprisonment as a deterrent: according to the Joint Council for the Welfare of Immigrants more than 10,000 people are imprisoned each year without trial, charge or conviction under the immigration laws. These people include refugees, asylum seekers, students, and residents accused of breaking immigration rules (Ashford, 1993).

Similar developments have occurred in France. The conservatives elected in 1993 had pledged to tackle crime and immigration. The Interior Minister Pasqua had already in the period of cohabitation in 1986 brought in a law which made it more difficult to obtain residence permits, gave greater powers to prefects to order expulsions, abolished rights of appeal and gave the police more powers to check identity and residence rights. The socialists subsequently modified the law, but once back in power the conservatives reintroduced the legislation tightening frontier controls, extending police powers to check identities, withdrawing the right to nationality by birth in France, and giving mayors powers to refuse marriages where they suspect they are marriages of convenience (some parts of the nationality and immigration legislation are currently being challenged by the French Constitutional Council as contravening the supranational EU law). There has been extensive protest from both Catholic and Protestant Churches, from socialists and communists who all see the new measures as only increasing exclusion and tension, and creating a climate of fear.

In Germany, despite protest from the Left, a constitutional amendment in 1993 tightened the previously liberal asylum laws. Germany has taken more refugees and asylum seekers than any other member state, particularly from the East/Central European countries, but had been under pressure to come into line with the rest of the EU as its policy on asylum meant an open door to the EU. But citizenship in Germany is notoriously difficult to acquire, and its 6 million 'foreigners' include people who may have worked and lived with their families in Germany for twenty years. As a *quid pro quo* for the tightening of asylum laws, the German government is considering extending dual nationality to those with work and residence rights.

In member states then there is a deliberate convergence of policies. While nationality is a fact for many settled ethnic minorities and may become more so for the Turks and other settled groups in Germany, there are others who are increasingly losing their limited rights to residence, to unite their families or to move within the EU as is guaranteed for EU nationals. Those in the 13th State are then excluded from the 'people's Europe', and from the protection of the European Court of Justice as the third pillar is an intergovernmental, not EC, institution. Even those who are member state nationals but from ethnic minorities will feel the pressures of increased policing.

Racism and xenophobia are increasing across Europe. Although the European Parliament has expressed concern at the discriminatory effects of policing produced by immigration policies and at the lack of democratic control of the Trevi and Ad Hoc Groups in determining policies (Bunyan, 1991), MEPs could not agree with Glynn Ford's (Leader of the Labour Group) anti-racism proposals in 1990, fearful of the consequences back home (Ford, 1992; Baxter, 1990). Tara Mukherjee, President of the European Migrants' Forum, suggests that, rather than treating immigration as a law and order issue, the EU should create a Commissioner for Racial Affairs (*The Independent*, 18th July, 1992). The law and order institutions should concentrate on controlling racists and the extreme Right, not immigrants, while the new Commissioner could open up debate on race and immigration issues. These matters could also be part of the brief of the Commissioner for Social Affairs who has after all taken debates and initiatives on sex equality significantly forward.

Despite calls for measures to protect non-EU migrant workers and to combat discrimination in every form in, for instance, the Social Chapter and by the European Commission, there has been no substantive action to protect the rights of 'immigrants' or to act on racism and xenophobia. In general EU social policies will further the citizenship of member state workers and their families, and put effort into social programmes for indigenous workers displaced from employment. Workers and their dependents in the 13th state are in a precarious position. Stronger policing will protect the external borders of Fortress Europe, defining European identity against 'the Other', whether on the outside looking in or inside but excluded from citizenship and its rights.

EUROPEAN MODELS OF WELFARE: SOLIDARITIES AND EXCLUSIONS

As we have seen, in the heyday of the social dimension, policies and programmes did broaden their focus, to those excluded, to the new poor, women, disabled people and those in declining regions. It is notable, however, that these measures are work focused: they emphasise the right to participate in the workforce, they define social integration as labour market participation, and they provide the means of doing so via retraining and other support measures. Social policy consisted of extending workplace protection measures, of job creation and training, and of broadly conceived measures to counter segregation in the workplace or marginalisation from it.

Some on the left in the UK poverty lobby have dismissed such policies. Townsend (1990), for instance, argues that they do nothing for the poor because there is a workerist assumption that social rights rest in employment. Piachaud (1991) asks:

who is a worker of the European Community? Employed nationals of Community nations obviously qualify. But does a retired worker or an unemployed person? Are those working at home caring for young, old and disabled people classified as workers? ... None of these questions is answered, perhaps because the Charter is the product of a corporatist, employer-trade union mentality which sees work and the world in narrow terms.

The dominant continental European model of social policy is a form of industrial citizenship (Room, 1991), and of male industrial citizenship (Langan and Ostner, 1991). This conservative-corporatist model (Esping-Andersen, 1990) sits, uneasily, alongside a liberalism in the principles of free competition, and a hitherto strong position of social democracy as represented in the Commission by Delors (influenced by the French socialist government in the eighties) and in the dominant socialist grouping in the European Parliament. The Social Charter combines the conservative-corporatist model with the workerism of social democracy. Thus EU social policy has both right and left versions (Room, 1991). The right version is in the Bismarckian tradition (found also in France, Austria and Italy) of buying off class conflict and preserving status differences based on occupation. It is predicated on full male employment, and a strong influence of the Church over the family and social life. There is an assumption that men will have wives for caring services and that women will acquire benefits through their roles as wives and mothers. The subsidiarity principle limits the role of the state and heightens that of the family and independent associations. There are few services, but there are generous financial benefits which reward motherhood, marriage, and an uninterrupted work record. The pooling of risk only within insured occupations means that the egalitarianism and universalism in Beveridge's model is absent.

Although the Social Charter looks 'socialist' it also draws on this divisive and hierarchical tradition, which currently in Germany is fostering resentment among Westerners in the enforced burden sharing with the eastern population:

the system is work-centred and creates in its members a strong orientation towards norms of reciprocity and equivalence: those who contribute 'deserve' the benefits. Conversely, it is considered illegitimate to let people who have not been part of the contributors' 'risk pool' share the benefits. (Ganssmann, 1993)

Countering such divisions, the left version emerges partly from the older universalistic, social democratic models of social policy seen in Scandinavia, and from aspects of the British welfare state and the general post-war influence of Beveridge (Esping-Andersen, 1990; Cannan, 1992). It has been replenished by eighties optimism, a high point of radical and creative thinking in several European countries (Chamberlayne, 1991/92). Decentralisation, participation, and attempts to overcome old divisions of insurance and assistance, which impact particularly on women, disabled people and migrant and ethnic minority workers, were seen in Germany, France, Italy and the Labour boroughs of the UK. The French social action involved a move to extend the basis of social rights from employment to membership of *le social*. It created more means for the marginalised to exercise citizenship, partly by providing spaces and networks in which all could participate, to provide the social rights *for* citizenship (Lister, 1990). This, like some of the EU poverty programmes, and the Greater London Council initiatives which provided the means for participation of groups of people - service users, workers and local residents (Croft and Beresford, 1990) - challenges the advantage of the worker over the non-worker, the citizen over the non-citizen, the man over the woman. At the same time these initiatives have emphasised the need to make employment more accessible to women and disabled people by the provision of childcare, training, adaptations to the workplace and so forth.

Social policies then can complement the policing of Fortress Europe by resting entitlements in employment, nationality or family roles. They thus create and reinforce hierarchies and divisions, with segregated groups increasingly reluctant to share with those 'others' who are viewed as having failed or performed poorly in the workplace. Or they can challenge social divisions and assert the justice of needs-based, egalitarian benefits and services, creating and fostering a civil society in which citizenship can be based and exercised and discrimination outlawed. As we have seen, EU social policy uneasily combines these two traditions, and the attack by the British neo-liberals is weakening the position of the social democrats. In Benington and Taylor's (1993) view, the point at which the Social Chapter emphasised employment-based entitlements rather than citizenship rights may come to be seen as a 'critical moment', and certainly a new political consensus or coalition will be needed to take forward and to develop progressive social democratic policies.

CONCLUSION

Eighties optimism and creativity has given way to a new realism in the face of massive criticism of welfare state systems, especially since the collapse of the former state socialist regimes. Yet I would like to end on an optimistic note. Social democratic theories of welfare need to be redrawn in the face of demographic changes, growing unemployment and changes in the political culture.

I have referred to social programmes which have aimed to find new ways of meeting social needs and to create new bases for citizenship and its entitlement. There have been many recent attempts to link the politics of choice with participation in social policy, in creating new social rights and relations of welfare. Some of the user-led approaches such as that of the international movements of people with disabilities, and of people affected by HIV and AIDS have shown how social movements can offer opportunities for political participation, for the articulation of needs and for their resolution (Bynoe et al., 1991; Croft and Beresford, 1990). In considering how a modern welfare system could take account of these principles, Pfeffer and Coote (1991) argue that a democratic approach must recognise that the main purpose of a modern welfare system is equity, an equal chance in life, which rests on two further goals: responsiveness to individual needs and making the public more powerful, as citizens and as customers. Empowerment is both an end and a means, through public participation in defining needs and planning services, rights for service users and citizens, and through public accountability.

At the point where the social policy role for the EU has become widely drawn there is doubt as to the model and direction it should take. There is a danger of a pessimistic slide to limited state intervention resting on social policies which benefit only nationals (and their dependents) in employment or with strong work records, reinforcing the social divisions created by Fortress Europe. There was no golden age of the welfare state, but the visions of Social Europe as a counter to nationalism, war and the abuse of human rights, of policies based on need and social justice, offer a counterpoint to the new (and old) conflicts within Europe.

REFERENCES

Ashford, M. (1993), *Detention without Trial,* Joint Council for the Welfare of Immigrants, London.

Baxter, S. (1990), 'Jeux avec Frontières', *New Statesman,* 16 October, pp. 15-16.

Benington, J. (1991), 'Local strategies to combat poverty: lessons from the European programmes', in *Critical Public Health,* no 1, pp. 23-29.

Benington, J. and Taylor, M. (1993), 'Changes and challenges facing the UK welfare state in the Europe of the 1990s', in *Policy and Politics*, 21 (2).

Brewster, C. and Teague, P. (1989), *European Community Social Policy: its impact on the UK*, Institute of Personnel Management, London.

Bunyan, T. (1991), 'Towards an Authoritarian European State', in *Race and Class* 32(3).

Butt Philip, A. (1992), 'European Social Policy after Maastricht', in *Journal of European Social Policy* 2 (2).

Bynoe, I., Oliver, M. and Barnes, C. (1991), *Equal Rights for Disabled People: the case for a new law*, IPPR, London.

Cannan, C. (1992), 'Active and Inactive Citizens in Europe's Welfare States: the legacy and contribution of Beveridge', in Jacobs, J. (ed.), *Beveridge 1942-1992*, Whiting and Birch, London.

Cannan, C., Berry, L and Lyons, K. (1992), *Social Work and Europe*, Macmillan, London.

Chamberlayne, P. (1991/92), 'New directions in welfare? France, West Germany, Italy and Britain in the 1980s', in *Critical Social Policy*, 33.

Cecchini Report (1988), *The European Challenge: 1992, the benefits of a single market*, Wildwood House, Aldershot.

Commission of the EC (1987), *The Community Combats Poverty*, Brussels.

Commission of the EC (1989a), *The EC and Human Rights*, Brussels.

Commission of the EC (1989b), *Employment and Insertion: Project Profiles* (ELISE) DG5, Brussels.

Commission of the EC (1990), *Community Charter of Fundamental Social Rights of Workers*, Brussels.

Croft, S. and Beresford, P. (1990), *From Paternalism to Participation*, Open Services Project/Joseph Rowntree Foundation.

Dennett, J., James, E., Room, G. and Watson, P. (1982), *Europe against Poverty: the European Poverty Programme 1975-80*, Bedford Square Press, London.

Delors, J. (1985), Preface to Vandamme, J., *New Dimensions in European Social Policy*, Croom Helm, London.

Doyle, L. (1993), 'Drug Tourism: side effect of Maastricht', in *The Independent*, 6 May 1993.

Esping-Andersen, G. (1990), *The Three Worlds of Welfare Capitalism*, Polity Press, Cambridge.

Ford, G. (1992), *Fascist Europe: the rise of racism and xenophobia*, Pluto Press, London.

Ganssmann, H. (1993), 'After Unification: problems facing the German Welfare State', in *Journal of European Social Policy*, 3 (2).

Gordon, P. (1989), *Fortress Europe? The Meaning of 1992*, Runnymede Trust, London.

Gordon, P. (1991), 'Forms of exclusion: citizenship, race and poverty', in Becker, S. (ed), *Windows of Opportunity: public policy and the poor*, Child Poverty Action Group, London.

Hillestad Thune, G. (1987), 'Human Rights in International Law', in *Proceedings of the Joint Meeting on Human Rights and Social Workers*, Council of Europe, Strasbourg.

King, M. (1988), *The French Experience: how to make social crime prevention work*, Nacro, London.

Langan, M. and Ostner, I (1991), 'Gender and Welfare', in Room, G (ed.), *Towards a European Welfare State?*, SAUS, Bristol.

Lister, R. (1990), *The Exclusive Society: Citizenship and the Poor*, London, Child Poverty Action Group.

Mayer-Fabian, G. (1987), 'Social Assistance and social welfare services in the Caselaw of the European Social Charter', in *Proceedings of the joint meeting on Human Rights and Social Workers,* Council of Europe, Strasbourg.

Moss, P. (1988), *Childcare and Equality of Opportunity,* Consolidated Report to the European Commission, Brussels.

Paul, R. (1991), 'Black and Third World People's Citizenship and 1992', in *Critical Social Policy,* 32.

Pfeffer, N. and Coote, A. (1991), *Is Quality Good for You? A Critical review of quality assurance in welfare services,* IPPR, London.

Piachaud, D. (1991), 'A Euro-Charter for Confusion', in *The Guardian,* 13 November.

Rifflet, R. (1985), 'Evaluation of Community policy 1952-1982', in Vandamme, J.(ed.), *New Dimensions in European Social Policy,* Croom Helm, London.

Room, G. et al. (1989), 'New Poverty in the EC', *Policy and Politics,* 17 (2).

Room, G. (1991), 'Social Policy and the European Commission', in *Social Policy and Administration,* 25 (3).

Room, G. (1993), *Anti-Poverty Action-Research in Europe,* SAUS, University of Bristol.

Taylor, D. (1991/2), 'A Big Idea for the nineties? the rise of the citizens' charters', in *Critical Social Policy,* 1 (2).

Thevenet, A. and Desigaux, J. (1985), *Les Travailleurs Sociaux,* Presses Universitaires de France, Paris.

Townsend, P. (1990), 'And the Walls came Tumbling Down', in *Poverty* (Child Poverty Action Group), no. 75, September, 1991.

Webber, F. (1991), 'From Ethnocentrism to Euro-Racism', in *Race and Class,* 32 (3).

11. The European Community and the Problems of Economic Transition in Central and Eastern Europe

Alasdair Smith[1]

INTRODUCTION

A stable and successful economy provides an environment in which civic society can flourish, but the economies of Central and Eastern Europe are not yet stable and successful. In this chapter, I argue that while economic liberalisation is a necessary condition for economic success, we also need a political framework that supports the liberalisation by providing mechanisms for income redistribution and by safeguarding the liberalisation from being subverted by special interests. The relationship with the European Community is central to the success of the economic reform in Central and Eastern Europe.

In the early days of transition there seemed to be a widespread optimism about the process and effects of economic reform, even if few imagined that it would be exactly easy. There was optimism that there were benefits for all, perhaps based on the view that the elimination of the enormous economic misallocations and obstacles in the pre-reform economies would generate sufficiently large aggregate gains that there would be benefits for everyone. There was also optimism that the transformation of Central and Eastern Europe was part of the wider reconstruction of all of Europe, a reconstruction at whose heart would be the European Community.

As things have turned out, it is impossible to argue that the economic transformation has brought unambiguous gains for all; and there is increasing awareness both of the importance and of the difficulty of creating the collective institutions needed to support the market economy. Also the EC has acquired a somewhat mixed reputation in its relations with Central and Eastern Europe. I wish to argue that the early optimism both about the ease of transition and about relations with the EC were misplaced but that there are still grounds for optimism about the economic transformation and about the possibilities of cross-European economic integration.

OVER-OPTIMISM ABOUT THE ECONOMICS OF TRANSITION

There is much disagreement about the true economic costs of the transformation process. Measured unemployment has greatly increased across most of Central and Eastern Europe, measured industrial output has fallen sharply in many sectors, and measured real wages have fallen also. In each case, the qualification 'measured' is important. Some people who register as unemployed have not previously been employed; the measured growth of private sector industrial output is likely to be an underestimate of actual growth, given the incentives for private entrepreneurs to avoid tax by misreporting; and the measured real wage makes no allowance for the substantial gains to consumers (especially women) from the elimination of queues and probably makes inadequate allowance for the change in quality and choice of goods available. The figures quoted by Balcerowicz (1993) for the increase between 1989 and 1991 in Polish household consumption of meat and fruit, and in ownership of colour TVs, VCRs, washing machines, and cars are difficult to reconcile with macroeconomic statistics which suggest large and widespread falls in overall household income, even allowing for the possibility that the acquisition of consumer durables may reflect a one-off change in saving behaviour. Like the elimination of queues, the acquisition of some kinds of consumer durables may be of especial relevance to the standard of living of women.

There is also disagreement about the connection between the recession in Central and Eastern Europe and the economic reform. The changes in measured output and measured real wages in all of the countries have been remarkably similar. Yet their starting-points were remarkably different: Poland had a debt problem, a long experience of attempted liberalisation and an incipient hyperinflation; Czechoslovakia had little debt, no liberalisation and no inflation. It is also interesting to compare Finland, which too has had a very sharp recession but no transformation because it was already a market economy. These comparisons suggest that much of the explanation of recession may lie in the one factor which was common to Poland, Czechoslovakia and Finland, the collapse of trade relations with the Soviet Union, rather than in economic reform.

Whatever doubt can be cast on the reported estimates of the aggregate costs of the economic transition, there is no doubt that some have suffered. Workers who have lost previously secure jobs and failed to find alternative employment, or farmers who have suffered large real income reductions (as has happened in Poland), or those dependent on services such as health care whose costs have rocketed, will provide eloquent testimony of the failure of economic reform to deliver gains for all.

But the implicit or explicit promise of gains for all should never have been made. It is true that the simple economics of comparative advantage, going back to Adam Smith, demonstrates that domestic and international market liberalisation will lead to resources being allocated more efficiently. In real world conditions, the theoretical argument needs to be hedged around with cautious qualifications about unemployment, environmental effects and other continuing inefficiencies in resource allocation. The removal of some barriers to efficiency will not increase society's income if the effect is to worsen other inefficiencies. Such qualifications lie behind many of the commonly expressed concerns about the effects of market liberalisation.

The central point, however, is that even the most purely theoretical economic discussion of liberalisation does not reach the conclusion that liberalisation will automatically benefit all members of society. On the contrary, in the standard textbook model of international trade, one of the key propositions, the Stolper-Samuelson theorem, demonstrates that those income-earners whose resources are tied up in import-competing activities will suffer income reductions as a result of trade liberalisation. Later analytical developments have shown that under very general conditions, there must be *some* losers in any liberalisation. This does not contradict the earlier proposition that liberalisation raises national income; it adds the rider that income must be redistributed to such an extent that there are some losers.

It is not necessary that the income redistribution associated with economic liberalisation must be in an inegalitarian direction; liberalisation of the EC's agricultural policy, for example, would raise aggregate EC income and redistribute income from large farmers and landowners to poorer consumers. However, in the case of the Central and Eastern European countries, where the starting-point was one of much greater equality of income than in market economies, it was predictable that the income distribution should move in an inequalising direction, so the losers would be among the poorer members of society.

Some losers in the Central and Eastern European transformation are easy to identify: armaments and other military-related sectors, those sectors which produced low-quality manufactures for the Soviet market, those sectors which depended on low-price energy. Studies by Hughes and Hare (1991, 1992) have attempted to find out in greater detail who are the likely winners and losers in sectoral terms but have not succeeded in deriving any very general predictions, whether because of the limitations of their methods or because there are no generalisations to be made.

In principle, the correct response to concerns about income distribution is straightforward. It is better to develop a system of redistributive taxation, or to arrange specific compensation programmes for the losers from particular reforms, than to maintain uneconomic activities into the indefinite future. Here then is one of the crucial issues for the establishment and maintenance of 'civic society': economic reforms may be generally acceptable and compatible with an open and democratic society only if there are mechanisms for dealing with income redistribution; but there are severe limitations on the administrative machinery of the transforming economies and great difficulties in designing and operating redistributive tax and social security systems.

This leads into a broader area of misplaced optimism. The market system is based on individualism, but paradoxically even the purest of 'free' market systems relies on collective support through the legal system, and through social understandings and compacts. Problems in Central and Eastern Europe arise from the inadequacy of social institutions to support the market. Accountancy skills and rules, competition laws, bankruptcy laws and conventions, private property laws are all examples of problem areas. In all these areas it is not only the law that may be deficient, as the law can only function if its principles command general understanding and assent. In Central and Eastern Europe and especially in the former Soviet Union, the absence of a firm and consensual governmental grip on the institutions of the market economy has led to such governmental functions as income redistribution, taxation and planning permission being partly taken over by the private sector in the form of theft and of protection rackets.

THE EC-CEE RELATIONSHIP IN THE SHORT RUN

Trade between the Central and Eastern European countries and the European Community has grown rapidly during the period of transition. Table 11.1 shows CEE manufactured exports to the EC rising by 80 per cent, and imports from the EC rising by 87 per cent in the three years from 1989, admittedly from a small base. (The CEE is defined as the five countries: Poland, Hungary, Czechoslovakia, Bulgaria and Romania.) In spite of this growth in trade, there is disappointment that the EC has not given a warmer welcome to the Central and Eastern Europeans as full participants in the wider European economy. Much of the disappointment focuses on the negotiation of the Europe Agreements, which on the one hand open up freer trade with Central and Eastern Europe, but on the other hand qualify the liberalisation by retaining protection in 'sensitive' areas such as agriculture, food, clothing and textiles, and further by retaining the powers of 'contingent protection', in the form of anti-dumping and 'safeguards' actions which can be deployed against unacceptable import surges in such products as steel, chemicals and footwear (Messerlin, 1992; Rollo and Smith, 1993).

Table 11.1: EC, CEE trade in manufactures, 1989-1992

	CEE imports		CEE exports	
	% share 1989	% growth 1989-92	% share 1989	% growtl 1989-92
Ores and metals	15.4	-2.8	6.1	49.9
Non-metallic minerals	4.3	72.5	2.2	132.5
Chemical products	11.8	24.3	19.1	50.5
Metal products	3.2	178.2	2.6	228.2
Agric. and ind. machinery	5.9	44.0	25.1	86.5
Office machines	0.5	128.6	3.7	193.3
Electrical goods	5.0	144.7	8.7	116.3
Transport eqpt	3.7	391.2	3.8	174.1
Food, beverages, tobacco	13.7	64.3	8.3	12.2
Textiles, clothing, leather	19.3	134.0	11.5	112.9
Paper products	2.6	164.4	2.1	47.5
Timber and other nes	2.1	131.1	3.8	65.0
Rubber and plastic prods	2.1	140.1	3.0	99.4
Total		87.3		79.9
France	11.3	86.7	9.7	19.1
Germany	46.3	94.5	54.4	129.2
Italy	13.0	100.2	12.5	67.0
UK	10.3	35.0	7.7	-2.9
Rest of the EC	19.2	77.8	15.7	49.3
Total		87.3		79.9

Source: EC COMEXT database.

Given the past record of the European Community in trade policy, the qualified nature of its welcome to the Central and Eastern Europeans was probably to be expected. The Common Agricultural Policy could not admit Eastern European farmers and survive in its present form, the budgetary cost of subsidising the sales on world markets of European surpluses would become unsustainable. It is, unfortunately, unrealistic to expect the EC to allow the CAP to collapse. Equally, given sensitivities throughout the Community, in Germany as well as in the poorer regions, about iron and steel, and in Portugal and Greece in particular about clothing, it is unrealistic to expect the EC to have liberalised unconditionally in such areas.

Table 11.1 shows that in 1989, the four largest categories of CEE exports to the EC (leaving aside the catch-all class 'timber and other not elsewhere specified') were textiles, clothing and leather; ores and metals (mostly iron and steel); food, beverages and tobacco, and chemical products. Together these four sectors accounted for just over 60 per cent of CEE exports of manufactures to the EC. Apart from chemicals they are all treated as 'sensitive' products in the Europe Agreements, and chemical exports from Eastern Europe have in the past been the frequent target of EC anti-dumping actions and may well continue to be so in the future. Of these four sectors, only food, beverages and tobacco shows above average growth. This could be interpreted as showing that the competitive advantage of the Central and Eastern Europeans is already diversifying away from traditional areas, or it could be evidence of the difficulty of penetrating EC markets in sensitive products. (The other interesting breakdown provided by Table 11.1 is by EC country: Germany which already has a large share of EC-CEE trade has seen its trade with the CEE grow faster than other EC countries' trade. By contrast, the UK, whose rhetoric about opening EC markets to Eastern Europe has been loudest, has seen a slight contraction of imports from the CEE countries!)

However trade will develop in the longer run, in the short run the promising areas for the Central and Eastern Europeans must surely include those where their competitive advantage is created by low wages: basic industries, agriculture and food, clothing and footwear. The more successful they are in these areas, the better off will be their lower-paid workers. Thus the single factor with most potential influence on the distribution of welfare in Central and Eastern Europe is access to EC markets.

The EC has been cautious in its approach to trade liberalisation in sensitive products. However, the caution has to be understood and evaluated against the extraordinarily rapid growth in trade shown in Table

11.1. There remain substantial barriers against Eastern products, but there are three reasons to be optimistic.

The first is that trade is a two-way process. Table 11.1 shows that the sectors in which CEE exports to the EC have grown fastest are also those for which CEE imports from the EC have grown fastest, including textiles, clothing and footwear. Only in a single sector, that including iron and steel, have CEE imports from the EC fallen, and it is surely not coincidental that this is the area in which protectionist pressure in the EC has been strongest. As sectoral interests within the EC recognise that Central and Eastern Europe is a market as well as a source of competition, the forces for protection may diminish.

Second, the EC will realise that trade may be a substitute for migration. The more we buy the products of Central and Eastern European workers, the more jobs will be created for lower-paid workers in the East and the less will be the pressures to migrate.

Third, the fact that the starting-point is one of such low levels of EC-CEE trade implies that very large proportionate increases can be absorbed by the EC economy without undue disruption.

THE FUTURE OF THE EC-CEE RELATIONSHIP

Whatever the current disappointments, the relationship with the EC remains at the heart of the transition problem for the Central and Eastern Europeans. The estimates of Hamilton and Winters (1992), based on the existing pattern of trade among market economies and the relationship of that pattern to the geographical and economic proximity of countries, suggest that the trade expansion that has taken place between 1985 and 1992 (of which the larger part is the post-1989 expansion shown in Table 11.1) is only the beginning of a process that could see CEE-EC trade rise by 400-500 per cent over 1985 levels. Will this expansion be based on the Central and Eastern Europeans' low wages, concentrated in 'traditional' sectors, and awkward for the EC to accommodate? Or will we see a move up-market, towards more advanced products?

One of the early studies of the impact of the Central and Eastern European transition on the EC, CEPR (1990), attempted to infer the future trade pattern mainly from information on resource endowments. Given the degree of misallocation of capital, the technological backwardness of much Central and Eastern capital investment, and the failure to maintain the capital stock, it seems that Central and Eastern Europe is very short of physical capital. With respect to human capital endowments, however, some data suggest that the Central and Eastern European economies lie somewhere between the richer and the poorer members of the European Community in both the occupational distribution and the educational qualifications of the labour force. There are special features of the occupational distribution: relatively few workers with commercial and service skills; and a rather large proportion of scientific and technical workers. This suggests that Central and Eastern Europe's competitive advantage in manufactures may therefore not be particularly concentrated at the labour-intensive end of the spectrum but rather may display strength in high-tech products; and the scope for expansion of high-tech production is reinforced by the very sharp decline of military employment.

This conclusion is reinforced by the statistics quoted by Hamilton and Winters (1992) on the quality of education in Poland and Hungary. According to cross-national studies the Polish education system does relatively well in comparison with many other countries, while on some measures Hungary's education system is of top quality by world standards. Given the pressures on public finances in Central and Eastern Europe, one might worry that shortage of funds for education will drive Poland and Hungary quickly down the international league tables, but the factors that lead a country to do well in this kind of international comparison may be robust enough to survive a period of inadequate funding.

This suggests that we could look at the successful economies of East Asia as providing a possible pattern for the Central and Eastern Europeans. The origins of the economic success of Japan, Korea, Taiwan, Hong Kong and Singapore are controversial; but human capital has played a central role in their development from a starting-point in which their competitivity was based on low wages. Can the Central and Eastern Europeans emulate the East Asians in attuning their human capital resources to the international market? If they can, then the EC will face on its doorstep not a set of low-wage developing countries, but rather countries which can realistically aspire, over a twenty year horizon, to the status of the existing middle-ranking EC members such as Spain, Italy and the UK. From the EC point of view this is an optimistic conclusion: trade with similar countries in products similar to the ones we produce ourselves seems to cause much less political tension than trade with countries whose competitivity in labour-intensive products is based on low wages.

THE ROLE OF INTERNATIONAL AND EUROPEAN INSTITUTIONS

Central and Eastern European industries, at the start of the reform process, displayed a very much higher degree of concentration than Western industry. Successful reform will change this picture, as small and medium private enterprises emerge, the capital market develops, and multi-plant public enterprises are broken up as they are privatised. History matters, however, and long after economic reform the Central and Eastern economies will have relatively concentrated industrial structures in which the public sector will continue to have a significant stake.

These observations could lead to pessimism about the degree of competition that will be attainable in the Central and Eastern European economies in the medium term, but such pessimism may be misplaced. To focus on the structure of industry within a single economy is to ignore the important role that international trade can play in relaxing the trade-off between scale and competition. In the larger market of the international economy, the behaviour of firms facing weak domestic competition may be disciplined by competition from importers and the fear of competition from potential importers. Thus even if Central and Eastern European market structures remain relatively concentrated for some time, they need not suffer the ill-effects of monopoly if they are genuinely open to foreign competition. Indeed, given the high initial levels of concentration and of public ownership and the incapacity of the civil services to administer an effective competition policy, a liberal international trade regime is arguably the *only* effective competition policy on offer.

All changes in trade patterns, however, cause problems for some, notably those producers who face intensified competition. The policy challenge is to cushion the transitional effects and to contain the political pressure for protectionism. The changes in trade patterns outlined above will give rise to protectionist pressures in Western Europe. As always, it is impossible to be optimistic about the containment of protectionist pressures in agriculture, but developments in EC policy-making subsequent to the negotiation of the Europe Agreements give some grounds for cautious optimism in other areas of trade policy.

There will inevitably be pressures in the reforming economies too to protect declining and moribund industries from the effects of competition, and so long as much industry is concentrated and publicly owned, those pressures will be particularly strong. Successful reform, however, requires that most of these pressures be resisted. Governments will need to make credible commitments to an industrial policy that severely limits state intervention. External obligations are a powerful aid to credible commitment, and acceptance of the full obligations of GATT membership gives governments the ability to resist protectionist pressures by pointing to the GATT-illegality of proposed interventions.

The GATT rules, however, limit governments' freedom only with respect to trade policy.   Interventionist industrial policies such as tax concessions and state subsidies are more important than interventionist trade policies.   A government seeking to bind itself so as to resist siren voices needs the restraints of an externally-imposed set of rules.   The competition policy of the EC is the most suitable set of such rules.   This is the rationale for the provisions in the Europe Agreements which aim to bring the Central and Eastern European within the rules of the EC's competition policy.

At present, the use (and the threatened use) of anti-dumping actions is a major instrument which the EC uses to protect its producers from foreign competition.   This provides another very strong incentive for the Central and Eastern countries to come within the EC's competition policy.   When a country's producers become fully subject to the 'domestic' competition policy of the EC, they should become immune from the anti-dumping and countervailing duty actions that are used against the 'anti-competitive' behaviour of foreign firms and governments.   The adoption by the reforming economies of the EC's competition policy thus amounts to substituting the disciplines of a rule-based regime overseen by the European Court for the vagaries of the EC's trade policy and the sectional pressures to which it responds.

ENLARGING THE EUROPEAN COMMUNITY

Full participation in a European-wide market economy is needed to allow the reforming economies of Eastern and Central Europe to attain the full benefits of their economic reforms.   The reform process also needs, as I have argued above, a firm institutional basis of credible policies on trade, competition and foreign direct investment.   Only the European Community can provide this framework.   Further, the bringing of the reforming economies under the umbrella of the Community will shield them from the worst excesses of the Community's own trade policies.   This adds up to a strong case for widening the Community to encompass the reforming economies.

It is not hard to understand why the Community is being cautious about the prospect of eventual membership for the Central and Eastern Europeans. Membership would imply membership of the CAP, which would be problematic as we have already seen. It would also imply eligibility for 'structural funds'. The current beneficiaries of these funds, such as Spain, Portugal, Greece and Ireland, will not be enthusiastic about their being diverted eastwards, but Germany, France and the UK are unlikely to be keen to enlarge the fund for redistribution. A third economic obstacle to CEE membership of the EC is equally formidable: Western fear of migration from the East. Finally, if monetary union remains on the Community's agenda, it is clear that a monetary union encompassing the Central and Eastern Europeans is a distant prospect.

The terminology of 'widening' and 'deepening' suggests a conflict between the opening of the Community to the East and the continuing integration of the existing Community. The single market programme is the deepening process, and it will certainly lead to adjustments and reallocations of resources within Western Europe, spread over the next decade or more. It might seem foolish to add to this the further adjustments associated with the integration of the Eastern economies. However, the combined changes in economic growth and in the allocation of resources are surely much smaller than the continuing changes associated with technical change, structural unemployment, innovation and international trade. Successful reform in Central and Eastern Europe and the former Soviet Union could well have a larger aggregate impact on Western Europe than '1992', but the impact will be spread over an even longer period of years; so even together the two sets of effects are likely to be a modest and gradual addition to the changes that would have been happening in any event. Furthermore, even the combination of two sets of gradual and partially predictable changes will give rise to much less severe adjustment problems than unpredictable shocks, such as those that emanate periodically from the world oil market.

Even though there are formidable barriers to full membership of the Community, the arguments presented above give a clear picture of how the association with the Community *should* develop prior to full membership. The reforming economies need full membership of the European market economy, and they need the rules and disciplines of the Community's competition policy. The problems of agriculture, of the structural funds and of migration prevent full membership of the Community from being a realistic immediate objective. This then gives a clear and simple definition of the form of association that is desirable; and it suggests a relationship at least as close as the European Economic Area which now joins the Community to most of the EFTA countries.

The European Community retains a central role in the transition not just to a market economy but also to an open, stable and democratic society in Central and Eastern Europe and it still has much to do to fulfil this mission.

NOTE

1.   I am grateful for the comments of the editors and of Mick Dunford and Helen Wallace.

REFERENCES

Balcerowicz, Leszek (1993), 'Common fallacies in the debate on the economic transition in Central and Eastern Europe', European Bank for Reconstruction and Development, London, Working paper No. 11.

CEPR (1990), *Monitoring European Integration: The impact of Eastern Europe*, Centre for Economic Policy Research: London.

Hamilton, Carl and Winters, Alan L. (1992), 'Opening up international trade with Eastern Europe', *Economic Policy*, 14, 77-116.

Hughes, Gordon and Hare, Paul (1991), 'Competitiveness and industrial restructuring in Czechoslovakia, Hungary and Poland', *European Economy*, special edition no. 2, 83-110.

Hughes, Gordon and Hare, Paul (1992), 'Trade policy and restructuring in Eastern Europe', in Flemming, John and Rollo, J.M.C. (eds), *Trade Payments and Adjustment in Central and Eastern Europe*, Royal Institute of International Affairs: London.

Messerlin, Patrick A. (1992), 'The Association Agreements between the EC and Central Europe: trade liberalization vs constitutional failure', in Flemming and Rollo, *op. cit.*

Rollo, Jim and Smith, Alasdair (1993), 'The political economy of Eastern European trade with the European Community, why so sensitive?', *Economic Policy*, 16, 139-81.

PART III

12. Steering the Public Sphere. Communication Policy in State Socialism and After

William Outhwaite

However unsuccessful were the language and communication policies of 'communist' regimes, their intentions were broadly speaking totalitarian in the sense of George Orwell's *Nineteen Eighty-Four*, involving:

1. a party/state monopoly on the provision of information;
2. explicitly tendentious presentation of information, in a system where 'agitation' and 'propaganda' were positive terms, supplemented by
3. widespread organised discussion of media output, ostensibly free but in reality highly structured, with the intention of securing positive feedback and the isolation of hostile opinion which
4. in any case could not be legally expressed, due to (1).

Western students of communist regimes conventionally argued that the term 'totalitarian' fits the heyday of Stalinism, with its visible use of terror ('administrative measures') but not the post-Stalinist decades.[1] In the case of communication policy, what is striking is the continuation of features of classical Stalinism, with its constant mobilising appeals. This, however, coexisted with a substantial weakening of other aspects of the mobilising project of the 'construction of socialism' and the more terroristic elements of Stalinism. Without this support the official discourse of post-Stalinist regimes became increasingly ritualistic, and the declarations of loyalty more and more perfunctory.

One of the many ways in which state socialist societies diverged from the 'Western' pattern of post-war European development is in the sphere of ideology and communication policy. For more than twenty years, Western social scientists have played down the importance, in their own societies, of formal ideological appeals embedded in constitutions like the Federal German *Grundgesetz* or the more diffuse notions of Queen and Country, freedom and democracy and so on to be found in the UK. They have stressed instead the inexplicit or tacit understandings which stabilise and reinforce the sociopolitical status quo in the liberal democracies: you can't change human nature, there'll always be rich and poor, there's good and bad everywhere, and there's no such thing as a free lunch. A growing awareness of the mass media as the prime source of ideological messages for most people in the advanced societies, and perhaps more widely, contributed to this direction of analysis: the ideological messages of *Coronation Street*, *Chateauvallon*, *Schwarzwaldklinik* or *Dallas*, however insidious, could hardly be unpacked into precise political messages; nor, so far as could be ascertained, did they emanate from some coordinated ideological offensive on the part of a capitalist ruling class.

Many thinkers otherwise sympathetic to a Marxist perspective questioned the existence or significance of a 'dominant ideology' of the kind initially postulated by the young Marx and further developed by Herbert Marcuse (1964) and André Gorz (see Abercrombie et al. 1980). As Michael Mann put it in an influential article (1975), the ideologies of intellectuals should not be conflated with those of 'other people'.

Work of this kind, focusing on advanced capitalist societies, tended to pass over the highly centralised and coordinated communication and ideological policies and institutions which were an important part of state socialist societies. Here one *did* have an explicit state doctrine, what the Russian exile Alexander Zinoviev simply called the 'ism', justifying the historical mission and current policies of the CPSU and its sibling parties, and a deliberate attempt by the ruling groups to control all public expressions of opinion. There was a direct line of command from the ideology and propaganda sections of the central committee secretariats to the editorial offices of the leading newspapers and broadcasting organisations and hence to the rest of the media. The exclusion of alien media sources by customs checks or electronic jamming closed the system in many countries; in East Germany in the 1970s, with characteristic absurdity, the authorities gave up the attempt to keep out West German broadcasting but continued to exclude newspapers. Along with the permanent and pervasive surveillance by the secret police forces, communication policy was the most visible expression of a genuinely totalitarian aspiration on the part of the ruling parties.

Language policy played a particularly important role here, both in the prescription and proscription of particular terms, such as the use of the term 'anti-fascist protective barrier' rather than 'wall' to refer to what the rest of the world called the Berlin Wall, and, more generally, in the use of a specific form of public language which in English and German tends to be called party jargon or *Parteichinesisch*, in French *langue de bois* or in Russian *dubovy yazik*.

This is a language form based on heavyweight ideological abstractions such as 'construction of socialism', 'assimilation of conditions of life', 'complete and all-sided realisation' of this or that plan, 'fraternal relations' between the USSR and its allies, and so forth. Adjectives are coupled to abstract nouns in links as firm and apparently unbreakable as the fraternal relations themselves, forming a system of blocks combined by relatively unimportant connecting verbs. The verbs, however, provide the dynamic element (struggle, fight, advance, and so on) in a language otherwise characterised by bureaucratic stasis. As Agnes Heller has written,

> The language of the doctrine is constructed from different clichés, like those of television advertising. At the same time it has a menacing tone, for it is the language of domination and power. (Fehér, Heller and Márkus, 1983, p. 196)

George Orwell in *Nineteen Eighty-Four* (1948) fictionalised an analysis of political language which he had already sketched out in 'Politics and the English Language' (1946).

> In our time, political speech and writing are usually the defence of the indefensible... Thus political language has to consist largely of euphemism, question-begging and sheer cloudy vagueness.

In *Nineteen Eighty-Four*, the totalitarian party has introduced a simplified language, Newspeak, which

1. excises words such as 'free' except in everyday contexts such as 'the dog is free of lice';
2. contributes to the mindless repetition of hackneyed phrases by Party speakers ('duckspeak') and
3. contributes to the Party's promotion of 'doublethink' (believing what is politically correct despite knowing it to be false) and 'crimestop' (preventing oneself in advance from thinking a criminal thought).

> The purpose of Newspeak was not only to provide a medium of expression for the world-view and mental habits proper to the devotees of Ingsoc [the Newspeak term for English Socialism] but to make all other modes of thought impossible. (Appendix, p. 241)

This is of course a fantasy,[2] but it is not too difficult to find examples of such an aspiration and of such practices in the language policy of state socialist countries.

One important element was the stipulative redefinition of central ideological terms such as 'freedom' and 'democracy'. Here, the starting-point was the Marxist insight that freedom and democracy are necessarily limited by the social relations of capitalist societies: socialist freedom and democracy are supposed to go beyond what Marx called 'the narrow horizon of bourgeois right'. This formed the basis of an apologetics of real socialism which justified restrictions on the press, on party competition and so on. Dictionaries and other works carefully distinguished between bourgeois and socialist forms, playing down any 'abstract' common features. As Erich Honecker put it, with reference to freedom of the press: 'freedom is always something concrete. There is bourgeois freedom and proletarian freedom, capitalist freedom and socialist freedom. One cannot unite the two' (*Neues Deutschland* 7 July 1978, cited in Gudorf 1981, p. 26).

Another GDR author wrote in similar terms about democracy:

As is well known, the state form of the bourgeois and the socialist world termed democracy have different characteristics ... Thus the term must be specified by corresponding additions (bourgeois, socialist) if one wants to operate without misunderstandings. In everyday political practice, of course, this does not always happen. Often the fact that this single expression has quite different referents is used to discredit socialist democracy among naïve listeners, because it is implicitly measured by the standard of bourgeois democracy. (Wilhelm Schmidt, cited in Gudorf, p. 186)

Qui s'excuse, s'accuse: it would never have occurred to Marx that communist democracy would be put on the defensive in the way described here. It may be noted in parenthesis that this redefinition of democracy is not dissimilar to the operation performed by conservative social theories in the West, where democracy is identified with electoral competition between political elites (see Bachrach and Baratz, 1970). In the socialist countries, however, the process was more self-conscious and more deliberately defensive.

Another characteristic feature was the stereotyped repetition of hackneyed phrases, familiar to readers of the state socialist press. (In the People's Republic of China, where the language creates obvious difficulties for the typesetter, they were able to cut corners by keeping entire blocks of type for the more commonly used phrases.) A GDR philosopher, Franz Loeser, published a schema of ten adjectives, adjectival nouns and nouns which could be combined to form the basis of any official speech. More interesting than this satire were the explicit justifications (without apparent irony) of this practice in the state socialist literature: it is held both to facilitate communication and to strengthen feelings of solidarity between speaker and hearer (see Reboul, 1980, ch. 5).

The notions of 'doublethink', 'crimethink' and 'crimestop' might seem the most utopian elements of *Nineteen Eighty-Four*. Here too, however, quite aside from explicit censorship (documented for example by the Polish censorship instructions reprinted by Cygan and Fernandez, 1978-79), there were interesting examples of a possibly more informal practice of self-censorship. In the years following the construction of what is generally known in the West as the Berlin Wall, one finds the GDR media avoiding the term 'wall' even in its general sense (Gudorf, 1981, p.245, note 58); the same was true in the USSR of 'archipelago' after the publication of Solzhenitsyn's *Gulag Archipelago*.[3] Even more interesting, communications theory was used to revamp the traditional notion of ideological vigilance in the face of the class enemy. As the GDR philosopher Georg Klaus put it:

> A politically mature and enlightened person, a politically mature and enlightened group or class reject information which is harmful to them. They do not allow it to influence their consciousness, i.e. the information store with its existing content, or to be incorporated into it. (Klaus, 1972, p. 145)[4]

If this was the policy, how successful was it? The short answer is 'not very'. Even wholly loyal writers such as Hermann Kant in East Germany tended to be ironical in their novels about the use of party jargon. It seems to have been viewed as at best a necessary evil, at worst as one of the visible and audible tips of the great iceberg of a frozen ideological system, boring its victims to death or perhaps dissent. This seems counterproductive: as the American sociologist Robert Nisbet noted: 'A secret weapon against [Marxism-Leninism] is the stupefying boredom that this creed induces in the minds of the second and third generations brought up under it' (cited in Smith, 1987, p. 34).

On the other hand, perhaps these phenomena of rejection, boredom or disbelief, are less significant than what Pierre Lorrain (1982) called 'ideological pressure' in daily life, the constant weight of, in Hélène Carrère d'Encausse's words, 'a weighty apparatus that directs, educates and reassures society, and keeps it constantly in contact with the certainties which are the basis of power' (Carrère d'Encausse, 1982, p. 16). This ideological pressure, Lorrain insists, is not the same as propaganda. Whereas propaganda imposes or seeks to impose certain kinds of ideas, ideological pressure aims to create an underlying attitude: 'What really counts is to impose ideologically correct behaviour' (Lorrain, 1982, p. 94, my translation). This may favour the acceptance of certain specific beliefs, but this is of secondary importance: 'The aims of pressure are broader than simply to serve as a launching-base for propaganda'.

Seen in this way, the role of language becomes even more crucial. It is not merely the more or less effective vehicle of an ideology and the filter which removes alien elements; the more the ideology is reduced to pure performativity, in Lyotard's sense of the term, the more the specifically linguistic element is all there really is. And this is even more so if the ostensible referents of the whole system of discourse are imaginary or imprecise. As in theological discourse, in the absence of any reference to a real world there is nothing to constrain a debate on how many 'socialist personalities' could fit on a pinhead.

> In order to safeguard the legitimacy of the Party, there is no point in imposing a *belief* in the truth of the doctrine which justifies it (as propaganda would attempt to do); it is enough to extend and to perpetuate the use of the *langue de bois*, which is a much simpler task. (Lorrain, p. 99)

This means that the efficacy of state socialist communication policy is hard to measure directly. Viewed as propaganda, and assessed in terms of direct impact on belief and practice it does not look particularly successful, though as David Wedgewood Benn (1989) points out in his judicious assessment of Soviet propaganda (emphasising its failure in particular to make use of psychological theory), it was after all operating in a context in which *nothing* worked terribly efficiently. But the more one broadens the focus to totalitarian culture as a whole, the more important communist 'newspeak' may seem.[5] Why this 'newspeak' remained in use (and could even occasionally be used by oppositional intellectuals for strategic purposes, however much the corruption of language otherwise inhibited their activity) is a question which has to be asked in the context of state socialist ideological policy as a whole.

Who, for example, were the addressees of this language? Were they the masses, the 'proles' as Orwell called them in *Nineteen Eighty-Four*, or the Party rank-and-file (the outer as distinct from the inner Party)? Probably mainly the latter - middle management as we might say in the West. But it was also seen as important that this discourse be publicly displayed, as part of what the Polish sociologist Jadwiga Staniszkis called the 'magical' illusion of a socialism in which things really were wonderful and getting better all the time. We now wonder how all this could have survived for so long, yet without the accident of Gorbachev's appointment it might very well have remained at least until the end of the twentieth century.[6] More to the point here, how can we theorise this form of ideology and political language?

The French social and political theorist Claude Lefort distinguishes usefully between three forms of ideology in modern societies (he restricts the application of the term to modernity, where societies are understood in their own terms and no longer in relation to 'a transcendent order' (Lefort, 1974, tr. 1986, p. 184). For Lefort (p. 190), ideology involves the denial of class divisions, the temporary nature of social arrangements and the division between knowledge and practice. Traditional bourgeois ideology is written in capital letters: Humanity, Progress, Science, Property, Family. It is however condemned to fragmentation, since the social order can be described in different ways, and its basic values contested and differently interpreted. 'Totalitarian' ideologies play for higher stakes, claiming a monopoly of authority in both the political and the cultural sphere. Here the contradiction is correspondingly sharper: 'on the one hand, power is doubly masked therein, as representative of the society without division and as agent of the rationality of the organization, whereas, on the other hand, power appears there, as in no other society, as an apparatus of coercion, the bearer of naked violence' (ibid., p. 221).

The 'invisible ideology' characteristic of modern Western democracies by contrast incorporates diversity into a new and imaginary representation of social unity:

> With the constant staging of public discussions turned into spectacles, encompassing all aspects of economic, political and cultural life ... an image of reciprocity is imposed as the very image of social relations. ... The neutrality of the chairperson dissimulates the power of the organization and, in the end, those who hold the power are presented on the same level as those whose fate they decide behind the scenes (ibid., pp. 226-7). [In contrast to totalitarian ideology] the closure of knowledge is not represented, nor does it have to be. If everything can be said, that which is said will be marked by indeterminancy; hence its perpetual novelty. (ibid., p. 233)

Lefort's ideal type of totalitarian ideology can be usefully broadened out into a model of the form of socialisation characteristic of state socialist societies. Unlike most right-wing dictatorships (National Socialism was a partial exception), these were participatory regimes which, for a long time at least, demanded more than just acquiescence on the part of their subjects. I shall focus here on the *moralising* quality of the Stalinist and post-Stalinist party-state, in all its incarnations from the most benevolent nursery teachers through to the KGB. Moral appeals or interpellations and their internalisation by their audience surely played an important part in keeping the system going. And moreover there seems to have been a genuine attempt to secure agreement, documented even in the absurdity of the confessions which victims of the purges were forced to sign. If the homely British bobby is not above fabricating confessions, we must ask why the NKVD did not do so more casually. My hypothesis would be that this is the homage that vice pays to virtue, that even in its most terroristic aspect the system could not give up the illusion that it represented a consensus. The Spanish Inquisition of course displayed a similar concern.

What I want to stress is the paradox by which a system was imposed which was both extremely dogmatic, authoritarian, even totalitarian, and which however included at least lip service to norms of discussion and agreement at every level. Descriptions of this form of regime such as consultative authoritarianism fail to capture the sharpness of this unity of opposites, which was also a unity of politicisation and depoliticisation (see Rutlewski, in Burkhardt and Fritzsche, 1992). Theorists who spoke (a little easily) of Marxism-Leninism as a religion and of the ruling party as a priesthood were perhaps closer to the mark; the populace had to be converted and incorporated, as well as simply mobilised. Thus a certain brusqueness of interpersonal relations in state socialist societies which was shocking in relation not only to American but even Western European norms of politeness was paralleled by an openness to a kind of dialogue which may be the paradoxical product of the absence of binding market or administrative norms. 'Rules are made to be broken', as we say, and this was surely the charter of the ruling communist parties, to override considerations of market or administrative rationality in order to get things done (whether for personal advantage or *pro bono publico* as they conceived it, or some combination of the two). Similarly, there had to be a public sphere, but it also had to be controlled.

One aspect of this at-least-simulated openness to dialogue is what Wolfgang Kraus (1966, 1990) aptly called the 'intellectualization' of the East:

> An observer coming from the West will be struck by the pronounced intellectualization which is a direct and indirect consequence of the politicization of all spheres of life. The constant emphasis on political positions and an inevitable stubborn, though often concealed opposition demand a technical virtuosity in argumentation with ideological theory (1990, p. 38). The communist states were not gradually emerging organisms but ... intellectual constructions. In such constructions a crucial role is played by those who know how to construct, and those who know how to popularize these constructions. Such people are indispensable both for the Party leadership and also for the masses. (pp. 84-5; my translation)

As Kraus notes, this gave intellectuals a particularly crucial role in anti-communist opposition movements, strikingly symbolised since he wrote by the abrupt elevation of Vaclav Havel to the Czechoslovak presidency. To say that intellectuals were prominent in state socialist societies does not of course mean that they should be seen as sites of a communicative rationality in which public affairs were governed by open discussion, though it does qualify the notion that all that counted was the Russian Knout and its local equivalents. I want to suggest that European state socialist societies were not so much a rejection of, as a sort of distorted image of enlightenment, democracy and communication. They were, in some respects at least, regimes of inverted communicative rationality, which however were neither rational nor genuinely communicative, just as the Holy Roman Empire was neither holy, nor Roman, nor an empire.

The concept of communicative rationality is borrowed from Jürgen Habermas's model of communicative action (1981), which points both to the way in which communicative relations have spread through many areas of modern societies, and also to the enormous possibilities for what, in the context of state socialism, he described as the 'shamming' of communicative relations (Habermas, 1982, p. 283). To summarise in a few words a rather complex analysis, Habermas argues that, with the decline of traditional justifications for political rule and other aspects of the coordination of action, members of modern societies are thrown on to their own capacities for communication and cooperation, via processes of argument and agreement. Seen from this perspective, the most obvious feature of state socialist societies was their distortion and restriction of communication, the centralisation of authority and the denial of responsibility.

> The close connection between an autonomous society of citizens and an intact private sphere is clearly shown in the contrast with totalitarian state socialist societies. Here a panoptical state not only immediately monitors the bureaucratically desiccated public sphere, but it also undermines the private basis of this public sphere. Administrative interventions and permanent surveillance destroy the communicative structure of everyday interaction in family and school, commune and neighbourhood. The destruction of solidaristic relations of life and the crippling of initiative and autonomy in spheres which are also characterized by overregulation and legal insecurity, go hand in hand with the destruction of social groups, associations and networks, with indoctrination and the dissolution of social identities, and with the suffocation of spontaneous public communication. Thus communicative rationality is *simultaneously* destroyed in public and private relations of mutual understanding. The more the socializing force of communicative action is weakened, and the spark of communicative freedom extinguished in private spheres of life, the easier it is to form into masses and plebiscitarily mobilize in the confiscated public sphere the actors who have been so isolated and estranged from one another. (Habermas, 1992, p. 446; my translation)

So far so bad, but it would I think be a mistake to overlook the islands of communicative rationality which could be found in this cold climate, not just in the private sphere but in many areas of public life, albeit against a background of dictatorship, propaganda and a surveillance which was more extensive and intensive than most Western observers realised.

One possible way of theorising this complex relation between authoritarianism and simulated communicative rationality can be found in a model which the Dutch social theorist Harry Kunneman, in one of the most stimulating and creative commentaries on Habermas's recent work, has developed in relation to welfare-state agencies. Kunneman brings out very well the implications of Habermas's occasional remarks about, for example, the welfare state therapeutocracy for his work as a whole. Habermas tends to praise Michel Foucault's detailed analysis of communicative pathologies, while rejecting his allegedly nihilistic resignation in the face of the ubiquity of instrumental or strategic action.   Kunneman by contrast stresses the normality of what Habermas sees as a deviant and pathological category, that of latently strategic action, which simulates an open-ended discussion but in the service of some ulterior purpose, as when one of the parties will anyway impose their will, whatever the outcome of the discussion. This becomes increasingly important when, as in Western societies in the last twenty years, authority relations in organisations, or at least their expression in concrete interaction, have become ostensibly more democratic and egalitarian. As soon as communicative processes 'threaten to become dysfunctional for the goals of the organisation, sanctions which are not communicatively criticizable can be brought into play' (Kunneman, 1991, p. 212).

A similar process occurs in the caring professions where practitioners are structurally constrained both to identify with their clients and their own definitions of their situation and to override these identifications when they use their monopoly of specialised knowledge, usually in response to external constraints (ibid., pp. 232ff). Kunneman sketches out the ways in which the roles of client, consumer and citizen are affected by processes of pseudocommunication. It is because Habermas' conceptual scheme denies 'a structural role for latent strategic action in the symbolic reproduction of the lifeworld that he cannot recognise, at the empirical level, the important contribution of pseudocommunication to the colonization of the lifeworld' (ibid., p. 280; my translation).

We may seem to have come a long way from state socialism, but this model can perhaps be of some use in analysing the inverted communicative rationality of the state socialist dictatorships. It was after all common to treat socialist economies as a single firm in which all transactions were internal (and prices therefore arbitrary), and this can perhaps be extended to treat these states as a whole as operating in many ways like a single complex organisation, in which all roads of power led to the Central Committee or its Secretariat. And the concept of citizenship in state socialism had more in common with a Western employment contract than with our notions of citizenship. You were expected not just not to commit treason, but to be actively loyal like an American organisation man or a

Japanese salaryman. Within these limits, there was considerable freedom of movement, expressed for example in János Kádár's classic statement, after he had 'normalised' post-1956 Hungary, that 'he who is not against us is with us' or in Honecker's would-be magnanimous proclamation to GDR writers that as long as they stood firmly on the basis of socialism, there were no taboos, with the implication that anti-social(ist) elements could be booed and tabooed all the way to the Wall.

I do not want to claim for Marxism-Leninism the status which social science has in Kunneman's model of restricted communication, but it did act as a place-holder for a science which could defend the ultimately indefensible.[7] Hence the rather quaint practice of attaching ideological institutes to the ruling party's central committee, and the continued production, reproduction and dissemination of the 'ism' until overnight it became a 'wasm'.

This is of course yesterday's snow, on the Red, Alexander or Wenceslas Square. What is striking in the development of post-communist societies is not just the speed of the transition, nowhere more rapid than in the spheres of communication and ideology, but its apparent normality and taken-for-grantedness. Habermas' concept of a *nachholende Revolution* (1990), a 'catching-up' or 'rectifying' revolution, is an apt one. In many areas there has been an apparently unreflective quantum leap from the old state (of affairs) to the new one, strikingly illustrated, for example, by the case of school textbooks.[8] For many citizens of post-communist societies, the transition has however been experienced as an exchange of one set of arbitrary dictates for another, equally inscrutable one: that of unrestricted market mechanisms applying to ideas as well as to other commodities.[9] Many writers, like Habermas, have spelled out the theoretical desiderata for models of a democratic and critical public sphere and civil society in both East and West, but this does not mean that their implementation is any nearer.[10]

It remains to be seen whether 'the East', whether of Germany or of Europe as a whole, will develop patterns of political culture which differ in a lasting way from those familiar in the West. Nothing which can be observed so far, not even the phenomena of nostalgia or backlash (documented for Germany in *Die Zeit*, June 1993) can be confidently seen as evidence of anything more than contradictory symptoms of a difficult transition. The old question whether state socialism could be democratised has now become academic. A major obstacle to democratic control has been removed, but others, more familiar to Western readers, have not.

What remains a salient question, I think, is whether the estrangement in state socialism of political language and the whole political system, along with the transformation of politics into a religion and politicians into priests, does not have echoes in the increasingly manipulated politics of the old and the new capitalist democracies (see Debray, 1981/1983). Marx's conception of a better alternative to bourgeois democracy may be deeply flawed, but the diagnosis of its limitations which he offered in his essay *On the Jewish Question* contains much that is relevant today in both East and West.

NOTES

1. Since the term 'totalitarian' often carries with it an implied comparison with fascism, it is worth noting that even the far more terroristic Nazi regime did not have such a developed propaganda system as did Stalinism at its height.
2. Of the plethora of books on *Nineteen Eighty-Four* published in or around 1984, see in particular Aubrey and Chilton, 1983; also Howe, 1983, Shoham and Rosenstiel, 1985 and the special issue of *Sociolinguistics,* vol. XVI, no. 2, December 1986, in which I presented an earlier version of some of these ideas.
3. I am grateful to Robin Milner-Gulland for this information.
4. See the essays by Kapferer and Rutlewski in Burkhardt and Fritzsche, 1992. Loeser, 1984, gives some amusing examples of such 'guidance' (*'Argumentationshilfe')*: a circus group was discouraged from the traditional use of custard pies and balloons at a time when these were in short supply in the shops. On TV propaganda, see, for example, Ludes, 1992.
5. One way of getting at these issues would be to compare countries like Czechoslovakia and Germany with, say, Poland and Hungary, where communication policy seems to have been less crude and where the regimes were locked into a more pluralistic context willy-nilly in Poland, or through cautious adaptation, in Hungary, to an emergent civil society.
6. Susan Buck-Morss, in some recent work, has addressed these issues through the concepts of style and fashion.
7. For an analysis of the 'innovation potential' of Marxism - Leninism, see Ludz, 1980.
8. Fritzsche, 1992. On the process of linguistic change, see Burkhardt and Fritzsche, 1992, section 2 ('Sprache der Wende-Zeit'), especially Burkhardt's analysis of parliamentary speeches.
9. A good example for the GDR is Maaz, 1991. Maaz, 1990 is a superb psychological analysis of the GDR.
10. See, for example, the interesting analyses in Deppe et al. 1992.

REFERENCES

Abercrombie, Nick, Hill, S. and Turner, Bryan (1980), *The Dominant Ideology Thesis,* London: Allen and Unwin.

Aubrey, Crispin and Chilton, Paul (eds) (1983), *Nineteen Eighty-Four in 1984: Autonomy, Control and Communication,* London: Comedia.

Bauman, Zygmunt (1983), 'Ideology and the *Weltanschauung* of the Intellectuals', *Canadian Journal of Political and Social Theory,* (7), pp. 104-117

Bachrach, P.and Baratz, M. (1970), *Power and Poverty: Theory and Practice,* Oxford: Oxford University Press.

Bergsdorf, Wolfgang (1993), 'Die Wiedervereinigung der deutschen Sprache', *Deutschland-Archiv,* 26, (10), October, pp. 1127-37.

von Beyme, Klaus (1991), 'Politische Kultur und "Politischer Stil": Zur Rezeption zweier Begriffe aus den Kulturwissenschaften', in Klaus von Beyme (ed.), *Theorie der Politik im 20 Jhdt*, Frankfurt: Suhrkamp.

Burkhardt, Armin (1992), 'Können Wörter lügen?', *Universitas*, (9), pp. 831-40.

Burkhardt, Armin and Fritzsche, K. Peter (eds) (1992), *Sprache im Umbruch: Politischer Sprachwandel im Zeichen von 'Wende' and 'Vereinigung'*, Berlin and New York: de Gruyter.

Carrère d'Encausse, Hélène (1982), *Confiscated Power. How Soviet Russia Really Works*, New York: Harper.

Cygan, Piotr and Fernandez, Rubem (1978-9), 'Secrets of Censorship in Poland', *Telos*, (38), pp. 175-189.

Debray, Régis (1981), *Critique de la raison politique*, Paris: Gallimard; tr. as *Critique of Political Reason*, London: Verso, (1983).

Deppe, Rainer, Dubiel, Helmut and Rödel, Ulrich (eds) (1991), *Demokratischer Umbruch in Osteuropa*, Frankfurt: Suhrkamp.

Dieckmann, Walter (1969), *Sprache in der Politik*, Heidelberg: Carl Winter.

Fehér, Ferenc; Heller, Agnes and Márkus, György (1983), *Dictatorship over Needs: An Analysis of Soviet Societies*, Oxford: Blackwell.

Fritzsche, K. Peter (1992), 'Auf der Suche nach einer neuen Sprache'. Schulbücher in der DDR', in Burkhardt and Fritzsche (1992), pp. 199-208.

Gadet, Françoise and Pêcheux, Michel (1981), *La Langue Introuvable*, Paris: Maspero.

Goldfarb, Jeffrey (1989), *Beyond Glasnost*, Chicago: Chicago University Press, 2nd edn. 1991.

Gudorf, Odilo (1981), *Sprache als Politik*, Cologne: Verlag Wissenschaft und Politik.

Habermas, Jürgen (1981), *The Theory of Communicative Action*, Cambridge: Polity, reprinted 1984 and 1987.

Habermas, Jürgen (1982), 'A Reply to my Critics', in David Held and John Thompson (eds), *Habermas. Critical Debates*, London: Macmillan.

Habermas, Jürgen (1990a), *Die nachholende Revolution*, Frankfurt: Suhrkamp.

Habermas, Jürgen (1990b), 'The Rectifying Revolution', *New Left Review*.

Habermas, Jürgen (1992), *Faktizität und Geltung*, Frankfurt: Suhrkamp.

Hellmann, Manfred (ed.) (1973), *Bibliographie zum öffentlichen Sprachgebrauch in der BRD und in der DDR*, Sprache der Gegenwart, Düsseldorf: Schwann.

Hellmann, Manfred (1984), *Ost-West-Wortschatzvergleiche*, Tübingen: Narr.

Hellmann, Manfred (1985), 'Sprache', in *DDR-Handbuch*, Cologne: Verlag Wissenschaft und Politik.

Howe, Irving (ed.) (1983), *1984 Revisited: Totalitarianism in our Century*, New York: Harper & Row.

Ivanov, V.N. (1983), 'The Sociology of Propaganda', *Soviet Sociology*, 25 (1), 1986. Original in *Sotsiologicheskii Issledovaniya* (3).

Joas, Hans and Kohli, Martin (eds) (1992), *Der Zusammenbruch der DDR*, Frankfurt: Suhrkamp.

Klaus, Georg (1972), *Sprache der Politik*, Berlin, GDR: Deutscher Verlag der Wissenschaften.

Korn, Karl (1958), *Sprache in den verwalteten Welt*, Frankfurt: Verlag Heinrich Scheffler.

Kraus, Wolfgang (1966), *Der fünfte Stand: Aufbruch der Intellektuellen in West und Ost*, 2nd edn, Bern: Scherz 1966, Frankfurt: Fischer; 1990.

Kunneman, Harry (1991), *Der Wahrheitstrichter. Habermas und die Postmoderne*, Frankfurt: Campus.

Lefort, Claude (1981), *L'Invention démocratique*, Paris: Fayard.

Lefort, Claude (1986), *The Political Forms of Modern Society. Bureaucracy, Democracy, Totalitarianism* (Tr. and ed. J.B.Thompson), Cambridge: Polity.

Lewis, Paul (ed.) (1984), *Eastern Europe: Political Crisis and Legitimation*, London: Croom Helm.

Loeser, Franz (1984), *Die unglaubwürdige Gesellschaft: Quo vadis, DDR?*, Cologne: Bund-Verlag.

Lorrain, Pierre (1982), *L'Évangile selon Saint Mar. La pression idéologique en URSS*, Paris: Belfond.

Ludes, Peter (1992), 'Fernsehnachrichtensendungen als Indikatoren und Verstärker von Modernisierungsprozessen. Probleme eines interkulturellen Vergleichs zwischen den USA, der Bundesrepublik und der (ehemaligen) DDR', in Stefan Müller-Doohm and Klaus Neumann-Braun (eds), *Öffentlichkeit, Kultur, Massenkommunikation*, Oldenburg: Bibliotheks- und Informationssystem der Universität Oldenburg (BIS)-Verlag.

Ludz, P.C. (1980), *Mechanismen der Herrschaftssicherung. Eine sprachpolitische Analyse gesellschaftlichen Wandels in der DDR*, München/Wien: Carl Hanser Verlag.

Maaz, Hans-Joachim (1990), *Der Gefühlsstau. Ein Psychogramm der DDR*, Berlin: Argon.

Maaz, Hans-Joachim (1991), *Das gestürzte Volk*, Berlin: Argon.

Mann, Michael (1975), 'The Ideology of Intellectuals and Other People in the Development of Capitalism', in C. Lindberg et al., *Stress and Contradiction in Modern Capitalism*, Lexington, Mass. and London: D.C.Heath.

Marcuse, Herbert (1964), *One Dimensional Man*, London: Routledge & Kegan Paul.

Meuschel, Sigrid (1992), *Legitimation und Parteiherrschaft in der DDR*, Frankfurt: Suhrkamp.

Mueller, Claus (1973), *The Politics of Communication: A Study in the Political Sociology of Language, Socialization, and Legitimation*, New York: Oxford University Press.

Nikolov, Lyuben (1991), 'Everyday Values vs. Over-Socialization', *International Sociology*, 6, pp. 375-9.

Orwell, George (1948), *Nineteen Eighty-Four*, London: Penguin, 1954.

Orwell, George (1971), 'Politics and the English Language', in *The Collected Essays, Journalism and Letters*, London: Penguin.

Pêcheux, Michel (1975), *Language, Semantics and Ideology*, translation of *Les Vérités de la Palice*, Paris: Maspero.

Picaper, J-P. (1978), *Kommunikation und Propaganda*, Stuttgart: Bonn-Aktuell no. 26, 2nd edn.

Pankoke, Eckart (1966), 'Sprache in sekundären Systemen', *Soziale Welt*, (3).

Reboul, Olivier (1980), *Langage et idéologie*, Paris: P.U.F.

Reich, H.H. (1968), *Sprache und Politik: Untersuchungen zu Wortschatz und -wahl des offiziellen Sprachgebrauchs in der DDR*, Münchener Germanistische Beiträge 1, München: Max Hueber Verlag.

Ritsert, Jürgen (1972), *Inhaltsanalyse und Ideologiekritik*, Frankfurt: Athenaum Fischer.

Rossbacher, Peter (1966), 'The Soviet Journalistic Style', *Gazette*, 2/3.

Rühle, Jürgen (1981), 'Sprache als Form von Herrschaft und Widerstand', *Deutschland-Archiv*, 14 (10), pp. 1058-66.

Schaffner, Christina and Porsch, Peter (1993), 'Meeting the Challenge on the Path to Democracy: Discursive Strategies in Government Declarations in Germany and the former GDR', *Discourse and Society*, 4 (1), pp. 33-55.

Shoham, S. and Rosenstiel, F. (eds) (1985), *And He Loved Big Brother: Man, State and Society in Question*, London: Macmillan.

Smith, Tony (1987), *Thinking Like a Communist: State and Legitimacy in the Soviet Union, China, and Cuba*, New York and London: W.W. Norton.

Staniszkis, Jadwiga (1985/6), 'Forms of Reasoning as Ideology', *Telos,* 66, Winter.

Taras, Ray (1984), *Ideology in a Socialist State*, Cambridge: Cambridge University Press.

Thom, Françoise (1987), *La langue de bois,* Paris: Julliard.

Thompson, John B. (1984), *Studies in the Theory of Ideology,* Cambridge: Polity.

Wedgewood Benn, David (1989), *Persuasion and Soviet Politics*, Oxford: Blackwell.

Die Zeit (1993), 'Sehnsucht nach der DDR?', Nr. 23, 4 June.

13. The Ideology of the End of Marxism/End of Socialism Thesis: A Critical, Global Perspective

John MacLean

INTRODUCTION

Recent events in Europe, more precisely the so-called revolutions of 1989-90 in East and Central Europe, the break up of the former USSR, and the still continuing open warfare and growing misery within Bosnia, seem momentous. They appear to many as great historical ruptures, and as representative of fundamental social change, with global as well as local and regional implications. Collectively, this set of apparently stupendous events have come to be called the 'problems of transition'. They are constructed by statespersons, academics and business people alike as calling into question long-established assumptions, for example about socialism, revolution, the state and security, civil society and citizenship, democracy and participation, nationalism, ethnicity and identity, and also about investment, markets, and the business ethic generally. At the same time, these events, 'problems of transition', are seen as offering unexpected opportunities for developing new forms of political, social, economic, security, civil and business practices, and more generally, for establishing a more peaceful and cooperative new world order. That is, these apparently momentous events are simultaneously constructed as representing both a site of danger and insecurity, and also a site of triumphal success and potentially enhanced security within the global political economy.

What is striking about these events is the high degree of convergence of views about what they in general represent. There seems to be widespread agreement, not only amongst Western academics, but among participants and activists too, whether of the conservative Right, liberal Centre, or radical Left, that these events represent either the end of Marxism, the end of Socialism, or the end of both (Kumar, 1990, pp. 2-8). One now notorious commentator saw the changes in the USSR in the late 1980s, and the revolutions in East and Central Europe in 1989, as representing the end of history (Fukuyama, 1989). Another, that they represented the end of the Cold War, in terms of 'nothing less than the defeat of the communist project as it has been known in the twentieth century, and the triumph of the capitalist' (Halliday, 1990, p. 12). If we suppose that on the face of it, the differing explicit ideologies of activists or participants on the one hand, and the usually implicit ideologies of interested academics on the other, allow this agreement about the events in question as representing significant interconnected 'endings', whilst still allowing different views about whether such 'endings' are good or bad, or about what their likely consequences are, then there must be some heavily obscured but relevant item which binds them together in a deep, unspoken but also unrealised alliance.

For the moment, I will call this an alliance of epistemology, but in doing so, I do not wish to imply that it occupies only the meta-theoretical domain. The core element in this alliance is the assumption that theory and practice (events, outcomes, facts) are differentiated. I will return to this point in more detail later. By establishing the content and operation of this widespread but tacit orthodoxy about significant 'endings', we might then be able to expand the boundaries of what it is that is problematic (or in need of explanation) about these recent events. This is not an idiosyncratic, or purely philosophical view about the end of Marxism/end of Socialism thesis. If one is concerned, as part of an analysis of social events, to identify the possibilities for real alternatives in the world so that an emancipatory project might be developed, then it is important to be as clear as one possibly can about whether or not 'actually existing Capitalism', or 'actually existing Socialism' (or 'actually existing anything else' for that matter) do face each other as real, that is equally available, alternatives. The possibility is always present in social formations that apparently alternative modes of existence (for example capitalist/socialist; developed/underdeveloped; employed/unemployed; rich/poor; order/chaos; or aggressive/peaceful) or apparently alternative social concepts or categories (for example theory/practice; objective/subjective; scientific/mystical; rational/emotional; public/private, or male/female) are actually in an hierarchical relation, wherein one of the 'alternatives' is privileged over the other from the start. This is usually an implicit privileging, which is taken for granted, but it has an important consequence, for both theory construction and social practice, which is that the privileged alternative often determines the potential of the non-privileged, in that the former contains the core conditions, concepts and practices in terms of which the latter (as 'other') is evaluated, generally found lacking, and thus of less worth (MacLean, 1981a, 1984, 1988a; Coole, 1988; Peterson, 1992).

However, there is perhaps nothing more compelling about empirical social events than those rare occasions when they appear as compelling, in the sense of seeming themselves, and unaided, to determine views about them through convergence, or minimal contestation about what they mean. This is not to say that everyone holds strictly identical views about the meaning of these recent events, or the 'problems of transition'; they do not, as I hope this chapter will itself demonstrate. However, it is the argument here that a dominant view was quickly established. What variance and dispute there is has become located much more with views and speculation about the likely consequences of, and possible future developments out of these events, than with evaluation about what the events themselves signify.

In my view, this is deeply problematic in at least three important respects. First, so far as explanation of the emergence of these events is concerned. Second, in relation to what might be considered as real, practical (that is, equally available) alternatives to the social, political and economic practices called into question, overturned, or rejected by these events. And third, with respect to the relationship between the necessarily local, geographical sites of the events, seen as purposive actions, and the structure of the global political economy. I will return to these points more fully later (see below, next section). For the moment, I want to set out in broad terms what my thesis in this chapter is. I also want to establish the initial grounds for problematising not so much the events of 1989-91, as if to offer simply a different account of their emergence or what they represent, but more precisely, the widespread convergence of views about what 'endings' these events represent, and what theoretical and practical problems they appear to have generated. To put this another way, what I intend to do is to interrogate and displace the assumptions about the relationship between specific, observable and historical social events, and thoughts about them which underlie this particular convergence of views. This agreement about 'endings' has in my view, already acquired the status of being taken for granted, and as such, is established as part of a dominant discourse. However, I will argue that the discourse of the 'ending' of Socialism (and consequently of Marxism) while seen as inevitable and a simple matter, is actually a complex misrecognition of the arbitrary conditions of social exchange. It is the conditions (meta-theoretical, theoretical and subjective) necessary historically for this to occur which interest me, not only in terms of their complex abstract nature but, more importantly, in terms of the extent to which they can be shown to already reside within the events in question. My proposition here is that these theoretical conditions, usually seen as external in some important sense to the events in question, are already constitutive of the events themselves, and are consequently, internal to them. This is not to say that there is no difference between social theory, and social events (facts) but rather, that a categorical differentiation cannot be sustained (MacLean, 1988(b)).

My central thesis here is that the widely accepted view, namely that certain observable events in the former USSR and East and Central European states (as cause) have led to the end of Marxism/end of Socialism thesis (as effect) is mistaken, although there clearly is some connection between them. I am not supposing either here that the recent epidemic of claims about the end of Marxism/end of Socialism, or about other endings, are the first to emerge historically, for they clearly are not. Indeed, the first coherent and important set of claims about the end of classical Marxism, both as a set of theories and as a basis for explicit political and economic practice, emerged as the central plank in the development of the Frankfurt School's articulation of critical social theory in the 1920s (Jay, 1973; Slater, 1977; Roderick, 1986). However, this was in the form of a critical engagement with classical Marxism, and was not part of an anti-Marxist discourse. Other important articulations of endings have emerged since, including the well-known end of ideology thesis of Bell, as a distinctive feature of post-industrial society (Bell, 1973, 1976), leading to the contemporary almost overwhelming discourse of post-modernism or post-structuralism. One commentator has recently felt able to go so far as to declare 'The End of Geography' (O'Brien, 1992). The crucial difference between this more recent end of Marxism/end of Socialism thesis and earlier and later claims about other kinds of endings, is the high degree of convergence in the former as to the determining role of the inescapable facts, or events that occurred in East and Central Europe, confirmed partially since in the massive conversion from socialist command economy principles to capitalist private enterprise and market principles in the People's Republic of China. However, there is in my view an important indirect link between the extensive contemporary discourse of post-modernism, and the specific end of Marxism/end of Socialism thesis I am analysing in this chapter. This link has two important dimensions that I would highlight here. First, both developments have something to do with the deep contradictions of the late twentieth century, or late modern world, and second, both represent concrete conditions of the process of globalisation within the global political economy. It is this latter aspect that I will now turn to.

THE ANTI-MARXIST DISCOURSE: THEORETICAL CONDITIONS

The substantive aspects of globalisation will be developed more fully in the next section. For the moment I want to assert, against the specific 1989-90 end of Marxism/end of Socialism thesis, that *prior* to the events in question, there was already in place in the world a complex, sometimes implicit anti-Marxist/anti-Socialist discourse, with a sophisticated and effective theoretical and practical content. By discourse here, I refer not only to language, but to the total ensemble of phenomena (including language) in and through which the social production of meaning, and the social production of what is real, and what is ideal (not real) is established, and which constitutes society as such (Laclau, 1980). Furthermore, I assert that although the observable, or behavioural dimension of social meaning takes place necessarily in specific three-dimensional territorial spaces, for example in Moscow in 1986, or 1989, in Czechoslovakia in 1989, or Romania in 1990, *explanation* of the emergence of these events, and of the convergence of view as to what they represent, is not reducible to the events themselves. That is, part of the discourse of the late modern age is located in, and mediated through global structures, which are themselves non-territorial, non-three-dimensional, and not directly observable. Some aspects of this global structure, relating to the post-Socialist dash to marketisation and privatisation are considered elsewhere in this volume by Sonia El Kahal. I am more concerned to identify its general implications for explanation, and for the process in and through which a dominant discourse is established, and possible emancipatory alternatives are at best subordinated, and at worst continuously deferred from thought and practice. This discourse does not operate to predetermine social outcomes. My argument here has nothing at all to do with claims about historical inevitability or necessarily progressive history, in relation either to the 'failure' of Socialism, or the 'success' of Capitalism. But, the discourse does generally operate to set the conditions and criteria of evaluation, and the range of policy choices available to be apparently freely chosen by actors.

What is important here is that these criteria are also seen as impartial, and independent of, any particular mode of social, political and economic organisation. In this way, for example, international trade liberalisation, in detailed commodity terms through the GATT institutional framework, becomes seen as invested with an expert, objective and non-ideological character, while protectionist policies, even in the minimalist form of infant-industry protection, become seen as self-interested, subjective positions, and as dangerous for the well-being of the global whole, if extended. Similarly, policies of marketisation and privatisation, and of general structural adjustment, are advanced through private business leaders and expert economists, and mediated also through global public organisations such as the International Monetary Fund (Bierstecker, 1990). This discourse has become so powerful as to be seized upon not only by the transitional states of East and Central Europe, but also by other less developed states in the international system, although all have quite different levels of economic development, resource endowment, and different political, cultural and social histories. In other words, the very conditions which, once established as a partly global discourse and which on my argument constitute part of the explanation for the failure of local political economies, become translated into the conditions for a 'new' success. What we have witnessed recently is a 'distinct emergence of patterned regularity in foreign and domestic economic policy, facilitated by the major international economic institutions that have dominated the international political economy since the end of World War II' (Biersteker, 1992, p. 104).

Biersteker goes on to assert that in order to obtain membership in these institutions, and indeed to engage effectively in international trade, socialist economies have been forced to make significant changes in their foreign and domestic economic policies, and that this has had important consequences not only in respect of global governance, but for domestic political choices too. He describes the sudden and dramatic transformation of economic policy throughout the developing world in the 1970s and 1980s as 'the triumph of neoclassical economics' (Biersteker, 1992, p. 105).

I would argue in extension to this that the post-1989 transformations of political economy in East and Central Europe confirm this 'triumph' as a global causal mechanism, which must be set alongside the specific internal conditions of Socialism (as actually existing Socialism), whether in the former USSR, the Czech Republic, Hungary or Romania, if we are to properly understand both the emergence of the events themselves, and the convergence of views that they represent the end of Marxism/end of Socialism. At the same time, we must note that large-scale failures of living standards, of political participation, increasing local forms of poverty, starvation on a global scale, abuses of human rights, or large-scale repeated recession (although not of capital accumulation) in capitalist political economies, have not and do not now lead to widespread convergent claims about the end of Liberalism/end of Capitalism. Indeed, as revealed in the specific examples referred to in the opening pages of this chapter, claims about the 'success' or 'triumph' of Capitalism depend upon claims about the 'failure' of other alternatives, in this case Socialism, for their articulation and consensual receipt.

By examining in a severe manner the intimate causal relationship between (i) the theoretical conditions of what is in the late modern world a partly global discourse, (ii) the observable and thus usually privileged status of the events of local, territorial sites in East and Central Europe during the late 1980s, as the apparently secure basis for the convergence of views concerning the end of Marxism/end of Socialism thesis, and (iii) the substantive conditions of globalisation, I will aim to show in the rest of this chapter first, that the claim that certain recent events signify the end of Marxism as a coherent and relevant system of explanation cannot be sustained. Second, I will show that the claim that these events also signify the end of Socialism as a coherent and practical political economy alternative with counter-hegemonic origins and possibilities, cannot be sustained. Finally, I will argue that the end of Marxism/end of Socialism thesis, rather than signifying a purer, transcendent mode of politics, 'politics as practical morality, as service to the truth, as essentially human as care for our fellow humans' (Havel in Vladislav (ed.), 1989, p. 55) in its deep alliance of epistemology with concrete subjective and unequal interests in the global political economy, is itself heavily ideological.

These arguments will together present a substantiation for the central proposition of this chapter which is this: the view that certain observable events in the former USSR and East and Central Europe, as facts, entail the widely accepted end of Marxism/end of Socialism thesis, or the view that the events in and of themselves are synonymous with this thesis, or both together, is mistaken. Against this composite view, I am asserting that the global anti-Marxist discourse I have posited, especially in its implicit aspects (which are quite different from explicit anti-Marxist statements) contained within it from its inception a latent end of Marxism thesis. Consequently, my argument is that this thesis of finality (as theory) has not emerged simply as an inescapable consequence of a set of observable, antecedent events (as practice), but is actually part of the cause of the events in question, prior to its explicit articulation. I will try to show how this argument can be sustained, and that it offers the possibility of a more complete holistic explanation of (i) the events themselves, and (ii) the explicit emergence of the end of Marxism thesis as chronologically subsequent to those events. This argument may also allow the possibility of reinstating Marxism as a coherent alternative methodology for social analysis, which is also the most searching critique of the now dominant Liberal/Capitalist discourse. This might appear a difficult argument to make, especially to those who take the view that social events, or 'facts', constitute an external and thus objective universe of raw data, whose complicated relations and origins can be directly understood through careful analysis, on the basis of the assumption that social events are impartial in respect of thought about them (Bourdieu, 1977; MacLean, 1988b; Sayer, 1992).

It is important to acknowledge that the widespread observable rejection and reversal of Marxism, both as an intellectual system and as a basis for political and economic organisation, that these events represent, does constitute an apparently strong case for the demise of Marxism or Socialism generally. This is made even stronger if we include here the reversals and transformations also taking place in the People's Republic of China, Tanzania, Angola, Jamaica, Nicaragua and, most recently, in Syria. As Biersteker has pointed out, it is difficult to find examples today, with the possible exceptions of Cuba and North Korea, where there is any attempt to counter nationally the hegemony of a relatively borderless, heavily governed and global capitalist political economy (Biersteker, 1992; Ohmae, 1991). However, I am not attempting here to deny that these dramatic and large-scale transformations in previously socialist political economies are taking place. Nor am I denying that the oppressive experience of 'actually existing Socialism' has been an important causal element in this movement. Internal conditions in the former socialist republics were (and remain) properly condemned as disabling of some of the minimum requirements of democratic participation, accountability and individual autonomy. My position here is that first, it is not the case that only socialist political economies reveal oppressive and exploitative detailed conditions of everyday life, and second, in terms of problems of explanation, the rejection of socialism in these named and observable cases is not reducible to local conditions, forms of assistance and local struggle in and through which they took place. My aim here is to bring more clearly into the picture those conditions of the global political economy, theoretical and practical, which, while not predetermining local outcomes, none the less do powerfully affect the range of options available to actors, individual and collective, even if not consciously realised by the participants themselves.

It is a separate question whether or not the simultaneous and equally widespread acceptance of 'actually existing Capitalism' will provide the benefits and solutions expected of it. Developments in the newly unified Germany since 1990, or the more recent Yeltsin interpretation of democratic participation in government might provide grounds for a pause in judgement on this. In any case political enclosure, racism, gender subordination, human and civil rights abuses, unemployment, poverty, starvation or homelessness are neither distinctive of, nor specific to socialist political economies, as any World Bank, or Amnesty International, annual report of the last ten years will comprehensively reveal.   However, important as these facts may be, I am not primarily concerned here with counterfactual argument.   What I am claiming is that it is not at all surprising that Socialism has been found wanting, nor that Liberal political and economic ideology has been almost universally seized upon as the answer to 'the problems of transition'.   This repeated choice has not only occurred in specifically East and Central European locations, but elsewhere in the world too, where 'the problems of transition' have a much longer, non-European history of decolonisation, within structured conditions of dependency and underdevelopment.   The negative evaluation of Socialism, and positive evaluation of Capitalism, a recent example of which is the paper on 'Economic Justice in Eastern Europe' (McAuley, 1993), is not surprising, indeed it is almost inevitable, if each is supposed to be a quite separate, alternative, and equally available form of political economy. However, a quite different analysis is available if we construct it instead as interconnected (although different) responses to the problems of modernity, but where one of these responses, Capitalism, has become transformed particularly since the Second World War, from its historically subjective, self-interested, politically contested, Western European location, into a global structure.   This structure, because it now presents itself as the objective conditions of global interaction, is also a causal mechanism, which mediates and is simultaneously reproduced through, the concrete policy choices of individual or collective actors in the world, and it is necessarily anti-Marxist. There are a large number of theoretical conditions necessary for the achievement of this transformation. In my view, three of them are of primary importance:

1. the categorical separation of theory from practice, that is, of explanation from social events or facts,
2. the categorical separation of politics from economics, allowing the historical development and specification of the public-private dichotomy,
3. the transformation of particular subjective interests into the universal objective conditions of social exchange.

The distinctions here are analytical only, but I will deal briefly with each in turn.

1. The view that theory on the one hand, and observable social events (or practice) on the other, are categorically separate is universally dominant in

academic practice, and in political, economic and business practices too. It depends upon a widespread inter-subjective agreement that there is a logical distinction between statements of fact, and evaluative statements, such that the latter can never be strictly derived from the former. In practice, though, it is difficult to see that any evaluation, or conclusion, could be at all meaningful without direct or indirect reference to some set of observable facts or events. More importantly, the distinction rests also upon the assumption that events or social facts are strictly raw data, and as such, are themselves utterly non-theoretical (MacLean, 1981(b); Bhaskar, 1986; Bourdieu, 1977; Sayer, 1992). This assumption cannot be sustained. Unfortunately, this is less important than the concrete consequences which the belief that practice is non-theoretical has in the world. First, it allows the view that social practices, say Capitalism, are not dependent upon thought about them, but constitute an external reality. Second, it allows the view that proposed or attempted alternative practices, say Socialism, not already a part of social behaviour, are not realistic, and are thus utopian or idealistic, and not available in the present. Third, it allows the view that what is claimed to be the reality of social exchange at any point in time is objective in the sense of being impartial with respect to any specific subjective interest in the world, say a multinational firm. These three consequences together allow a significant convergence of view, which cuts across the academic-participant divide, that the explicit articulation of the end of Marxism thesis, because it emerged chronologically after the specific events in East and Central Europe, is both an effect of those events, and is also confirmed or validated objectively by those events. They also make the depiction of Capitalism as a partly global structure difficult to perceive, but easy to reject, in that it is not directly observable, or reducible to a specific set of events or facts. This further makes the argument I am making (namely that there is a concrete global anti-Marxist discourse in existence, and that it is causal in relation to the events in question), difficult to comprehend and accept, not least because it has to be constructed explicitly in opposition to the core theoretical and meta-theoretical assumptions of the dominant orthodoxy, and thus in relatively complex and unfamiliar terms.

2. The view that politics and economics are categorically different, like the view that theory and practice are separate, is historically specific. Both views developed as part of the social construction of scientific reason and the Enlightenment during the seventeenth and eighteenth centuries. However, as with the view that theory and practice are separate, the grounds for asserting that politics and economics are separate and quite

different kinds of activity are constructed in universal and ahistorical terms. The core difference offered is that economics is a natural phenomenon, and subject therefore to objective laws, while politics is not natural, but wholly social, and necessarily evaluative. It is, therefore, not objective. The argument here is clearly specious, and itself value-laden. Again, and unfortunately, this is less important than the concrete consequences it has. First, it allows the theoretical and empirical development of society into the spheres of public and private domains, without supposing that the content of either is fixed or constant. Second, it allows the strict but false association of economics with the private, and politics with the public. And, because economics is constructed as a natural objective phenomenon, then the private sphere itself is seen as a set of objective conditions, often collectively referred to as the market. Any model of political economy, say Capitalism, which matches these abstract conditions of the separation of politics (the public) from economics (the private) in terms of observable behaviour, is consequently deemed to be an objective and inherently impartial, thus non-ideological model of political economy. Conversely, any model of political economy, say Socialism, which disrupts the distinction between public and private, or politics and economics, is thereby deemed as subjective, inherently partial and thus an ideological model of political economy. Given the privileging of objective over subjective, facts over values, impartiality over partiality, and non-ideological over ideological, then it is not at all surprising that Capitalism can be apparently objectively evaluated as superior to Socialism, especially if, as I am asserting here, it has acquired a global content and is consequently a world universal rather than simply a national universal.

Third, it allows economists to become constructed socially as human expert knowledge systems, whose theories and analysis, and crucially in this context, their advice, is thus seen as objective and impartial. This is so however, if and only if the content of their economics accepts and reproduces the assumed separation of economics from politics, and of the private from the public sector. So, that which has come to count in the world as the dominant form of objective, impartial academic economics is actually and intimately the development of particular capitalist economics into a universal form of economics. In this process, the historical and subjective interest of capitalist economics becomes detached and embedded. Conversely, any form of economics, say Marxist economics, which refuses the separation of politics from economics is thereby constructed as value-laden, partial, and therefore ideological.

Fourth, and connected to this, the establishment of capitalist economics, as the dominant form of academic economics, allows the development of indices of comparative evaluation and measurement which are seen as objective and impartial, and separate from any specific model of political economy, including the capitalist model, and also reinforce and reproduce a conception of the world as composed of separated units, states, firms, social groups and so on, in interaction. This is a daring and staggering social achievement, not the least because it is not at all a conspiratorial one. What is interesting is that those, like capitalist economists, who have a monopoly on some discourse about the social world, as Bourdieu has recently argued

> think differently when they are thinking about themselves, and about others... This is seen in economics, where writers oscillate between the tendency to credit economic agents, or rather the 'entrepreneur', with the capacity to assess objective chances rationally, and the tendency to credit the self-regulation mechanisms of the market with the absolute power to determine preferences. (Bourdieu, 1992, p.80)

These developments, in conceptions of theory and practice, and conceptions of politics and economics, in so far as I have argued them as essential to the construction of the end of Marxism thesis in its dominant convergent form, are consequently established also as the basis for substantiating my earlier claim (see pp. 77-79 above) that the end of Marxism/end of Socialism thesis, constructed as an objective conclusion based on observable facts, is actually itself ideological.

3. The basis for the effective transformation of particular subjective interests, with universal and objective conditions of social exchange has already been established in my discussion above in respect of the separation of theory from practice, and the separation of politics from economics, in particular the establishment of capitalist economics as the 'pure' objective form of academic economics. However, I want to add two further points here. First, the development of a global anti-Marxist discourse, as part of the general global political economy, carries a much broader content than simply the universalisation of a particular form of economic theory and practice. It includes the universalisaton of particular views about politics, law, culture, business ethics, sexuality and parenting; it is in other words, socially comprehensive. It is important to note here that universalisation, to be confirmed, does not require strict evidence that everyone everywhere holds the same view, merely that there is a dominant view or practice in terms of which other views or practices are evaluated and analysed. Second, this process of transformation of subjective ideological interests into apparently objective, non-ideological conditions of the global political economy, is also an essential element in the development and reproduction

of hegemonic power in the world. I have argued this more fully elsewhere (MacLean, 1988b, pp. 76-81).

In relation to my argument about the nature of the content, and causal status of the anti-Marxist discourse embedded in the global political economy, the distinctive element of hegemonic, or structural power is the condition within which already subordinated groups freely choose options which they believe to be rational (in the sense of consistency with their subjective self-interests), but which can be shown to be actually in the interests of the dominant group. This is clearly quite different from coercive power, or explicit persuasion either through incentives or disincentives. It is also much more sophisticated and efficient, particularly where large-scale subordination is concerned, which it is in the global system. This does not of course mean that coercive power is never utilised in the global system. From time to time it is, as the United Nations attack upon Iraq in 1991, but the failure to attack Israel or Indonesia for similar behaviours, clearly demonstrate. However, it is also the case that power in the global system could not be for long maintained on the basis of continuous and explicit coercion. This feature in my view is an important element in explaining not only the repeated failure of Socialism, but the consequent headlong dash to Capitalism.

THE ANTI-MARXIST DISCOURSE: SUBSTANTIVE CONDITIONS

I hope it is clear by now that the basis of the distinction I have offered in terms of sections in this chapter, that is 'theoretical conditions' and 'substantive conditions', is severely called into question by my own arguments about theory, practice, facts, objectivity, subjectivity and so on, and the relation between them. However, we can construct this as a purely analytical distinction for the moment. In this section, I will be very brief, and offer only some indicative examples of what I see as the core observable conditions of the anti-Marxist discourse embedded in the global political economy.

There are two main reasons that allow me this brevity. First, empirical conditions in the world seem inherently easier to comprehend because of their initial immediacy of access as sense-data. This quality of availability for observation, directly or indirectly, makes them appear as relatively simple, in comparison with theoretical and conceptual statements. And in one sense, they are, because they seem immediately real, and indeed to constitute reality itself. Second, and more importantly, I have taken up the great bulk of this chapter in dealing explicitly with the theoretical conditions of the end of Marxism thesis as a global discourse, which might appear to the reader an unbalanced distribution of both effort and space, and to privilege theory over practice. However, what I have been trying to argue throughout is that observable, empirical events in the world are not only *not* independent of thought about them, but further, that all social practices, or reality, are actually theory-laden. That is, theory does not reside only in the subjective domain of mental states, but is embedded, usually implicitly within, and is thus an integral part of apparently objective reality. If this is correct, then what is real is not synonymous with what is empirical. This does not matter very much in terms of our ability to perform day-to-day social practices. If our aim however is to *explain* observable social practices, then exposure of this necessary internal relationship between theory and practice becomes essential for any fully holistic account.

This is not in any sense an argument that there is no difference between theory and practice; they can and must be capable of initial separate definition. Nor is it an argument that social events can be wholly understood in purely theoretical terms. However, the relationship between forms of social theory and social events is an extremely complex one, partly because it is not obvious, nor itself directly observable, and partly because dominant systems of intellectual thought and practice not only deny such an intimate link, but also actively (although not necessarily intentionally) operate to render it invisible (MacLean, 1981b). Consequently, exposure of this intimate reciprocal causal link requires an equally complex language of analysis, unfamiliar aspects of social behaviour cannot readily be expressed in familiar language. Bourdieu has put this point rudely. He says

> I am not out to make my writing clear and simple, and I consider the strategy of abandoning the rigour of technical vocabulary in favour of an easy and readable style to be dangerous. This is first and foremost because false clarity is often part and parcel of the dominant discourse, the discourse of those who think everything goes without saying, because everything is just fine as it is. Conservative language always falls back upon the authority of common sense. And common sense speaks the clear and simple language of what is plain for all to see. ... I am convinced that for both scientific and political reasons you have to accept that discourse can, and must be, as complicated as the (more or less complicated) problem it is tackling demands. (Bourdieu, 1990, p. 52)

Turning now directly to the substantive conditions of the anti-Marxist discourse embedded in the global political economy, I will offer some indication of where this might be located concretely.

First, a major site of embedded liberal political and economic ideology is to be found in the constitutions, institutions, decision-making practices, conditions for membership, and definitions of competence, of the extensive, and still growing United Nations Organization and its specialised agencies (Ruggie, 1982; Taylor, 1993).   The UN Charter, the IMF Articles of Agreement, the 'free-flow of information' principle in UNESCO, the limiting of the ITU's regulatory competence to standard-setting, the elimination of concepts of socialised medicine from the constitution of the WHO, and most recently the establishment of a new specialised agency in 1984, The World Intellectual Property Organization, all articulate and reproduce Liberal/Capitalist concepts and assumptions.   Furthermore, the very separation of the United Nations system into the UN as a political institution, the IMF as an economic institution, the UNESCO as an educational and cultural institution, the ITU as a scientific/technical institution, both depends upon, and reproduces concretely, the theoretical separation between politics and economics to which I referred at some length in the previous section.   Second, politics and economics are again reproduced and separated through the apparently separate empirical development of states and firms.   It is states who are the main (and only legally legitimate) holders of instruments of coercion, while firms, especially today's global firms, are the major holders and movers of capital and credit (Dunning, 1993). The content of international and regional human rights legislation privileges a Western Liberal/Capitalist conception, namely a concern with political and civil rights rather than socio-economic rights.   International law is itself strikingly divided into international private law, and international public law.   International trade, either as embodied in the GATT or in the Treaty of Rome, offer Liberal/Capitalist conceptions as the basis for global exchange. At the same time, international business, both as a discipline and as a concrete practice, articulates capitalist enterprise as the 'pure' form of business. There are many other possible examples available.   What is important to note here is that the theoretical conditions posited in the previous section as being part of the observable, substantive conditions of the global political economy cannot be fully exposed without detailed concrete historical analysis.   The grounds for doing so I hope are now established.

CONCLUSIONS

What I have tried to argue in this chapter is complex and difficult, but I hope also clear and coherent.   It has been necessarily complex because I have sought to overturn the widespread and dominant view that the end of Marxism/end of Socialism thesis arises almost inescapably, as a matter of common sense, out of the events, particularly in East and Central Europe, which did represent the ending of particular state Socialist political economies. Against this, I have argued that although these events do enhance the simple power of the anti-Marxist discourse, the latter existed *prior* to the occurrence of the events in question and indeed, is part of the cause of them. I have also argued that in the late modern world, this anti-Marxist discourse is embedded in the structures of the global political economy, but that the latter consists of liberal political and economic, that is Capitalist, theory and practice transformed into the universal objective conditions of social exchange.

If the argument is at least coherent, it leads to some striking conclusions. First, that socialist political economies are almost certain to fail in a globalised world, quite independently of evaluations of their internal characteristics. Second, that although social events necessarily occur in specific geographical locations, part of what the events actually are, at the level of explanation, is, in the modern world, located within global, non-territorial structures. Third, the repeated choice of Capitalism as the answer to the problems of transition, when it is actually the cause of the demise of Socialism and of 'the problems of transition', is no longer surprising, indeed no real alternative is seen as available. Fourth, the events in question do not represent fundamental change or historical rupture in the world. Indeed, the contrary appears to be the case, that is, they represent more clearly historical continuity and an even greater disciplining strength to the dominant orthodoxy of Capitalism. Fifth, that apparently objective conditions of the world are deeply ideological. Finally, if the argument in this chapter is persuasive as well as coherent, then it denies in and of itself the end of at least one aspect of Marxism, namely Marxism as a critical methodology, capable of developing radical alternative accounts of why the world is like it is.

REFERENCES

Bell, D. (1973), *The Coming of Post-Industrial Society: A Venture in Social Forecasting*, New York: Basic Books.

Bell, D. (1976), *The Cultural Contradictions of Capitalism*, New York: Basic Books.

Bhaskar, R. (1986), *Scientific Realism and Human Emancipation*, London: Verso.

Biersteker, T. (1990), 'Reducing the Role of the State in the Economy: A Conceptual Exploration of IMF and World Bank Prescriptions', *International Studies Quarterly*, Vol. 34, pp. 477-92.

Biersteker, T. (1992), 'The Triumph of Neo-Classical Economics in the Developing World: Policy Convergence and Bases of Governance in the International Economic Order', in Roseman, J. and Czempiel, E.O. (eds), *Governance without Government: Order and Change in World Politics*, Cambridge: Cambridge University Press.

Bourdieu, P. (1977), *Outline of a Theory of Practice*, Cambridge: Cambridge University Press.

Bourdieu, P. (1990), *Woman in Political Theory*, Sussex: Wheatsheaf Books.

Cox, R. (1983), 'Gramsci, Hegemony and International Relations: An Essay in Method', *Millennium*, Vol.12, No.2, pp.162-75.

Dunning, J. (1993), *The Globalization of Business*, London: Routledge.

Fukuyama, F. (1989), 'The End of History?', *The National Interest*, Vol. 3, pp. 3-18.

Halliday, F. (1990), 'The Ends of the Cold War', *New Left Review*, No. 180, March/April.

Jay, M. (1973), *The Dialectical Imagination*, London: Heinemann.

Kumar, K. (1990), *The Revolutions of 1989: Socialism, Capitalism and Democracy*, Paper to the International Cultural Foundation Conference, Sofia, Bulgaria, 24-27 November.

Laclau, E. (1980) 'Populist Discourse and Political Rupture', *Screen and Society*, Vol. 4.

MacLean, J. (1981a), 'Marxist Epistemology, Explanations of Change, and the Study of International Relations', in Buzan, B. and Jones, R.J. (eds), *Change and the Study of International Relations*, London: Pinter, pp. 46-67.

MacLean, J. (1981b), 'Political Theory, International Theory and Problems of Ideology', *Millennium*, Vol. 10, No. 2, pp. 102-25.

MacLean, J. (1984), 'Interdependence: An Ideological Intervention in International Relations?', in Jones, R. J. and Willets, P. (eds), *Interdependence on Trial: Studies in the Theory and Reality of Contemporary Interdependence*, London: Pinter, pp. 130-66.

MacLean, J. (1988 a), 'Marxism and International Relations: A Strange Case of Mutual Neglect', *Millennium*, Vol. 17, No. 2, pp. 295-319.

MacLean, J. (1988b), 'Belief Systems and Ideology in International Relations: A Critical Approach', in Little, R. and Smith, S. (eds), *Belief Systems and International Relations*, Oxford: Blackwell, pp. 57-82.

McAuley, A. (1993),'Economic Justice in Eastern Europe', in Ringen S. and Wallace C. (eds), *Societies in Transition: East-Central Europe Today*, Prague, Central European University, pp. 29-44.

O'Brien, R. (1992), *Global Financial Integration: The End of Geography*, London: Pinter.

Ohmae, K. (1991), *Borderless World: Power and Strategy in the International Economy*, London: Collins.

Petersen, V. S. (1992), 'Transgressing Boundaries: Theories of Knowledge, Gender and International Relations', *Millennium*, Vol. 21, No. 2, pp. 183-206.

Roderick, R. (1986), *Habermas and the Foundations of Critical Theory*, London: Macmillan.

Ruggie, J. (1982), 'International Regimes, Transactions and Change: Embedded Liberalism in the Postwar Economic Order', *International Organization*, Vol. 36, Spring.

Sayer, A. (1992), *Method in Social Science: A Realist Approach*, 2nd Edition, London: Routledge.

Slater, P. (1977), *Origin and Significance of the Frankfurt School*, London: Routledge & Kegan Paul.

Strange, S. and Stopford, J. (1991), *Rival States: Rival Firms*, Cambridge: Cambridge University Press.

Taylor, P. (1993), *International Organization in the Modern World*, London: Pinter.

Vladislav, J. (ed.) (1989), Vaclav Havel: *Living in Truth*, London: Faber & Faber.

14. 'Public Service' and 'Collectivism': the Place of Gender and Voluntary Work in Different European Traditions

Jenny Shaw

INTRODUCTION

The years following the collapse of the socialist states in Europe seemed to offer a field day for social science and social scientists working in the West. The revolutions of 1989 came as near to a social experiment as any generation was likely to witness. The social, political and economic transformations appeared so fundamental that they offered a once-and-for-all chance to challenge or confirm many of the basic tenets of Western social theory. These included such questions as the relative place of agency or structure in social explanation (see Collins, 1992), the nature of social solidarity and, of course, the future of capitalism (see Fukuyuma, 1989). For a while the revolutions revitalised 'grand' social theory, enabled the boldest to make predictions, and made comparative studies respectable once more. Moreover, change was so fast that studying it did not require a lifetime's dedication.

However the speed of change also created problems and, almost before some questions could be formulated, the conditions that threw them up changed again. Without efficient and effective monitoring of the changes, many of the most interesting questions could not be answered directly. Paradoxically, as the desire to study the countries of East Central Europe and reanalyse Western social science grew, the feasibility of much of the necessary empirical research actually worsened. Funds were short, especially for expensive comparative research, and much of the data was either non-existent or unreliable. Thus many of the questions that bubbled forth in the immediate aftermath of 1989/90 have been left stranded. One of these concerns the role of values and whether the moral order underlying the ex-communist and socialist countries has really changed. Of course, such a large question is difficult to study directly and any stab at it is bound to be tentative and preliminary. However, because some of the market-inspired reforms have already been tried out in Great Britain, an indirect way of considering the impact of values is through a loose comparison between states at different stages in the neo-liberal experiment. In practice this means comparing Great Britain with a number of East Central European countries. The broad question is further narrowed down by taking the two, superficially distinct, notions of 'public service' and its counterpart 'collectivism' and comparing their legacies or fate(s) in the changed social, economic and political conditions of Europe and looking at how they might affect future provision of welfare. If the rejection of socialism entailed a rejection of everything to do with 'fraternity' or 'solidarity', then much of the talk of regenerating 'civil society' is likely to come to nothing, unless responsibility for others in a general sense is spelt out and facilitated.

As countries throughout the developed world face, or perceive themselves as facing, a need to cut back on welfare expenditure, the issue of caring and voluntary work has come to the fore (see Balbo and Novotny, 1986; Deacon and Szalai; 1990, Deacon, 1992). Explicitly or implicitly, greater community involvement and voluntary work are seized upon as a way of making good the shortfall in services that are expected to be withdrawn or truncated and of making unemployment 'legitimate'. The practical aspects of some of the scenarios tend to be rather hazy and the issue of everyday life overshadowed by the grand-sounding debates about citizenship and civil society. Gender does not figure especially prominently in most of these debates, though feminists working in social policy have been quick to point out that calls for the community and the family to play a larger part in 'active citizenship' usually skate over the implication that it is mainly women who are expected to supply the unpaid labour. In fact the changes in both East and West Europe, as they polarise those in and out of work, increase wage differentials and lengthen working hours, have a profound impact on both the direction and willingness of ordinary people to give to charity and undertake voluntary work. Britons give less to charity than they once did and the rate has declined throughout the Thatcher years (see Saxon-Harrold and Carter, 1987). This can be interpreted as a weariness, as individualism or as protest against the government-led intention to shift expenditure away from the centre. Whatever, it needs explanation; as does a report from a Czech delegate to a 1991 conference on the implications for gender relations following the political changes in East Central Europe and the Soviet Union.[1]

Hana Navarova reported a newspaper survey which had asked female respondents whether, if they left the labour force, they would consider voluntary work. The response was overwhelmingly negative. Without further details of the survey it would be a mistake to build too much on it, and quite wrong to generalise across all of the ex-socialist states, or even the Czech Republic and Slovakia. However it alerted the conference audience to the question of whether, in one way at least, women in East Central Europe were unlike those in the West in being unprepared to carry the bulk of voluntary and charitable work (see HMSO/OPCS, 1990-93, Hollis, 1987), and whether this was a sign that Communism had either got rid of the idea that caring was women's work or created a profound expectation of collective provision?

There are, of course, many ways of characterising the 1989 revolutions. It is stating the obvious to call the transition a 'legitimation crisis' after Habermas (1976) but there are clearly parallels between events in the ex-socialist societies and the debate on the shaky moral order underlying capitalism that has preoccupied writers such as Offe and Keane (1985), Hirsch (1977) and Bell (1979) in which a tension between the deep moral order and the surface institutions is a key structural feature. Whatever happens in Europe in the long run, in the immediate future the societies in transition are highly likely to be characterised by an acute crisis of responsibility, especially in the basis for communal action. Who, now, should do what, for whom?

Although 'needs' are notoriously difficult to define, and therefore to cater for, the immediate question is whether the ideology of collectivism in East Central Europe has muddied the historical perception of individual needs? If its recent demise has taken away some of the bases and organisational infrastructure for responding to social need, what of its effect over the last forty or so years? Could it still be acting to inhibit an 'alternative' or latent social capacity to respond to needs at any level, individual or collective? At root, the issue is whether the demise of socialism has created a moral vacuum around the very notion of 'need'. There clearly are plenty of individual 'needs' left, but there may be little or no social capacity in the sense of a tradition and set of organisations able to respond to them in ways that are seen as fair and appropriate. On this much of the debate about 'civil society' depends, for the other side of 'need' is 'duty' and 'responsibility'.

The impulse triggering the 1989 revolutions is widely thought to stem from individual aspirations for higher living standards and more consumer choice as much as from a desire for democracy *per se*. However, after decades of official 'comradeship' it is unclear whether there is anything more than pent-up and selfish values to shape the direction taken by the ex-state socialist countries, especially as they unpack their versions of the welfare state? No society can change totally, and if it is possible for remnants of pre-socialist society to reemerge, then it may also be possible for some aspects of a socialist society to survive; though how we would recognise them in the current context may be more difficult.

The emotions that underpin what might be called fraternity, solidarity, caring, or an impulse to act altruistically for the 'greater good' are ones that all societies need to mobilise and promote. In the West the term 'public service' more or less does this job, whereas in the ex-socialist countries it was the ideology of 'collectivism' and 'international solidarity'. Both are obviously simplifications (as are capitalism and socialism) but each are, or were, key ideological components of their respective political systems. Moreover each draws on social structures and value systems that are far deeper, or older, than the political ideologies to which they are currently attached. If 'collectivism' was grafted on to pre-socialist values it is hard to know whether to expect it, and its associated impulses to meet the needs of strangers (Ignatieff, 1984), to go down with the demise of socialism, or to be enthusiastically retrieved and recovered? Much will turn on the motives publicly ascribed to explain individual behaviour (see Blum and McHugh, 1971) and on the meaning which the two ethics, of public service on one hand and collectivism on the other, give to such motives.

'PUBLIC SERVICE' AND 'COLLECTIVISM'

Whatever their formal ideologies, all countries depend on some system of unpaid (or underpaid work) work and voluntary work; and most countries attempt to organise and co-opt such work as part of a wider social policy. As a way of acting, 'public service' draws its meaning largely from a contrast with activity that is not public-spirited, namely that which is selfish and profit-inspired. In the British context this 'public service' tradition is associated with a history of colonial administration, with liberal ideology, with a particular system of private schooling, and with the growth of professionalism. Delving further back its meaning can be traced to feudalism in which service to God and to a Lord were fused and in which reciprocity, or duty, to both those 'above' and 'below' played a part.

Over time the service ideal lost some of its religious tone and the element of reciprocity became more abstract. It also became somewhat less hierarchical and more closely attached, through such notions as the 'Commonwealth', to a broader notion of the 'public' and, incidentally, more racist. Today it has a fusty image. Often rather absurd or pompous it covers behaviour as various as a willingness to participate in voluntary organisations and/or seek work in the generally lower paid public sector, give to charity, set up self-help groups, newsletters and organisations, run jumble and car boot sales and write to the newspapers frequently (Baczynski, 1988). From one angle it may be seen as empowering, evidence of 'active citizenship' as it tips over into lobbying and pressure group politics. At the other end, where it merges with 'charity', it is often seen as demeaning, patronising and 'disempowering'. Whatever, it is complex and not only is Britain frequently cited as being unusual in its tradition of voluntary work (see Handy, 1994), this feature is singled out as something other countries could do well to copy. As a nation Britain still has more registered charities than any other nation of a comparable size. Over a quarter of a million exist and new ones are formed at the rate of 4,000 each year. Some of these, no doubt, are tax dodges but not all. We may joke about losing an empire and needing to find a role, but many ex-colonialists indeed became the mainstay of the parish councils, rotarians and rose-growing clubs. This wealth of administrative expertise was part of the fall-out from the Empire and has contributed directly both to the numerous charities and voluntary organisations in Britain and to a culture in which an obligation to serve remains marked.

The effects of such a culture or ethic are bound to be various. Amongst them, conceivably, is the very direction of a nation's occupational structure and economic growth. A popular account of Britain's economic and industrial decline in the period 1850-1980 (Weiner, 1981) stresses the corrupting part played by the middle classes and their snobbery in shifting energy, commitment and money away from manufacturing. They are charged with betraying their historical role by preferring gentrification and the professions to trade and industry. Yet it could be argued that the reason the 'brightest and the best' did not go into industry was because they chose to do something else which they saw as equally, if not more, worthwhile. They went off to run the Empire. Most biographies and autobiographies of such people make it pretty clear that this was generally not a very comfortable or attractive life. Staying in England and running a factory must have been easier and pleasanter. That so many people joined the Indian Civil Service and its equivalents in Africa made sense only if they believed in Imperialism and the need to 'serve' for it. Nowadays this all seems misconceived and patronising, but it needs understanding: after all they were not conscripted. Thus the growth of professionalism and a commitment to public service, including public administration as a career, may not only be an alternative explanation for under-investment in trade and industry, but evidence of a public service ethic which partly stemmed from a reaction to the market and capitalism.

To take another example, the broad sociological importance of volunteering was demonstrated by Titmuss (1970) in a study of blood donors, blood collection and distribution. In that pre-HIV/AIDS time there were several systems. Some countries, such as Britain, used unpaid volunteers, whilst others used the market. Titmuss found that where blood was collected from volunteers, the blood was 'better', that is, there was little waste, it came from the healthiest section of the population and was not infected. Where blood was sold for money there was more waste, more shortages, and it came from the poorest and sickest people who sold it, and their hepatitis, to scrape a living. Titmuss explained the difference in terms of an altruism embedded in the social structure and embodied in the idea of free medical care. Hence his title, *The Gift Relationship*. This, he argued, created a desire amongst the healthiest to give something of themselves for those less fortunate, for a greater good. The giving of blood was empowering to those who gave and to those who received. Whilst the donors made it clear that they gave blood as a sort of social insurance, in the hope that 'it' might never happen to them, they also believed that giving entitled one to receive and demonstrated that charity and public service are never altogether disinterested. Still the system made available the chance to 'give'. The moral imperative to do so came from the abstract sense of being treated well and, perhaps, from a widespread sense of the need to limit the rule of the market. It is significant that Titmuss did this study in the 1960s, a period that now looks like the high point of twentieth century capitalism. Clearly Titmuss had some such idea for he explicitly places himself in theoretical allegiance with Durkheim and Mauss and the insight that even the most contract-based of social relationships rely on a non-contractual element to maintain their very existence.

In his book, *Social Limits to Growth*, Hirsch (1977) argued that most exponents of free market economics recognised areas of social life where market principles were inappropriate. Published shortly before the Thatcher experiment in monetarism was introduced to Britain, it was prophetic. Hirsch argued that the principle of self-interest was incomplete as a social organising device and could only operate effectively if combined with some supporting social principle. This fundamental characteristic of economic liberalism, though taken for granted by Adam Smith and John Stuart Mill, had been lost sight of by their more recent followers who neglected the need for stringent qualifications to self-interested behaviour (see especially Gilmour's 1992 'insider' critique). An attempt to erect an explicitly *laissez-faire* social organisation, without a supporting social morality, had been made; and the result was structural strain on both the market and the political mechanisms designed to regulate and supplement it. Hirsch noted that even when the market 'succeeded' many of the 'successes' were misattributed as they really stemmed from remnants of a pre-market social ethos. What is especially useful about this account is not so much Hirsch's pessimism over capitalism's capacity to satisfy an ever-growing demand for goods, but his explicit concern with the dependence of one system on the values of another, and the potential for confusion that such a situation produces.

In a similar vein Marquand (1991) draws a distinction between 'civic republicans' and 'liberal individualists' in a discussion of citizenship that takes off from Douglas Hurd's (1988) call to build active and responsible citizenship on the 'centuries-old English tradition of voluntary service'. For getting people to work for nothing is clearly a great way out of economic difficulties and compensating for cuts in government support for social welfare. However, as Marquand points out, liberal individualism affords rights to citizens not to do something, that is, it is a negative freedom whilst civic republicanism, an altogether rarer and harder creed, enjoins the citizen to be 'active', and is a positive freedom. It stresses an obligation to contribute, especially to government. These two distinct models are often fudged and confused. Whilst the new Right wants more volunteers, they do not want more participation in government and to this end restricted unions, hence they are selectively appealing to two quite different traditions. As Marquand notes, working for nothing is a monarchical or feudal concept of service, not a civic one. For it to appeal it needs a widespread support for traditional values. This, even in Britain, looks increasingly less likely as the boomerang effect of Prime Minister John Major's call for a programme of 'Back to Basics' in 1993/94 has shown. Just as the women of East Central Europe are perhaps unwilling to be rolled out to fill the gap left by the state's withdrawal of public provision, so too the people of Britain may be said to have demonstrated a sea change in attitudes in their rejection of certain interpretations of 'Back to Basics'. Many were worried about the hidden economic agenda behind the decision to dismantle large mental health hospitals and develop the theory of community care. Despite evidence (Rogers and Pilgrim, 1986) that such programmes had very different effects in Italy and Britain (with Britain producing homelessness and suicide more than integration), it took the murder of a bystander by a prematurely discharged patient to focus this concern in political terms.

Pairing 'collectivism' with 'public service' may seem a touch forced (especially if the coercive and alienating elements of 'collectivism' are ignored), but the point of the comparison is to explore how the impulse towards altruistic social behaviour is accommodated and channelled. Just as the ethic of 'public service' can take a conservative or radical form, so too can 'collectivism'. Disentangling the motives for giving or engaging in 'public service work' under either type of political regime is bound to be complex. Sometimes ambition will be more important than altruism, especially as individual motives are generally easier to perceive than the structures in which they are embedded. Whatever, it is easy to misinterpret.

WELFARE AND CHARITY IN CAPITALIST AND NON-CAPITALIST SYSTEMS

At the individual level, doing something for nothing depends for its impact, and capacity to generate private satisfaction, on the contrast with activity that is clearly for profit. In nineteenth-century Britain philanthropy was the other side of capitalist exploitation and, for individuals worried about the hereafter, its antidote. The comparatively high levels of charitable giving displayed by contemporary Americans (almost four times as high as for Britons, according to Saxon-Harrold and Carter, 1987) and the frequency with which American business gurus profess their Christianity, is, similarly, closely linked to the more aggressive form of capitalism that flourishes in the United States. Such charitable giving can, of course, be superficial. Eva Hoffman's (1989) autobiographical account of emigrating from Poland to North America in the fifties repeatedly describes her shock at finding that, beneath their wide smiles and apparent friendliness, her American peers really did not believe they had an obligation to help others. This served to emphasise for her just how deep her Polish and socialist heritage was.

If we consider countries where capitalism and its associated institutions have been absent, or have taken a different form, where there is not a well-developed voluntary sector or where the activity of the Churches has been curtailed, then the prospect of alternative sources to government welfare may look quite different. Who, or what agency, might be expected to step into the breach and look after the elderly, the sick, the young and the unemployed? Will appeals for voluntary work fall on deaf ears? Is there an implicit assumption that 'the family' as a 'pre-socialist' form will do the job? Or might a commitment to communality and collectivism survive as both separate from, and deeper than, the commitment to socialism?

Some hint of the uncertain future to come was garnered by Deacon (1987) in a study of Hungarian attitudes to welfare and sensitivity to need and reward for effort. He argues that a shift in explanations of poverty, away from individualistic and towards more structural ones, was detectable around 1984. Stressing that the relevant context for this shift was a political system where the state was supposed to have solved all social problems and the only politically endorsed explanations of poverty were personal ones, Deacon interprets the shift as a form of resistance to socialist attempts to increase labour productivity and not as support for the socialist ideology and honour of labour. The existence of such feelings, carried over into a situation of state cuts in welfare, and a debasement of existing political rhetoric (communism and 'solidarity') poses a question which goes well beyond the practical side of providing welfare. This is simply whether citizens of the ex-state socialist countries, having enjoyed good levels of public provision for more than two generations, can reorganise and provide it on a non-state, non-centralised basis without a widespread ethic to support a certain sort of altruism? A possible obstacle to such a reorganisation could be the discrediting of the individual impulses on which that sort of provision had always depended. If everything to do with welfare provision, central state employment and public service under Communism is reviewed as distorted and/or corrupt it might well be much harder to engage similar impulses in a new system.

In the immediate aftermath of 1989, euphoria quickly turned to recrimination and to how various forms of contact with the Stasi, Securitate and so on should be viewed. Skeletons were found in a lot of cupboards and many who had thought of themselves as 'victims' came to be viewed as 'collaborators'. Claiming that one was acting out of a sense of 'public service' is likely, now, to be met with scorn; though it raises the question of what exactly is or was 'public service' and what its role in different societies might depend upon. It may now seem far-fetched to think of working in intelligence activities or the secret service apparati as a form of public service akin to choosing to work in the 'public sector' in the West, but this thought may have once influenced decisions to do so.

In the past provision under collectivism was often related to party status rather than need. The legacy of this may be apparent in the contemporary interest in the relatively abstract concepts of citizenship and civil society which are similarly often insensitive to the detail of everyday life. The idea of rights (for example, to housing, jobs and other benefits) may seem central to the notion of civil society, but the wherewithal of providing them is left unspecified in the ex-socialist countries. The actual or threatened withdrawal of these rights, or their mutation into the far less secure charitable handouts, produces a violent reaction, precisely in proportion to how deeply taken-for-granted they have become.

This is acute in East Central Europe where it is not clear that an adequate number of charities exist to give handouts and violent reactions, born of frustrated expectations, feed the revival of ethnic nationalism as a form of fall-back position. What we may be witnessing in some forms of conflict and 'ethnic cleansing' is the effect of decades of totalitarianism and the outlawing of non-governmental organisations. By removing a crucial level of organisation, or mezzostructure (see Hankiss, 1990), the opportunity of behaving in a public-spirited or altruistic way was also destroyed or attenuated. Of course, the ex-socialist countries vary in this as in all other respects, but differences according to whether, or how rigorously, intermediate or 'alternative' organisations such as the Church have been suppressed are crucial. The loss of the freedom to associate, and not to be seen as a threat if one did, was profound in its effects.

In some of the East Central European countries, where denominational and neighbourhood-based organisations survived (as in the ex-GDR), primary health care and facilities for children and the aged were often organised by the Churches. In these instances an alternative welfare structure existed, but it is stretched to breaking point and has yet to recover from the effects of central organisation (see Chamberlayne, 1992). If welfare needs are to be met on a secular or a denominational basis an infrastructure is necessary and neither the Churches nor the 'family' can provide it all. However, both in terms of its recent past in relation to 'Solidarity', and its future in terms of responses to welfare cuts Poland, with its strong Catholic Church, might be the exception that proves the rule. Though one recent commentator, Jerschina (1992), holds that Poland too is short on voluntary organisations and local links because it developed into a 'federation of families' which, though it offered a form of social insurance, also obstructed participation in political activities.

Although the Western way of doing things is not mandatory, the part played by organised religion in providing the practical infrastructure for giving both time and money should not be underestimated. In societies where religion has been suppressed or attenuated there may be grounds for doubting how quickly a voluntary sector organised around it could emerge. Religion may be reviving in the East, but its importance may be more ritualistic and expressive than practical, unless and until it successfully reclaims its own resources. For without them it is hard to see how religious organisations could become the mainstay of a post-socialist welfare state.

All of this relates to the broad issue of what has happened to the moral order underlying Communism. Was a commitment to collectivism only skin deep (see Szelenyi, 1988), as the speed of communist renunciation suggested, or was it very strong indeed, as a refusal to respond to appeals to supply welfare on an individual and voluntary basis might suggest? It is possible to see some of these issues as the same or similar to those which centre on nationalism and the revival of ethnic hostilities. All can be understood both as welfare issues, in so far as ethnicity, kith and kin are bases for providing welfare in emergencies, and as evidence of 'deeper' identifications. The re-emergence, or rapid rise, of Masonic lodges in Russia since 1989 has worried many and suggests, if not a total rejection of collective responsibility, then certainly a very narrow and very gendered interpretation of fraternity (see *The Guardian*, 29 February 1992 and *The Observer*, 7 June 1992). Such movements may be seen as backlashes to the immediate political situation, or as evidence of earlier moral orders. Both possibilities need exploring, especially as the latter is likely to have profound implications for gender relations.

THE BACKLASH TO INDIVIDUALISM

Commitment to the notion of a welfare state in the West has depended, historically, on an amalgam of different values and interests, from paternalism through to self-interest in insurance and to sophisticated views on the need to support the well-being of all (see Rustin 1979). The 'post-war consensus' was always a balancing act, based on a contingent equilibrium between the economic and moral systems, one that was surprisingly easily upset by the first years of the Thatcher administration, a defining characteristic of which was a determination to rid the country of its 'dependency culture'. Yet the seeds of its failure might have been present from the start. Charitable giving could hardly be expected to rise substantially if 'dependency' was an evil rather than a misfortune; if giving to charity was still 'good', but 'taking' from anyone was 'bad', nothing in between was left. There was no place for any notion of reciprocity or of a good that was not individual. It was a recipe that could not work in the long run and led to what may be interpreted as a defence of collectivism in the form of support for the welfare state.

Although many people played with Thatcherite ideas in the early 1980s, as soon as the practical implications of the policies became apparent the more general values of fairness and the responsibility of the state to its citizens either reemerged or were discovered as a reaction to the anti-collectivism of Thatcher (see Rentoul, 1989). Taylor-Gooby (1991) traces growing, rather than declining, support for the welfare state throughout the Thatcher era suggesting, in particular, a backlash against the aggressive individualism which had focused on institutions such as the National Health Service. It could almost be called a defence of collectivism. Similarly the failure, towards the end of Thatcher's premiership, of those who should have remained loyal needs explanation. The entrepreneurs, given the chance to reshape education in the form of the 1988 Education Reform Act and City Technology College programme, did not take it. Though the business community's lack of enthusiasm for the plan is usually put down to their narrow-mindedness, or to an understanding that corporate philanthropy is always self-interested (Vogel, 1991), it is clear that many despised the programme as a 'drop in the ocean' of educational need. Their unwillingness to have any truck with an inadequate and divisive scheme may be seen as part of the 'backlash' against individualism and the inappropriate use of private money where public money should be forthcoming. This may be taken as further evidence of a limit to how far charity or corporate philanthropy can be made to substitute for proper welfare state provision.

Another example of this backlash might be the reaction to the semi-official report *Voluntary Action* (Knight, 1993). This proposed a split within the British voluntary sector between campaign groups, which would lose their charitable status, and service providers, who would keep it. The rationale was a general belief in the market-based purchaser/provider model and its capacity to increase efficiency. Fairly obviously the proposed restructuring of the sector can be interpreted as a strategic preliminary to further cuts in welfare provision. From the British Government's view the 'problem' facing the voluntary sector was how to make it more productive: a particularly difficult problem when a high proportion of the labour it uses comes from people who already work for nothing. An incomes policy is clearly not an option. Not surprisingly, the proposal was received with almost complete dismay by those working within this sector (see *The Observer*, 20 February 1994). At present it is still under discussion. Whatever the final outcome, the point is that the proposal both rests on a tacit understanding of a connection between the traditions of charity and public service and the distinctive pattern of British capitalism, and seeks to exploit it further.

BACKLASH TO COLLECTIVISM OR GENDER AS A 'DEEP' MORAL CATEGORY

The currently fashionable term 'civil society' can mean all non-state activity, and in the East Central European context its potential for revival is regarded as one of the benefits of the changes. It stands for the people against a monolithic state and the activities that constitute it are generally viewed, unproblematically, as empowering. However this may be misleading precisely because much of what goes on under the heading of civil society means unpaid or voluntary work. A willingness to do something for little or no money needs explanation in any developed, monetised society. It is all the more urgent where the once forbidden 'profit motive' is suddenly and energetically promoted and the 'opportunity costs' of doing it are that much higher. In this context it is the idea of 'willingness' that needs attention.

If we look closely at the gendered distribution of unpaid work, that is, at housework and 'caring' on the one hand and political activism on the other, we may see a deepening of gender divisions in the post-transition societies, perhaps most marked in the decline of women in the post-1989 parliaments (see Einhorn, 1993). To understand this pattern the more coercive concept of patriarchy, and not the liberal one of civil society, which assumes an individual equality, is needed. However we understand patriarchy, as male power rooted narrowly in familial or tribal relations, or as a broader set of structures (see Walby, 1990) part of its value is its relative independence from both capitalism and socialism. In the post-socialist context we should not be so swayed by liberal, gender-blind concepts of citizenship (see Pateman, 1988; Meehan, 1993) that we confuse patriarchy with civil society-type activities.

At the conference mentioned at the start of this chapter there was a widespread expectation that the position of women would probably worsen and that, in addition to the loss of job security and rising pay differentials, many welfare provisions such as good maternity benefits, job protection, pre-school and other childcare provisions would be cut. The effects of a shift to market economies were assumed to follow the pattern of most capitalist economies and produce deeper and clearer gender divisions in the workforce and indeed a series of recent studies suggest that this is so (see Einhorn; 1993, Watson, 1993). Nevertheless many also expected women to experience relief at not 'having to go to work' and that this would converge with the 'need' to reduce and restructure the labour force with the result that a lot of women would quit paid work, 'voluntarily' or otherwise. The consequences of this were not necessarily attractive. Western feminists feared that women would be forced into a deeper economic dependency on men and, as a consequence, rates of personal violence would increase, as they do in the West (Hobson, 1990). Already there were signs that this was happening with people being frightened to walk alone in streets, an increase in pornography, prostitution and sexual harassment. Four years on, and most of these predictions have been fulfilled. Moreover, women have lost ground in political representation and are losing jobs faster than men.

As Einhorn (1991, 1993) has noted, these countries were striking in the developed world for the absence of Western-style feminism. This has puzzled many writers though some, such as Einhorn (1993) and Watson (1993), draw attention both to the role of the family as a site of resistance to state socialism and to the 'emasculation' of men under state socialism as conditions which lead both sexes to see a traditional gender identity as an achievement.   Whilst the chance to nest-build and home-make is understandable it does not translate immediately into a generalised desire to 'do good'. Having some time for one's family is one thing, spending time on good works in a broad sense is quite another.   The expectation that voluntary work will be forthcoming is based, implicitly or explicitly, on the traditional sexual division of labour and the semi-feudal values which underpin it, which is why the general failure to discuss how gender underpins many of the activities that comprise modern notions of citizenship becomes all important (see Yuval-Davis, 1991; Meehan, 1993).

No one seriously doubted that the shift into market societies in East Central Europe would have costs in the form of higher unemployment, reduced welfare and a series of political backlashes in all the countries undergoing transformation; or that many of these costs would fall on women.   But what was perhaps unexpected, was the interplay between values and gender, between deep moral categories and the social structures which support them and their expression in theories of citizenship.   If the women surveyed in ex-Czechoslovakia had been asked if they would care for their family, rather than 'do voluntary work', their answers might have been different (though there is still the problem of who 'counts' as family). With high rates of divorce and remarriage there is ambiguity about expectations and obligations towards an extended network of step-parents or ex-spouses and their wider kin.

The new language of citizenship, if it is to be put into practice, needs to be interpreted in terms of gender.   Though there is considerable similarity in the ideologies/ethics of collectivism and public service, especially as each are expected to play a critical part in the global dismantling and diversification of welfare state systems, neither will be fully understood if their gendered nature is left unexamined.   Gender relations were neither frozen nor absent under state socialism but they were less institutionalised around the public/private divide than in the West.   The rejection of voluntary work may be due to exhaustion but it may also be a refusal of self-sacrifice.   In the West much of the charitable tradition is intensely 'private'; many foundations are not 'listed', many donors refuse to be named. The private/public divide is crucial to both voluntary work and charity and gender relations.   In the long run the gender dimension, mediated by changes to the ethics of collectivism and/or public service and the attack on welfarism, may turn out to be more important in the East than the purely political revolutions which so captured the European imagination in 1989.

CONCLUSION

Bad as the increase in poverty in Britain has been in the 1980s, the absence of what I have called an ethic of public service would probably have made the situation far worse. It has been cynically exploited by the British government in recent years and may be on its last legs. But it has been an important dimension in the neo-liberal experiment and one that is worth bearing in mind if other countries decide to copy Britain. However, this public service ethic also depends on *unreconstructed* gender relations.

In East Central Europe where both the freedom for individual action and the development of non-state organisations have been curtailed for one to two generations, the outcome of privatisation may be far worse. The difference between Britain and East Central Europe may be that in one case too much has been expected to come out of public service impulses whilst in the other it is its virtual absence (or destruction after forty years or so of communist rule) that is crucial. Closely tied to this is what has happened to gender relations. In the West gender relations evolved continuously, the public/private divide remained strong and women's incorporation into the labour force was gradual. The possibility of part-time and voluntary work has long been 'available'. In the East, gender relations were abruptly disrupted. Forced into a double burden, women had neither the time to undertake voluntary work nor the intermediate organisations to coordinate their efforts. 'Relieved' of the double burden, the model of citizenship embraced by the women of East Central Europe may be the purely private one implied by liberal individualism, its strongest feature the right *not to do,* and not civic republicanism. If this is correct we should take care in interpreting the apparent desire of women of East Central Europe and the ex-Soviet Union to embrace traditional gender identities. This may not be anti-feminist because of the pull of the family and 'normalisation'. Their response may just as easily be interpreted in terms of the prevailing and individualistic model of citizenship and absence of an ideology and set of institutions which can underpin voluntary work whether that work is done by men or women.

NOTE

1. The ESRC workshop 'Gender Relations in East Central Eruope and the Soviet Union' was organised by B. Einhorn and held in Brighton in April 1991.

REFERENCES

Baczynski, R. (1988), *Discontent and Liberal Opinion. Non-Partisan Readers' Letters to British Local Newspapers since the Late 1960s*, London: Metaballon Books.

Balbo, L. and Novotny, H. (eds) (1986), *Time to Care in Tomorrow's World*, Vienna: European Centre for Social Welfare Training and Research.

Bell, D. (1979), *The Cultural Contradictions of Capitalism*, London: Heinemann.

Blum, A. and McHugh, P. (1971), 'The Social Ascription of Motives', *American Sociological Review*, vol. 36, no. 1, February.

Chamberlayne, P. (1992), 'Focus on Volkssolidarität', *Community Development Journal*, vol. 27, no. 2 pp. 149-155.

Collins, R. (1992), 'The Romanticisation of Agency/Structure versus the Analysis of Micro/Macro', *Human Relations*, vol. 45, no. 9, pp. 77-97.

Deacon, B. (1987), 'Opinion about Welfare Policy in Britain and Hungary', in M. O'Brien (ed.), *Comparative Social Research*, no.4, *The East-West Dimension*, Birmingham: Aston University.

Deacon, B. and Szalai, J. (eds) (1990), *Social Policy in the New Eastern Europe: What Future for Socialist Welfare?*, Aldershot: Avebury.

Deacon, B. (ed.) (1992), *Social Policy, Social Justice and Citizenship in Eastern Europe*, Aldershot: Avebury.

Einhorn, B. (1991), 'Where Have All the Women Gone?', *Feminist Review*, 39, pp. 16-36.

Einhorn, B. (1993), *Cinderella Goes to Market: Citizenship, Gender and Women's Movements in East-Central Europe*, London: Verso.

Fukuyama, F. (1989), 'The End of History?', National Interest, Summer.

Gilmour I. (1992), *Dancing with Dogma: Britain Under Thatcherism*, London: Simon & Schuster.

Habermas, J. (1976), *Legitimation Crisis*, London: Heinemann.

Handy, C. (1994), *The Empty Raincoat: Making Sense of the Future*, London: Hutchinson.

Hankiss, E. (1990), *East European Alternatives*, Oxford: Clarendon Press.

Hirsch, F. (1977), *Social Limits to Growth*, London: Routledge Kegan Paul.

HMSO/OPCS (1990-93), Social Trends, nos 20-23.

Hobson, B. (1990), 'No Exit, No Voice'. Women's Economic Dependency and the Welfare State', *Acta Sociologica*, 33.

Hoffman, E. (1989), *Lost in Translation: Life in a New Language*, London: Heinemann.

Hollis, P. (1987), 'Women in Council: Separate Spheres: Public Space', in Rendall, J. (ed.), *Equal or Different: Women's Politics 1800-1914*, Oxford: Blackwell.

Hurd, D. (1988), 'Citizenship in the Tory Democracy', *New Statesman*, 29 April.

Ignatieff, M. (1984), *The Needs of Strangers*, London: Chatto.

Jerschina, J. (1992), 'Polish Parents in the 1980's and 1990's', in Bjornberg, U. (ed), *European Parents in the 1990's*, New Jersey: Transaction Publishers.

Knight, B. (1993), *Voluntary Action*, London: Centris.

Marquand, D. (1991), 'Civic Republicans and Liberal Individualists: the Case of Britain', *Archives Européenes Sociologiques*, XXXII, pp. 329-44.

Meehan, E. (1993), *Citizenship in the European Community*, London: Sage.

Offe, C. and Keane, J. (eds) (1985), *Disorganised Capitalism: Contemporary Transformation of Work and Politics*, Cambridge: Polity Press.

Pateman, C. (1988), *The Sexual Contract*, Cambridge: PolityPress.

Rentoul, J. (1989), *Me and Mine: The Triumph of the New Individualism*, London: Unwin Hyman.

Rogers, A. and Pilgrim, D. (1986), 'Mental Health Reforms: Some Contrasts Between Britain and Italy', *Free Associations*, no. 6.

Rustin, M. (1979), 'Social Work and the Family', in Parry, N. Rustin, M. and Satyamurti, C. (eds), *Social Work, Welfare and the State*, London: Edward Arnold.

Saxon-Harrold, S. and Carter, J. (1987), *The Charitable Behaviour of the British People*, Tonbridge: Charities Aid Foundation.

Szelenyi, I. (1988), *Embourgeoisement in Rural Hungary*, Cambridge: Polity Press.

Taylor-Gooby, P. (1991), 'Attachment to the Welfare State', in Jowell, R. Brook, L. Taylor, B. and Prior, G. (eds), *British Social Attitudes*, Aldershot: Gower.

Titmuss, R. (1970), *The Gift Relationship: From Human Blood to Social Policy*, London: Allen & Unwin.

Vogel, D. (1991), 'Business Ethics. Past and Present', *Public Interest*, 102, Winter.

Walby, S. (1990), *Theorising Patriarchy*, Oxford: Blackwell.

Watson, P. (1993), 'Eastern Europe's Silent Revolution', *Sociology*, vol. 27, no. 3, pp. 471-87.

Weiner, M. (1981), *English Culture and the Decline of The Industrial Spirit 1850-1980*, Cambridge: Cambridge University Press.

Yuval-Davis, N. (1991), 'The Citizenship Debate: Women, Ethnic Processes and the State', *Feminist Review*, 39, pp. 58-68.

15. East Central European Media Systems in Transition

Nancy Wood*

INTRODUCTION

Anyone who witnessed television coverage of the 1989 revolutions in East Central Europe will have no difficulty acknowledging the importance of the role it played in mediating public perception and understanding of those tumultuous times. Not only did the media guide our vision and appraisal of events; it was clear that in East Central Europe, control of the media was itself a key factor determining the outcome of the political struggles taking place.

Now that these countries are in the throes of political democratisation and economic liberalisation, it is important to take stock of how their media systems have fared until now in this transitional period. Although freedom of expression was a fundamental goal of the 1989 revolutions, its achievement in practice is proving no easier than political and economic reform. This is partly a consequence of the entrenched media structures and practices bequeathed by state socialist regimes. However, it is also a result of fundamental changes taking place in the larger European and global media landscapes, developments which circumscribe to a considerable extent the paths the newly-democratised media systems in East Central Europe can follow.

This article maps out some general trends in the East Central European media in this period of transition, drawing in particular on developments since 1989 in Poland, Hungary and the Czech and Slovak Republics. Such a broad overview is plagued with problems from the outset. Extrapolating general trends from the specific circumstances of each country risks overshadowing important differences among their respective media systems. While all the countries of East Central Europe were dominated by state socialist ownership and control of the media, each country experienced that fact and the ensuing constraints differently. A thorough investigation would need to keep in play these similarities and differences both in the pre-1989 era and in the present, giving due weight to the relevant historical, political and cultural factors. Even where commonalities seem to outweigh the differences, it is important not to generalise from these to the whole of the East European region. In Bulgaria and Romania, for example, the pace of media democratisation is much slower and strewn with more obstacles of both a political and economic nature. Whether in attempting to reform their media these countries will merely follow some paces behind their East Central European counterparts, or be compelled by their specific circumstances to take different routes altogether, remains to be seen. Finally, any observations or analyses offered at this stage must necessarily be tentative in the light of the rapidity of change and the unpredictability of the current situation. All that can be highlighted here are the main contours of the East Central European media landscape as they appear at the time of writing.

MEDIA-STATE RELATIONS

Legislation enshrining freedom of expression and the formal independence of the media from political interference has been enacted in all the parliaments of East Central Europe. Moreover, the abolition, or at least the erosion, of state control over the production, distribution and dissemination of media messages and the expansion of independent media activity have been the ostensible aims of politicians and media professionals alike. And yet the media systems of East Central Europe remain highly politicised domains and the site of volatile, protracted and acrimonious dispute.

That the new dispositions of power in these countries, despite a professed commitment to media democratisation, should continue to view the media as an instrument of politics is not surprising given the legacy of state socialism. The common 'logic' of the former political systems, aptly characterised by Claude Lefort as 'the process of identification between power and society, the process of homogenizing the social space, the process of enclosing both society and power' (Lefort, 1986, p. 286), reached to the heart of political culture. Dislodging this logic and its effects, and instating a separation between power and society, including between the political sphere and the media, cannot be achieved by legislative means alone. For these reasons, struggles over the independence of the media assume a larger social significance, acting as a litmus test of the democratisation process itself. Indeed the perception that the media in a democratic society constitutes a 'public sphere' which interrogates and challenges political power rather than acting at its behest (cf. Habermas, 1989) has to be embraced not only by politicians and media professionals, but by the East Central European citizenry at large.

Polish media analyst Karol Jakubowicz lends substance to this perspective when he suggests that Poland's failure to achieve fundamental structural reforms within broadcasting institutions, and the delay in passing legislation designed to guarantee broadcasting's independence from the state, can partly be explained by every government's perception that it might need to use broadcasting in an instrumental way if its economic policies and austerity measures provoke dissent and unrest. He observes:

> Because of the political importance of broadcasting, parties in power seek to gain a measure of influence over television. Those in opposition do not oppose this as vehemently as could be expected, no doubt because they hope to do the same when they get into power. There is little real belief in the ideal of autonomous, impartial and politically-neutral public service broadcasting because it is quietly assumed that every government will seek to bring pressure to bear on it in any way it can. (Jakubowicz, 1992, pp. 5-6)

This said, Poland has taken some important steps to institute formal divisions between the state and media. A new Broadcasting Council has been established with the express aim of separating the regulation of broadcasting from broadcasting activity itself. Its members are nominated by both chambers of Parliament and the President but they must not have any direct involvement in government or broadcasting activity. It remains to be seen whether this initiative in structural reform will stave off political pressure but as Jakubowicz emphasises, the 'Council is the first administrative body in Poland situated outside the government, without direct subordination either to the Council of Ministers or to Parliament. To some extent it is a constitutional experiment which has no precedents in the postwar history of Poland' (Jakubowicz, 1992, p. 9).

Appointments to positions of power within broadcasting institutions have also been at the centre of the so-called 'media war' in Hungary. The struggles intensified in late 1992 when the Democratic Forum Prime Minister József Ántall suspended state television president Elemer Hankiss and brought state television finances directly under prime ministerial control because of a perceived anti-government bias in television coverage. In January 1993, Hankiss and radio chief Csaba Gombar resigned in protest at government interference, citing as the last straw the failure of the new media law to get through Parliament because of government opposition to the proposed method of hiring and firing the heads of TV and radio. The opposition Free Democrats favoured appointments made on the basis of a consensus of all parliamentary parties, but the ruling Democratic Forum wanted appointments to remain the prerogative of the prime minister's office (*Index on Censorship*, 2/1993, p. 20, July, 1993, pp. 23-4). The resulting stalemate has left the draft media law in tatters and the negotiating parties exhausted and embittered.

Perhaps the most ominous developments are taking place in the newly-independent Slovak Republic where personnel in both the press and broadcasting have been subject to direct state intimidation and manipulation. Since taking power, the nationalist government of Vladimir Méciar has sacked two leading newspaper editors, ousted the chief and news director of Slovak TV, installed government appointees in television administration, and subjected the constitutional guarantee of freedom of expression to the interests of 'state security, public order, public health and morality' (*Columbia Journalism Review*, March/April 1993, p. 46). These aggressive, interventionist measures have been matched by the proliferation of pro-government media outlets in radio and the press, and the consolidation of control over state television and the national news agency.

Such examples can serve to illustrate the general point that the logic of state socialist power has not yet been exorcised from the media sphere in East Central Europe and, as Jakubowicz points out, the philosophy of an independent and neutral public service broadcasting has few genuine adherents among the new powerbrokers. Many analysts would argue that only the public service broadcasting model offers a viable alternative to state-controlled broadcasting systems in East Central Europe. This is a case that cannot be made fully here. But in its essential outlines, it would maintain that public service broadcasting best furthers the aims of the democratisation of society because it addresses its audience primarily in their capacity as citizens, rather than as the consumers targeted by commercial broadcasting systems. This mode of address, it can be argued, is inscribed not only in the type of programme output, but also in the set of relationships established between the state, broadcasting institutions and audience. On the one hand, the ethos of public service broadcasting recognises broadcasting's necessary independence from the authority of the state; on the other hand, it aims to be responsive to the 'communicative entitlements' of ordinary citizens, central among these, their right of access to a full range of broadcasting services which, attuned to the needs, interests and desires of a wide citizenry, endeavours to enhance the character of both public and private life in the light of its own pervasive presence in these spheres (cf. Scannell, 1992). But even if the premise that public service broadcasting best serves the citizenship needs of East Central Europeans is accepted, developments are taking place at other levels of media activity which make its realisation an increasingly remote prospect.

MEDIA MARKETS AND THEIR VICISSITUDES

At the same time that the media systems of East Central Europe are re-defining their relationship to political power, they are in the throes of radical transformation of their media economies. Because of the compromised history of state monopoly media systems, many media practitioners are suspicious of any meaningful reform of this sector and view rapid and total commercialisation as the only antidote to state interference in media matters. The legislative delay in allocating new commercial broadcasting franchises by all the governments of East Central Europe has also produced frustration and impatience in a public eager to capitalise on an era that should usher in an expansion of broadcasting outlets. In Hungary and Poland in particular, a number of television and radio services have been operating illegally (and very successfully) for some time in protest at this protracted process. But if there is a pent-up, popular desire for accelerating the pace of commercialisation, there are already a number of casualties arising from the rapid marketisation which has occurred in several media sectors, and more ominous developments on the horizon because of the particular economic and cultural context in which this deregulation is taking place. These can be described and analysed at a number of levels.

(i) Loss of State Subsidies

Even those media sectors which can legitimately claim some measure of continued government subsidy in this period of transition, notably television and the cinema - have become casualties of the severe economic crisis that has accompanied rapid transition to free market economies in East Central Europe.

We can take cinema as a prime example since West European audiences who in the past were treated to a regular diet of films from this region now will be hard pressed to name any films on European circuits which have been made by the national industries of East Central Europe in the last few years. For domestic audiences the situation is no different, with a drastic decline over the last three years in the number of national products appearing on cinema screens. Poland is a dramatic case in point: in 1990, there were only three US films in the top twenty box office successes of that year, twelve of which were Polish films, including the top three. A year later, all of the top twenty films were from the USA. This trend has been repeated in the Czech Republic and in Hungary (*Financial Times Business Reports,* 'Screen Finance', 3 June 1992). With state budgets under severe strain and all industries in competition with each other for finance capital, few films are finding the necessary production funding.

In the spheres of domestic film distribution and exhibition, painful adaptation to free market conditions is compounded by rampant video piracy (also the scourge of American film export agencies). The rapid growth in VCR penetration and widespread availability of pirated film videos, combined with a lack of deterrent legislation or the concerted enforcement of existing piracy legislation, has created a situation where between 60 per cent (Czech Republic) and 90 per cent (Poland) of the video market deals in illegal copies ('Media climate briefing', Coopers and Lybrand, Issue 41/1993).

National film industries elsewhere in Europe, also in dire financial straits, have increasingly looked to co-production opportunities with other EC member states, but if co-production is proving a mixed blessing for European cinéastes, it is even more so for film projects which go into the co-production market-place without the means to attract European partners on equal terms. In effect, a form of European colonialism seems to prevail in which 'co-production' has recently meant using East Central Europe as a cheap production location for Western film companies, often offering significant margins of savings on Western competitors. There is a danger that East Central Europe will see its own national production base transformed into a service film industry for its richer European and US partners.

One small prospect for change appeared late in 1991 with a new trade agreement between the EC and Hungary, Poland and the former Czechoslovakia offering these countries association with 'MEDIA '95', the EC's five-year audio-visual programme. In principle, this means that the countries of East Central Europe could participate in a number of schemes designed to strengthen the film and television industries of Europe, and especially those of small European countries. The schemes range from support for script development, film and television co-production and film distribution to regional workshops and training. However, MEDIA '95 is underfunded, has experienced recession-induced cutbacks and requires of its non-Community participants financial contributions that East Central European governments are unlikely to be in a position to meet. In any event, the small scale of such measures cannot possibly hope to address the scope of the support required to ensure the viability of domestic audio-visual industries.

For both ideological and economic reasons, state subsidisation of other media sectors, like the print media, is no longer possible or desirable. Left to the early free market conditions of the post-1989 period, new newspaper and magazine titles proliferated and flourished, finding readers for a multitude of hitherto untapped opinions, tastes and interests. The insatiable market for pornographic magazines in East Central Europe is, predictably, the example of this boom that is most often cited by Western media analysts, but we should not ignore the range of new titles directed at women, young people, new political constituencies, interest groups, the hobbies of ordinary citizenry and the like. Moreover, styles of newspapers are changing radically, dictated by readers' seeming preferences for less political content, livelier formats and 'infotainment'-style coverage. This means not only that 'Sun'-style tabloids, featuring crime, sex and scandal have taken many newspaper markets by storm (the most recent success story being the Czech tabloid *Blesk*, with a circulation of 500,000 copies), but that the 'serious' newspaper market has undergone considerable revamping. Papers like Poland's *Gazeta Wyborcza* and Hungary's *Népszabadság* have been transformed into 'quality tabloids', providing news in more accessible formats and giving over much of the space hitherto devoted to political coverage to a wide variety of popular features (*New York Times*, 28 December 1992).

While the spectrum of opinion and 'taste publics' catered for by this expansion and transformation of the print media is an evident boost for the 'democratic public sphere' in East Central Europe, these euphoric days are clearly over. There is simply not enough room in the newspaper and magazine market to sustain the abundant array of titles (to take just one example: the city of Prague alone boasted 15 dailies by the end of 1992). Newsprint costs are high, advertising sales are precarious and consumers' disposable income is under increasingly severe constraints (*Presstime*, March 1991, p. 23). In this situation of fierce competition for readers, advertising revenue and foreign investment (of which more below), analysts predict that a radical 'shakeout' of the print media market is looming in which only a fraction of existing titles will survive (*New York Times*, 28 December 1992).

Of course, it can be argued that this is as it should be and that no market-based society will support newspapers or magazines that are unable to hold their own in a competitive environment on the sole basis that they enhance the communicative dimensions of the democratic public sphere. However, it is worth considering briefly the underlying and more general trends within media markets that these developments might represent.

In his book The *Media and Democracy*, John Keane argues that market liberalism has thus far conceived of censorship too narrowly, as the exercise of the monopoly power of the state to curb the exchange of opinions among various groups of citizens. However Keane believes that this liberal ideology must be revised to take account of the evident and increasing contradiction between freedom of communication and unlimited freedom of the market. Referring primarily to the situation in Western democracies, Keane charts the number of ways in which communication markets increasingly restrict freedom of communication: for example, by generating financial barriers to entry for new media concerns, by their tendency to create media monopolies, by forcing non-profitable concerns out of business, by restricting choice and 'by shifting the prevailing definition of information from that of a public good to that of a privately appropriable commodity' (Keane, 1991, p. 89). Certainly this prognosis rings true in Britain where the press is dominated by a small group of media concerns. (It is a well-known fact that Rupert Murdoch of News International owns a third of the country's national dailies, and a third of the Sunday newspaper market.) Keane and other media critics argue that, given the high costs of entry, and excessive dependency of newspapers on advertisers, only limited state and/or public intervention in the newspaper market can rectify this situation and widen and preserve the range of political opinion and sources of information essential to the functioning of democratic societies.

This view has not held political sway in Britain and it is certainly not likely to do so in East Central Europe where state subsidy of the print media is more often than not directly translated into political influence. Is Britain therefore holding up a mirror to the states of East Central Europe, showing the future for which the print media is destined by the very logic of unfettered free market principles? Part of the response to this question depends on the role we can ascribe to foreign investment in the process of media democratisation.

(ii) Foreign ownership and investment

The effects of foreign investment on the national media industries of East Central Europe are still extremely difficult to assess. On the one hand, it is evident that privatisation of media systems, backed by foreign investment, has helped to weaken the grip of state control over national media systems. Some analysts (*IPI Report*, February 1993) have pointed to the lack of foreign investment in the Slovak media as one reason for its susceptibility to government pressure. The cash injection provided by foreign investment has also largely funded the modernisation of the technological infrastructure of many media enterprises and the introduction of new media technologies. Despite legislative holdups in allocating new franchises, satellite and cable have made steady incursions into broadcasting territory in East Central Europe and virtually all the new services are financed by foreign consortia (even if they are fronted by domestic subsidiaries).

At the same time, weakened national media industries are easy prey for Western media monopolies whose primary interest is not the expansion of the range of political opinion, nor even the political influence they might wield in their new acquisitions, but an extension of their existing empires in order to obtain much-needed access to new media markets.

Thus far, the press has been the sector most rapidly and extensively privatised in East Central Europe and it has garnered a considerable amount of foreign investment from media heavyweights like Hersant, Springer, Bertelsmann, and Murdoch, and from middle-sized European media groups anxious to obtain a foothold in East Central European publishing markets. And in a saturated and cut-throat newspaper market, even those with aspirations to financial independence (like the Czech daily *Lidové noviny*) have had to seek foreign backing to ensure their very survival. However, despite the early period of intensive 'courtship' by Western interests, resulting in extensive foreign ownership of newspaper concerns, it is no longer certain that similar solicitations by failing newspapers will meet with success. As their own investment capacity is curbed by debt financing and the effects of recession, Western investors have shed the longer-term perspective on their investment returns in the Eastern newspaper market and now want hard evidence of tight economic management and shorter-term profitability (*New York Times*, 12 December 1992).

However it is the sphere of broadcasting that has attracted the most attention and controversy regarding foreign ownership. Rehearsing many of the debates that have taken place in West European broadcasting systems regarding limitations on foreign ownership, concern focuses on the point at which foreign presence in national broadcasting industries translates into a real threat to cultural self-expression and autonomy. Legislation restricting foreign ownership, control and investment has been enacted in most parliaments of East Central Europe but the length of time it has taken to see the light of day suggests that legislators are not only encountering great difficulty in identifying what constitutes 'dangerous' levels of foreign capital penetration of national media markets, but that they are also acutely aware of the implications of sending deterrent signals to prospective foreign investors.

In 1989, Hungary imposed a moratorium on the allocation of new broadcasting franchises to avoid hasty privatisations financed by Western interests at a time when the country was in a state of political transition. The new government elected in spring 1990 inherited the task of formulating press and broadcasting legislation which would institute rules regarding foreign ownership and acquisition. The draft broadcasting bill proposed to limit foreign investment but without specifying the exact extent. The legislative process then became embroiled in the above-mentioned political disputes over Hungarian television, and the process stalled, leading some foreign investors to abandon their investment plans and leaving others, like the US-owned cable operator Home Box Office, uncertain about the future of their already considerable scale of investment. In Poland, meanwhile, the new broadcasting law has set a limit of 33 per cent on foreign investment in a broadcasting company. However, even before the law's enactment in July 1993, and the allocation of private television franchises (scheduled for the autumn of 1993), Italian media mogul Nicola Grauso had moved in with both investment capital and a programming operation. Grauso has provided equipment, and (through a Berlusconi agency) substantial programming and advertising to the twelve local television stations in which he has bought a one-third share. The current transmission activities are technically illegal, but Grauso is confident of the government's tolerance in the short run and generosity in the longer run when commercial franchises are finally allocated. In the new media law of the Czech Republic, where there is no specified ceiling on foreign investment, major media groups like Canal Plus, Berlusconi and Bertelsmann, thwarted in the first allocation round of a private television franchise (which went to a Czech group backed by a former US ambassador to Hungary), are no doubt waiting in the wings for the next investment opportunity.

To encourage new entrants into the media scene and discourage concentration of ownership by a few media conglomerates, Poland and the Czech and Slovak Republics have followed the West European example of establishing legal limits which prevent any single media concern from becoming dominant (cf. Jakubowicz, 1993), though it is likely to be no easier to patrol the circumnavigating strategies of such concerns than it is elsewhere in Europe.

It is clearly too simple, and in the present situation unrealistic, to adopt an entirely favourable or hostile stance regarding foreign investment in East Central European media markets. In the light of the circumstances sketched above, there seem to be several (tentative) conclusions to draw. In the print media, foreign financing seems to be reaching levels that suggest not only that no newspaper can survive without it, but that the fate of any newspaper will be henceforth determined by the most stringent of economic calculations made by foreign investors. Political independence from the state may have been achieved, but seemingly at the price of financial dependence on Western paymasters. Regarding the broadcasting industries, there is still some scope for limiting the incursions of foreign capital by pleading defence of national cultures. However if the free market is going to be curbed in this way, it may be worth considering the recent experience of 'deregulation' in the broadcasting industries of Western Europe. There is another reason that this might prove instructive. Even while awaiting entry into EC membership proper, the media of East Central Europe are not immune from the pressures which the deregulated economic environment of the West European media has already generated. Thus they approach the task of transforming their own media economies in tandem with a West European media landscape marked by a decade of fierce deregulation and experiencing the contradictory forces attached to European economic integration.

'TELEVISION WITHOUT FRONTIERS'

Throughout the 1980s in Western Europe, institutions of the EC and governments of individual EC member states committed themselves to objectives intended to increase the trade in cultural goods and services among European countries and thereby break down restrictive national trade barriers. The impetus behind these objectives was primarily economic in origin, that is, to bring national cultural economies into line with the larger free trade objectives of the European market of 1992. The EC policy initiative which best embodied this aim was the Directive 'Television without Frontiers' which, focusing on the sphere of broadcasting, set out measures designed to increase trade in programming among European nations, limit their dependency on US television imports, encourage the emergence of new broadcasting services throughout Europe and across nation-state boundaries, especially by cable and satellite, and expand advertising-funded broadcasting channels (cf. Schlesinger, 1991).

It is still too soon to ascertain the full effects of the Directive, incorporated into EC legislation in 1990, but several outcomes are worth noting that carry implications for the media systems of East Central Europe in this transition period.

At a general level, the most far-reaching effect of deregulation has been the erosion of the power and financial well-being of European public service broadcasting. Public service broadcasters throughout Europe have been put on the defensive by the Directive's clear mandate in favour of commercial broadcasting systems. Once the unchallenged bastions of national culture, public service broadcasting systems have lost their privileged and protected status and are increasingly obliged to enter into fierce competition with commercial rivals. But their chief rivals are not the trans-frontier services envisaged by the authors of the Directive, and transmitted by cable and satellite technology, but new commercial channels operating primarily within nation-state borders and directed at national audiences. Rather than producing a popular demand for commercial, trans-European broadcasting services, the economic and policy measures accompanying 'Television without Frontiers' have paradoxically consolidated *national* broadcasting systems, although these are now increasingly dominated by commercial rather than public service interests. This demise of the public service broadcasting sector in Western Europe does not bode well for its supporters in East Central Europe hoping to emulate this model in order to curb the excesses of both state intervention and media marketisation.

However, the Directive itself manifested confusion about how to pursue its economic and cultural aims. For a start, it is clear that boosting the economic exchange of cultural products among EC member states cannot be achieved by restrictive measures alone. The Directive attempted to stimulate such an exchange (and a corresponding reduction in members' dependency on US programmes) by stipulating a voluntary quota of 50 per cent on non-EC television imports. But many countries have been forced to exceed the quota simply in order to fill the increased number of programme hours made available by new services and channels. In a situation where the supply of domestic programming is insufficient, broadcasters will turn to US imports as a cheap and readily-available alternative. Moreover, attempts to enforce the quota system threaten to undermine the very services the policies of deregulation have helped to create. For example, the French government set an obligatory quota of 60 per cent on EC programming on French channels, only to see one of its newer commercial channels, *La Cinq*, go under, citing the prohibitive demands of financing the quota as the main reason for its demise. But the quota is misguided in other respects in that it has assumed that reliance on US output translates simply into cultural dependency. However research shows that in many West European countries, audiences consistently demonstrate clear preferences for television programmes, especially fiction, produced in their own countries rather than US imports or imports from other EC countries (Biltereyst, 1991; Silj, 1988; Tracey, 1985). In short, the cultural preferences of national audiences are keeping US cultural dominance at bay and thwarting the economic objectives of increased inter-European trade in televisual products.

If we bring East Central Europe into this picture, the issue of the desired relationship between domestic, European and US programming is further complicated. State resources for the broadcasting sector in East Central Europe have been reduced by economic stringencies and/or political decisions. A form of licence fee payment continues to subsidise state broadcasting services but an economically-squeezed public cannot be expected to sustain rising licence fee costs. In this situation, commercial media interests, increasingly backed by foreign investors, look set to dominate the broadcasting systems of East Central Europe. And as is well-known, the primary target of commercial broadcasting systems is the advertising revenue they hope to generate by their delivery of audiences/consumers to advertisers. A 1991 forecast estimated the advertising market in Poland, Hungary and the former Czechoslovakia to be worth about $100 million, with television representing half of this predicted revenue (*Broadcast*, 9 April 1992). Advertising interests have swooped in to claim a share of this market, and tariffs have soared accordingly. Even with inflationary costs, for a recession-struck European advertising industry, this new market has appeared like manna from heaven. Audiences for television in East Central Europe are extremely high, relatively young and, in the eyes of advertisers, open to consumerist persuasion. At the same time, governments, mindful of the need to be seen protecting national broadcasting interests, have limited television advertising time on state channels, making prime-time advertising slots costly and difficult to obtain. In such a situation, the commercial broadcasting sector, that is private terrestrial, cable and satellite services, will clearly be the main beneficiary of advertisers' attentions, especially if these serve up the steady diet of American imports that are so much in popular demand at present in these countries.

While this arouses in some circles the same worries about a US onslaught on cultural autonomy and national sovereignty that inspired the Directive's protective guidelines, it is not clear how this worry might best be addressed. The majority of programming on terrestrial channels in East Central Europe is still home-produced, but this is partly due to the inflated cost of acquiring foreign imports. New legislation is following the West European example of imposing quota restrictions on acquired material (the Polish media law stipulated a 30 per cent quota on domestic output, the Hungarian draft broadcasting bill has proposed 51 per cent and the Czech media law 40 per cent (*New York Times*, 27 December 1992)). Even if sufficient programming can be generated domestically, and the irritation of foreign investors at the quota system appeased, such measures are hardly a filip to the cause of national identity if East Central European audiences would prefer the imported, especially American, fare. Meanwhile, the production of quality, domestic programming that might win over audiences is itself hindered by squeezed budgets and stalled in industries whose energies are often diverted from innovation by relentless political squabbles. The current high audience ratings achieved by *Dallas* and

Dynasty in East Central Europe may be distasteful for politicians and television practitioners eager to foster audience loyalty to a predominantly domestic output, but it is unlikely that quotas alone will achieve this result. Moreover, one should be careful not to over-react to the caprices of audience taste. West Europeans might recall that it was no so long ago that such programmes also riveted national audiences, only to be eclipsed by an insatiable audience appetite for domestically-produced drama.

CONCLUSION

In the analysis offered above, the process of media democratisation in East Central European countries is faced with a number of urgent tasks, and an array of seemingly insoluble dilemmas.

Certainly a radical reorganisation of media/state relations is necessary in order to ensure that the formal and constitutional guarantee of media independence from state interference becomes a practical reality. The establishment of independent broadcasting bodies is an important step in this direction, and the enlargement of a competitive, commercial broadcasting sector can also have the effect of diverting the obsessive attentions of both governments and journalists away from battles in the state broadcasting sphere. A culture of media autonomy cannot be legislated into existence, or ushered in overnight by structural reforms and by an influx of commercial rivals, but these measures are a precondition for any meaningful change (cf. Jakubowicz, 1993). (It is already evident that such independent bodies would have to cast a vigilant eye over the commercialisation process itself in the light of state attempts to manipulate broadcasting privatisation in favour of particular party-political interests.)

At the same time as the states of East Central Europe should be required to relinquish control over certain aspects of media activity, however, they are also faced with pressures to assume an enhanced regulatory role. Restrictions on foreign ownership, the imposition of programme quotas, limits on advertising and so forth are seen as necessary to curb the inevitable excesses of the free play of market forces. The state purse is also being called upon to sponsor or subsidise those media activities which may not be economically self-sufficient, but are nonetheless essential to the viability of national media industries and to the promotion of a diversity of opinion. Like elsewhere in Europe, the effects of deregulating media systems are generating demands for some measure of 're-regulation' by the state.

There are no easy solutions to these contradictory pressures and certainly no blueprints showing how they might be 'managed' democratically in the specific circumstances of the post-totalitarian states of East Central Europe. I have suggested, for example, that some of these regulatory initiatives aimed at protecting national cultural interests from the homogenising forces of the global media may in fact prove to be anathema to a public whose media consumption has for so long been steered away from Western cultural fare. Moreover, when 'national' interests are defined in restrictive, exclusivist and normative terms, and when the domain of broadcasting becomes subject to these definitions and/or attempts to patrol them, regulation can take on all the sinister connotations of its state socialist predecessor. Poland is a case in point: once the new media law stipulated that no programmes damaging to the state or offensive to 'Christian values' could be aired, the broadcasting sphere has come under increasing pressure from the Church to act as the national arbiter of (religiously-based) public morals, rather than functioning as a communicative space for contesting value systems (cf. Gross, 1993). In these situations, whose will should prevail in the interests of a democratic, national-popular culture? In a sense, the resolution of such quandaries hinges not only on the issue of the role the media can and should play in the democratisation process of East Central Europe, but on what role it actually plays in the everyday life of its citizens.

It is tempting to invoke once again the ideal of the media as a 'democratic public sphere' addressing individuals in their capacities as citizens of these newly-democratised states. However, apart from the fact that the prospects of establishing a public service-based media in the face of the current commercial onslaught are very remote indeed, the experience of transition in many spheres of life in East Central Europe is reminding us that in any event such goals cannot be imposed from above but must emerge as a demand from below, from the felt needs and desires of everyday life. If demands for the media to assume this democratic function have yet to be popularly expressed, then it is perhaps high time to investigate the reasons for this apparent reticence.

NOTE

*I am grateful to James Donald for his comments on an earlier draft of this chapter.

REFERENCES

Biltereyst, Daniel (1991), 'Resisting American Hegemony: A Comparative Analysis of the Reception of Domestic and US Fiction', *European Journal of Communication*, Vol. 6, No. 4.

Gross, Irene Grudzinska (1993), 'Broadcasting Values', *East European Constitutional Review*, Vol. 2, No. 3, Summer.

Habermas, Jurgen (1989), *The Structural Transformation of the Public Sphere: An Inquiry into a Category of Bourgeois Society*, Cambridge, MA: MIT Press.

Jakubowicz, Karol (1992), 'The Restructuring of Television in East Central Europe', paper delivered to a symposium on media developments in East Central Europe, organised by the Centre for Communication and Information Studies of the University of Westminster, London, 3 July.

Jakubowicz, Karol (1993), 'Freedom vs. Equality', *East European Constitutional Review*, Vol. 2, No. 3, Summer.

Keane, John (1991), *The Media and Democracy*, Cambridge: Polity Press.

Lefort, Claude (1986), 'The Logic of Totalitarianism', in *The Political Forms of Modern Society*, Cambridge: Polity Press.

Scannell, Paddy (1992), 'Public service broadcasting and Modern Public Life' in Scannell, P., Schlesinger, P. and Sparks, C. (eds), *Culture and Power*, London: Sage.

Schlesinger, Philip (1991), *Media, State and Nation: Political Violence and Collective Identities,* London: Sage.

Silj, Alessandro (1988), *East of Dallas: The European Challenge to American Television*, London: British Film Institute.

Tracey, Michael (1985), 'The Poisoned Chalice? International Television and the Idea of Dominance', *Daedalus*, Vol. 114 (4).

Index

Ad Hoc Group on Immigration, 141
advertising, 74, 167, 220, 223-24, 226-27
agency, 194, 197, 204, 217, 223
Agency of International Development, 130
agitation, 165
agriculture, 89, 92, 112, 121, 154-55, 158, 160
AIDS, 147, 202
altruism, 202, 204-55
Amnesty International, 20, 188
Anderson, Benedict, 11
Anderson, Sascha, 47, 49
anti-communist, 172
anti-dumping, 154-55, 159
anti-fascist, 166
anti-Marxist, 186, 188
anti-monopolist regulations, 112
apparatchik, 92, 99
Arendt, Hannah, 20, 23
armaments, 152
associationist system/economy, 96
associations, 20, 76-7, 114-15, 145, 173
Australia, 21-2
authoritarianism, 18, 22, 172-73
automobile market, 119
autonomy, 3, 10, 26, 70-72, 76-7, 90, 173, 187, 222, 226-27

balance of payments, 95, 98
Balkans, 17
Baltic republics, 89-90, 97, 99
banking system, 94, 119
bankruptcy laws, 119, 153
basic industries, 155
Belgium, 67, 142
Belgrade, 94, 101
Belohradsky, Vaclav, 35-6, 38
Belorussia (Belarus), 90
Berlin Wall, 166, 169
Beveridge Report, 136

Blesk, 220
Böhme, Ibrahim, 47
Bourdieu, Pierre, 187, 189, 191, 193, 195-96
Bretton Woods System, 125
Britain, 14, 16, 56-7, 60, 68, 76, 139, 142, 148, 198, 201-4, 211-13, 221
British Nationality Act, 1981, 142
Brubaker, William Rogers, 71, 84
Brussels, 58, 66, 99, 148-49
Bulgaria, 82, 119, 130, 153, 196, 215
Bush Administration, 119
business ethic, 118, 121, 123, 127-28, 180, 191

Canada, 21-2
capitalism, 12, 98, 197, 199, 200, 202-4, 208-9
capitalist, 1, 98, 134, 166, 168, 181, 183, 185, 187, 190-191, 194, 204, 209
capitalist democracies, 176
caring, 145, 174, 198-200, 209
Carrère d'Encausse, Hélène, 169, 177
cars, 114, 151
Catholic Church, 206
CDU (Christian Democratic Union), 41-3, 47-9, 52
Cecchini Report, 136, 148
censorship, 169, 220
Central and Eastern Europe, 39, 84-6, 117, 121, 123, 125, 127, 129, 131-32, 150-151, 153-57, 160-161
Central Asian region, 95
Central Committee(s), 92, 174
Central Europe, 34-5, 44, 70, 85, 118-19, 121, 131-32, 139, 159, 161, 180, 183, 185-86, 189, 194
central planning, 90-91, 95, 120
centrally planned economy, 28, 96
charities, 201, 205
Charter 77, 25, 81

Child Poverty Action Group, 148-49
childcare, 70, 73, 75, 138, 146, 209
China, People's Republic of, 168, 183, 187
Christian Democrat Popular Party, 111
Christian Democratic Union, *see* CDU
Christian Social Union, *see* CSU
cinema, 218
citizen, 3-4, 13, 22, 25, 35-6, 64, 71, 136, 140, 142, 146, 174, 203
citizenship, 3-6, 9, 11, 13, 22, 25, 27, 32, 35-6, 52, 55, 64, 69, 70-72, 74, 78-82, 134, 138, 140, 142-48, 174, 180, 198, 201, 203, 205, 209-11, 217
Civic Forum, 27, 29, 30-33, 36
civil society, 2, 4-5, 12, 17-19, 22, 27, 31, 35, 41, 44-5, 51-2, 70, 72, 75-7, 81, 125, 146, 175-76, 180, 198-99, 205, 208-9
class conflict, 145
class enemy, 169
Clausewitz, Karl von, 15
clientelist economy, 102
co-production, 219
coal and steel production, 135
Cohen-Tanugi, 62, 68
Cold War, 1, 5, 9, 17, 60, 181, 196
collectivism, 78, 198-200, 203, 204-7, 210
colonialism, 219
commercial banks, 107
commercialisation, 104, 218, 227
Commissioner for Social Affairs, 144
commodities/commodity, 175, 184, 221
Common Agricultural Policy, (CAP), 155
Common Market, 54, 56, 58, 60-61, 137
communication policy, 165-66, 176
communications, 17, 126, 169
communism, 1, 34, 37, 73, 92, 96-7, 99, 205
communist, 25, 28, 32, 41-2, 44, 91-2, 95-6, 98, 114, 168, 170, 181, 197, 206, 211
communist nationalism, 95
communist parties, 172
Communist Party of the Soviet Union, CPSU, 166

communist regime(s), 2, 24-7, 31, 34, 36-7, 165
communist state(s), 26, 98, 172
community, 4-5, 11-13, 41, 45, 48, 59, 72, 76, 83, 138, 140, 198, 208
community care, 203
Community Charter of Fundamental Social Rights of Workers, 137, 148
competition laws, 153
competitive markets, 119, 121
computer industry, 119
Conference on Security and Cooperation in Europe (CSCE), 19
conservative-corporatist model, 145
Consortia of American Businesses (CABNIS), 120
constitutions, 74, 165, 193
consumer, 4, 79, 119, 123, 133, 151, 174, 199
Council for Mutual Economic Assistance (COMECON), 120
Council of Europe, 21, 135-36, 148-49
Council of Ministers, Poland, 58-9, 63, 66, 216
critical social theory, 183
Croatia, Croatian, 21-2, 94, 97-8
Croatian League of Communists, 94
CSU (Christian Social Union), 42
culture, 2, 11, 14, 16, 21, 26, 41, 44-5, 47, 51, 72, 113, 122, 128, 135, 138, 140, 147, 175, 191, 201, 227-28
customs union, 135
Czech Republic, 24, 28-9, 35-6, 38, 82, 85, 103, 185, 199, 218-19, 223
Czechoslovakia, former, 5, 24, 26, 32, 35, 38-9, 82, 85, 89, 98-9, 115, 118-19, 130, 133, 151, 153, 161, 176, 184, 210, 219, 226

De Gaulle, Charles, 58, 61
de Maizière, Lothar, 42, 47
debt financing, 222
defence industry, 89
delegitimation, delegitimised, 13, 25, 29-31, 34
Delors, Jacques, 61, 63, 68, 136-37, 145, 148
democracy, 4, 17, 24, 27-9, 34, 36, 40, 69, 74, 81, 102-3, 109, 113, 120,

122, 125, 135, 145, 165, 168, 173, 176, 180, 199
Democratic Forum, Hungary, 74, 103, 111, 216
DEMOS, Slovenia, 91
Denmark, 14, 55, 142
dependency culture, 207
deregulation, 6, 117, 122, 127, 138, 218, 224-25
dictatorship, 44, 96, 173
Dientsbier, Jiri, 27
disabled people, employment of, 138, 141, 144-46
discourse, 2, 6, 12, 27, 29, 70, 74, 76, 79-80, 170, 182-86, 191, 193
discourse, anti-Marxist, 183-84, 186, 189, 191-93, 195
discourse, anti-Socialist, 184
discourse, dominant, 79, 182, 184, 193
discourse, official, 165
disintegration, 1, 24, 26, 31, 33, 35, 45, 52
dissent, 27, 41, 111, 169, 216
Dlouhy, Vladimir, 28-9, 118
doctrine, 59, 166-67, 170
doublethink, 167, 169
Drakulic, Slavenka, 73-5, 84
drug abuse, 139
Duchêne, François, 57, 60, 67-8

East Central Europe, 70-75, 77-84, 115, 197-99, 203, 205, 210-211, 214-15, 217-22, 224-29
East Germany, 42-4, 51, 53, 166, 169
Eastern Europe, 6, 11, 15, 17, 20, 23, 50, 53, 56, 84-6, 89, 90, 92-3, 96-7, 99-100, 102, 115-19, 121-22, 126-27, 129-33, 155, 161, 178, 188, 196, 212-13
economic growth, 93, 102, 113, 125, 160, 201
economic integration, 6, 62, 151, 224
economic liberalisation, 122, 150, 152, 214
economic management, 105, 222
economic transformation, 6, 29, 96, 99, 150-151
economic transition, 151, 161
  see also transition
economics, 123-27, 135, 152, 185, 188-91, 194, 202

economies, 15-16, 115, 120, 127, 150, 153, 156-60, 185, 187, 195, 209, 218, 224
EFTA (European Free Trade Association), 60, 160
emancipation, emancipatory, 4, 6, 20, 70, 72-3, 80-81, 181, 184
empowerment, 2-4, 9
Eppelmann, Rainer, 44
equality, 69, 72-3, 78-83, 152, 209
equity, 71, 124, 147
Estonia, 89-90, 92, 99
ethnic cleansing, 4, 206
ethnic identity, 100
ethnic minorities, 143-44
ethnic nationalism, 206
ethnicity, 17, 41, 82, 180, 207
ethnocentric, 52
Euro-Racism, 149
Europe, 4, 9, 12, 17-18, 27, 34-5, 53-4, 56, 63, 67-9, 84-5, 101, 115, 120, 130, 132, 134-35, 137-38, 140-144, 147-150, 154-55, 175, 180, 196-99, 212, 219, 223-24
Europe Agreements, 154-55, 158-59
European Central Bank, 63
European Coal and Steel Community, 57
European Community (EC), 5, 15, 54-8, 64-5, 67-8, 134-35, 145, 148, 150, 153, 155, 157, 159-161, 212
  see also European Union
European Convention on Human Rights and Fundamental Freedoms, 135
European Court of Human Rights, 136
European Court of Justice, 55, 58, 64, 143
European Defence Community, 57, 61
European identity, 140, 144
European Parliament, 55, 64, 137, 144-45
European Union, 6, 19, 54-5, 57, 60, 64-6, 134, 140
Europeanism, 3

fascism, 69, 136, 176
Faul, Erwin, 51-3
FDP (Free Democratic Party), 42
federalism, 93
finance capital, 219
Finland, 151

foreign assistance, 107
foreign capital, 222-23
Foreign Direct Investment, 106, 120
foreign investment, 130, 220-223
foreign ownership, 222, 227
Fortress Europe, 141, 144, 146-48
Foucault, Michel, 174
France, 16, 54-8, 60-63, 65, 67, 84, 135, 142-43, 145-46, 148-49, 154, 159
Frankfurt School, 183, 196
Free Democratic Party, *see* FDP
Free Democrats, Hungary, 42, 216
free market, 37, 79, 120-122, 127, 202, 218-19, 221, 223
free-trade agreements, 99
freedom of communication, 221
freedom of the market, 221
Freedom Support Act, 120

Gazeta Wyborcza, 220
GDR, 41-8, 51, 53, 75, 82, 84-5, 168-69, 175-78, 206
Gellner, Ernest, 11, 23
gender, 6, 20, 69-72, 74-81, 83, 187, 209-11
gender relations, 198, 207, 210-211
General Agreement on Trade and Tariffs, GATT, 19, 61, 158-59, 184, 194
Georgia, 99
Germany, 5, 40-41, 43-5, 47, 49-57, 60, 63, 65, 79, 84-5, 98, 142-43, 145-46, 154-55, 159, 175-76, 178, 187
global political economy, 117-18, 123-24, 126-29, 180, 182-83, 186-87, 191-95
globalisation, 4, 17, 123-24, 183-84, 186
Gorbachev, Mikhail, 90-93, 121, 132, 170
gray or black economy, 110
Greater London Council, 146
Greece, 60, 155, 159
Grundgesetz, 165
Gulag Archipelago, 169
Gypsies, 134
    see also Roma

Habermas, Jurgen, 51, 53, 173-75, 177, 196, 199, 212, 215, 229

Hankiss, Elemer, 206, 212, 216
hard budget constraints, 90
Havel, Vaclav, 20, 26-7, 31-2, 37-9, 172, 186, 196
Heller, Agnes, 167, 177
Helsinki Citizens Assembly, (HCA), 20
Hirsch, Fred, 122, 131, 199, 202-3, 212
HIV, *see* AIDS
Holy Roman Empire, 173
Honecker, Erich, 46, 168, 175
household income, 151
housing, 75, 139, 205
human capital, 156-57
Hungarian Investment Foundation, 108, 112
Hungarian minority, 34
Hungarian Socialist Workers Party, (HSWP), 114
Hungary, 6, 74, 79, 82, 84, 86, 99, 102-4, 107, 111-15, 118-19, 130-132, 153, 157, 161, 175-76, 185, 212-14, 216, 218-19, 220, 222-23, 226
hyperinflation, 151

identity, 3, 17, 22, 26, 32, 34, 40, 47-9, 51, 70, 76, 83, 93, 95, 129, 138, 140, 142-43, 180, 210
ideological pressure, 169
ideology, 3, 6, 14, 16, 26, 70, 73-4, 82-3, 96, 109, 123, 165-66, 170-171, 175, 183, 188, 193, 199, 200, 205, 211, 221
imagined communities, 16
immigration, 134, 140-144
Immigration Act, 1988 (UK), 142
independence, 32-3, 36, 38, 42, 67, 76, 82-3, 90-91, 209, 215-17, 222-23, 227
individualism, 34, 67, 83, 153, 198, 207-8
International Bank for Reconstruction and Development (IBRD), 117
    see also World Bank
International Chamber of Commerce, 127
International Monetary Fund, (IMF), 19, 117, 130, 185
international organisations, 9, 15-16, 19-21, 35, 117, 123, 126-28
International Telecommunications Union, (ITU), 123

international trade, 117, 152, 158, 160-161, 184-85
investment, 93-5, 100, 106, 112, 119, 156, 159, 180, 201, 221-23
investment banks, 119
investment capital, 107, 223
investment funds, 94, 103
Ireland, 142, 159
Italy, 135, 145-46, 148, 154, 157, 203, 213

Jakubowicz, Karol, 216-17, 223, 227, 229
Japan, 60, 157
job creation and training, 145

Kant, Herman, 169
Keane, John, 199, 212, 220-221, 229
Keynesianism, 1
KGB, 171
Kindleberger, Charles, 56-7, 68
Klaus, Georg, 169, 177
Klaus, Vaclav, 28, 31, 35-6, 38
Klinger, Fred, 44-6, 50-51, 53
knowledge, 5, 11, 19, 59, 123, 126, 130, 171, 174, 190
Kohl, Helmut, 42, 47, 49, 52
Kraus, Wolfgang, 172, 177
Kunneman, Harry, 174-75, 177
Kusy, Miroslav, 26, 39
Kuwait, 15

labour market, 138, 144
laissez-faire, 202
language, 6, 11, 14, 21, 27, 29, 34, 51, 71, 73, 78, 83, 165-68, 170, 175, 184, 193, 210
Latvia, 89-90, 92, 99
League of Communists, (Yugoslavia), 90-91, 94
Lefort, Claude, 170-171, 177, 178, 215, 229
legislation, 37, 55, 58-59, 68, 72, 74, 76, 79, 82, 109, 140, 143, 194, 216, 219, 222, 224, 226
legitimacy, legitimate, 2, 4, 9-10, 12, 15, 25-6, 30, 32, 35-6, 40, 50-51, 65, 95, 170, 194, 198
legitimate disagreement, 24
l'espace sociale, 137
Liberal, 42, 186, 188, 194, 212

liberal, 28, 35-6, 49-51, 55, 57, 62, 69, 76, 79, 83, 94, 123, 143, 158, 180, 193, 195, 200, 203, 209, 211, 220
liberal democracies, 166
liberal individualism, 78, 203, 211
lifeworld, 174
Lister, Ruth, 71, 79, 80, 82, 85, 146, 148
Lithuania, 89-90, 92, 99
Loeser, Franz, 168, 176, 178
Lorrain, Pierre, 169-170, 178
lustration, 34
Luxembourg, 68, 142
Luxembourg Compromise, 58, 61, 63

MacDonald's, 119
macroeconomic statistics, 151
Mafiosi, 110
    see also organised crime
Management By Objectives (MBO), 128
Management training, 121
Mann, Michael, 166, 178
manufacturing industry, 121
Marcuse, Herbert, 166, 178
market economy/economies, 24, 27-8, 89, 96, 99, 102-3, 106, 118, 120-121, 150-153, 156, 159-60, 209
market privatisation, 109
    see also privatisation
market socialism, 91, 94
Marody, Mira, 75, 85
Marx, Karl, 45, 166, 168, 176
Marxism, 6, 132, 180-189, 191, 193-96
Marxism-Leninism, 169, 172, 175-76
Marxist, 48, 166, 168, 190, 196
Marxist-Leninist ideology, 14
Meciar, Vladimir, 33, 38
media, 6, 21, 34, 165-66, 169, 214-229
media systems, 214-15, 218, 221, 224, 227
migration, 14, 156, 160
Miklosko, Jozef, 32
militarisation, 1
military employment, 157
minimum incomes, 139
Mitterrand, François, 60, 137
monetarist, 28, 67
monetary union, 55, 63, 160
moral order, 197, 199, 206
Moscow, 73, 101, 119-20, 131, 184

Moscow International Business
    Management School, 121
multicultarism, 14, 51-2
multinational companies, 14

Nagorny Karabakh, 92
nation, 10-12, 14, 16, 22, 26, 32, 34,
    37, 49, 51-2, 58, 70-71, 73-4, 76,
    79-81, 201
nation-state(s), 1, 5, 9-19, 21-2, 58, 67,
    71-2, 224-25
national communism, 95
    see also communism
national culture, 10, 13-14, 16-17, 21,
    81, 224
National Health Service, 207
national identity, 9, 32, 34, 51, 71, 77,
    92, 226
national minorities, 3, 34
national self-determination, 3, 9
National Socialism, 171
national sovereignty, 226
nationalism, 3, 9, 17-18, 21, 24, 32-4,
    36-7, 41, 48-9, 51-2, 56, 71, 77-9,
    83, 89, 91-6, 99, 100, 134-35, 139,
    147, 180, 207
nationalist clientelist system, 109
Nazi-Soviet Pact, 89
needs, 20, 46, 50, 65, 72, 82-3, 121,
    127, 134, 147, 152, 159, 198-201,
    203, 206-7, 209-210, 217, 228
neo-liberals, 3, 29, 36, 134, 146
Népszabadság, 114-15, 220
Netherlands, 14, 132, 142
networks, 11, 14, 43, 77, 81, 107, 113,
    146, 173
New Right, 18, 31, 203
new social movements, 2, 20-21, 134
new world order, 180
newspaper, 199, 217, 219-223
Newspeak, 167
Nineteen Eighty-Four, 16, 165, 167,
    169-170, 176, 178
Nisbet, Robert, 169
NKVD, 171
nomenklatura, 4, 92-3, 95, 98-9, 110
nomenklatura nationalism, 6, 96-9
nomenklatura nationalist(s), 95-7, 99
Non-Governmental Organisations
    (NGOs), 20
Nordic countries, 99

normalisation, 25, 211
normalised, 25, 175
North Atlantic Treaty Organisation
    (NATO), 22, 35
Northern Ireland, 15

On the Jewish Question, 176
    see also Marx
organic privatisation, 106
    see also privatisation
organised crime, 142
Orwell, George, 16, 165, 167, 170, 178

patriarchal, patriarchy, 71, 209
Paukert, Liba, 70, 82, 85
perestroika, 90
personal computers, 119
philanthropy, 204, 208
pluralism, pluralistic, 5, 90-91, 102,
    176
Poland, 21, 63, 79, 81-5, 98, 99, 101,
    103, 115, 118-19, 122, 124, 130-
    132, 151-53, 157, 161, 176-77,
    204, 206, 214, 216, 218-19, 220,
    223, 226, 228
policing, 140, 142, 144, 146
political culture, 4-5, 22, 32, 41, 61,
    215
political economy, 95, 118, 161, 185-
    88, 190-191
Poor Law, 136
pornography, 209
Porter, Bernard, 56, 68
Portugal, 60, 155, 159
Portuges, Catherine, 80, 85
post-communist, 2, 24, 27-8, 30, 37, 99,
    175
post-modernism, 183
poverty, 51, 122, 134, 137-38, 145-48,
    185, 187, 204-5, 211
power, 1-5, 9-10, 12, 15, 18-19, 24, 27,
    29-31, 33, 36-8, 49, 57-9, 61, 65,
    74-5, 92-3, 95, 98, 102-3, 105,
    107, 109, 113, 115, 126, 143, 167,
    169, 171, 174, 191-92, 195, 209,
    215-18, 220, 224
pre-privatisation, 105, 114
private enterprise, 90, 183
private ownership, 107
private property laws, 153
privatisation, 3, 6, 34, 90-92, 96-100,

102-115, 117-124, 126-28, 130, 184-85, 211, 221, 227
productivity, 83, 112, 205
profit motive, 209
profitability, 222
propaganda, 45, 48, 74, 165-66, 169-70, 173, 176
property rights, 112, 115, 126
Protestant Church, 43, 46
Public Against Violence, 30, 32-3
public good, 221
public opinion, 66, 90
public sector, 124, 158, 190, 201, 205
public service, 6, 198, 200-205, 208, 210-211, 224-25, 228
public service broadcasting, 216-17, 224-25, 229
public sphere, 6, 70, 72, 74, 76-7, 83, 172-73, 175, 215, 220, 228
public/private divide, 76, 83, 210-211

quotas, 227

R&D, Research and Development, 112
racism, 134, 144, 148, 187
Reagan Administration, 128
recession, 62, 66, 151, 185, 219, 222, 226
reform, economic, 28, 33, 93-4, 150-152, 158, 214
reform, political, 30
refugees, 50, 69, 134, 141, 143
representative democracy, 13
responsibility, 2-3, 9, 11, 18, 22, 25, 31, 36, 57-8, 69, 71, 74, 78, 81, 105, 139, 173, 198-99, 207
restructuring, 97-8, 104, 108, 112, 119, 128, 135, 161, 208
revolution, 24, 26-7, 42, 44-5, 47, 91, 96, 98, 125, 175, 180
rights, citizenship, 55, 71, 74, 78, 82-3, 146
rights, civil and political, 3
rights, economic, 59, 64, 140
rights, human, 19-20, 34, 46, 49, 135, 137, 147-49, 185, 194
Roma, 22, 113
Romania, 130, 153, 184-85, 215
Rosecrance, Richard, 57, 68
rule of law, 4, 12, 17, 22, 34
ruling class, 166

Russia, 92, 119-120, 129, 131, 177, 207

Schengen Accord, 142
Schengen Information Service, 142
Scott, Joan, 78-9, 85
second economy, 96
secret police, 166
security, 19, 22, 24-5, 53, 136, 140-141, 153, 180, 209
SED, Socialist Unity Party of Germany, 41-3, 45-8
self-censorship, 169
self-management, 97
self-privatisation, 105-6
    see also privatisation
sensitive products, 155
separatist nationalism, 96
    see also nationalism
Serbia, 94, 97-9
service sector, 106, 121
sex equality, 144
shock therapy, 99
Šiklová, Jirina, 81, 83, 85
Single European Act, 54, 62, 137, 140
single market, 61-2, 66, 137-38, 141, 148, 160
    see also Single European Act
Slovak National Party, 32-3, 37
Slovak Republic, Slovakia, 34, 217
Slovenia, 89-91, 97-8
Snitow, Ann, 78-80, 82-3, 85
social change, 180
Social Chapter, 137, 140, 144, 146
Social Charter, 136-37, 139, 140, 145, 149
social democracy, 1, 43, 145
Social Democratic Party of Germany, *see* SPD
Social Europe, 134-35, 137, 140, 147
social groups, 173, 191
social identities, 173
social justice, 2, 44, 71, 113, 134, 141, 147
social movements, 147
social policy, 6, 62, 78, 135, 137, 139, 140, 145-47, 198, 200
social rights, 36, 49, 80, 134-36, 138-39, 145-47
social science, 175, 197
socialism, 16, 31, 39, 44, 48, 52, 70,

73, 78, 94, 110, 168, 170, 173-75, 180, 187, 198-200, 204, 209
socialism, construction of, 165, 167
socialist democracy, 168
socialist economies, 174, 185
socialist political economies, 187-88, 195
Solidarity, 99, 134, 206
Solzhenitsyn, Alexander, 169
Southern Ossetia, 92
Soviet Union, 14, 16, 77, 82, 85, 89, 91, 95-6, 99, 100, 130, 132, 151, 153, 160, 179, 211
sovnarkhoz, 93, 95
Spain, 60, 157, 159
Spanish Inquisition, 172
SPD (Social Democratic Party of Germany), 43-4, 47, 50
spontaneous privatisation, 103-4, 116
    see also privatisation
Stalinism, 93, 165, 176
Staniszkis, Jadwiga, 170, 179
state banks, 108
state budget, 98, 103, 112
state capitalism, 94, 98
State Property Agency (SPA), Hungary, 103, 105-6
state security, 46, 217
state socialism, 6, 69-73, 76-8, 80, 173-75, 210, 215
state socialist countries, 70-71, 74, 167, 200, 205
state socialist dictatorships, 174
state socialist regimes, 69, 147, 214
state socialist societies, 80, 134, 165-66, 171-73
state socialist system, 1
state subsidies, 29, 120, 159
state-owned assets, 108
state-owned enterprises, 104-5, 108
stock exchange, 111
Stolpe, Manfred, 48-9
Stolper-Samuelson theorem, 152
structural funds, 159-160
structural unemployment, 160
    see also unemployment
subsidiarity, 5, 18, 64-6, 138-39, 145
surveillance, 17, 166, 173
Sweden, 99
Szalai, Júlia, 72, 81-2, 84, 86, 198, 212

tabloids, 220
taxation, 12, 94, 153
technical change, 63, 160
Thatcher, Margaret, 61, 139, 140, 198, 202, 207
Third World, 128, 134, 137, 149
Tilly, Charles, 12, 23
Titmuss, Richard, 202, 213
totaliatrian ideology, 171
totalitarian culture, 170
totalitarian ideology, 171
trade barriers, 224
trade liberalisation, 122, 152, 155
trade unions, 44-5, 137
Transcaucasia, 91
transition, 1, 5-6, 24-5, 28-9, 73-4, 83, 98, 115, 118, 120, 124-25, 127, 129, 131, 150, 153, 156, 160, 175, 180, 182, 188, 195, 199, 209, 214, 218, 222, 224, 228
transnational civil society, 17, 22
Transnational Corporations, (TNC's), 106
transparency, 110
Treaty of Rome, 57, 135, 140, 194
Treuhand, 98
Tudjman, Franjo, 97

Ukraine, 92-3, 97, 99
unemployment, 28, 50-51, 56, 71, 107, 122, 132, 134, 137, 139, 147, 151-52, 187, 198, 210
UNESCO (United Nations Educational, Scientific and Cultural Organisation), 117-18, 123, 127-29, 133, 194
UNESCO, United Nations Educational, Scientific and Cultural Organisation, 133
United Nations (UN), 19, 117, 128, 130, 133, 192, 194
United States of America, 14, 57, 60, 178, 218
urban renewal, 139
USSR, Soviet Union, former, 117, 121, 130, 167, 169, 180, 183, 185-86
    see also Soviet Union

visa policy, 141
vocational training, 136, 138
Vogel, Ursula, 72, 79, 86, 208, 213

voluntary work, 198-201, 204, 208, 210-211
von Weizsäcker, Richard, 49

Walser, Martin, 51
warfare, 15, 180
welfare, 3, 6, 22, 25, 72, 76, 82, 102, 112-14, 121, 134, 137, 147-49, 155, 198, 203-10
welfare state(s), 134, 136, 146-48, 174, 200, 206-8, 210
Wenceslas Square, 175
West Germany, 135, 148
Western Europe, 11, 16, 23, 35, 52, 57, 67, 72, 100, 129, 158, 160, 224-25
Wheaton, Bernard (and Kavan, Z.), 24, 27, 29, 32, 37, 39
Wolf, Christa, 47, 49, 53

women's movement, 72
worker participation, 139
World Bank, 35, 84, 123, 127, 188, 195
World Health Organization (WHO), 117

xenophobia, 50, 134, 144, 148

Yeltsin, Boris, 124, 187
Yugoslav army, 90-91
Yugoslav communism, 95
Yugoslav Federation, 95
Yugoslav state, 93-4
Yugoslav successor states, 98-9
Yugoslavia, former, 50, 89-91, 93-5, 97, 100, 119, 131

Zinoviev, Alexander, 166